FACTORY-ORIGINAL
FORD RS COSWORTHS

FACTORY-ORIGINAL FORD RS COSWORTHS

The originality guide to the Ford Sierra, Sapphire and Escort RS Cosworth

BY DAN WILLIAMSON
PHOTOGRAPHY BY SIMON CLAY

Herridge & Sons

Acknowledgements

Ford RS Cosworths might not be the most exotic supercars nor the most expensive classics. They may not be the fastest, and they're probably not the most amazing to drive. But even now, decades after launch, they still punch well above their weight, offering exhilaration that's unmatched by any other mainstream manufacturer's production saloon. They are simply thrilling.

RS Cosworths possess an incredible ability to get under the skin of their owners; a head-rushingly addictive relationship that means almost any foible may be forgiven. An RS Cosworth can empty an owner's wallet as quickly as it can reach 60mph, and it can choose to misfire depending on the direction of the wind. It always looks fabulous, even when it's parked alongside exotica or in pieces on the garage floor.

It's thanks to these owners that factory-original RS Cosworths are still in existence, and it's with special gratitude we'd like to thank the keepers of the cars used for photography in this book: Mark Barber, Marc McCubbin, Damon Sargent, Ben Corner, Chris Barlow, Mark Bailey and Neil Arnold.

Personally, I'd also like to thank the people and organisations who've helped to put this publication together: Karl Norris at Norris Motorsport (for sharing so many years of intimate mechanical insights), Paul Linfoot (for RS500 facts, encouraging the concept of this book and general straight-talking Yorkshireness), Clemens Rieg (the king of Ford chassis plate decoding), Andy Rouse (for recollections of Rouse Sport Sapphires), Paul Bury, the RS Owners' Club, Dave Hill at Ford's photo library, and Sarah Mortimer (for artwork on this book's chassis plate illustrations and high-speed memories of my own RS Cosworths).

Photography credits

Simon Clay, Ford Motor Company, Dan Williamson

Published in 2016 by
Herridge & Sons Ltd
Lower Forda, Shebbear
Beaworthy, Devon EX21 5SY

© Dan Williamson 2016

ISBN 978-1-906133-58-0
Printed in China

CONTENTS

INTRODUCTION

Ford and Cosworth. Two incredible brands. Two firms at the forefront of engineering innovation. Two words that when used together conjure the kind of sensational sights, sounds and smells that make European car enthusiasts go weak at the knees.

Ford and Cosworth are entwined by motorsport, enshrined in legend and unashamedly synonymous with success. And when the two join forces, they become unbeatable.

Add another phrase into the mix – Rallye Sport – and the knack for winning on racetracks translates into victory across the automotive board, from circuits to forests, from touring cars to rallycross.

And, most importantly for the purposes of this book, the words Ford RS Cosworth symbolise sovereignty of the everyman motoring world – the master of supercar-slaying saloon cars and king of the performance tuning market.

The Ford RS Cosworth is a competition champion that became a street-fighting legend. It's the moniker of an international blue collar hero. It's the star of road, track and posters on bedroom walls.

A legend of road and racetrack – the original Sierra RS Cosworth of 1985 set new standards in saloon car performance.

Indeed, the story has frequently been told. Cosworth Engineering was a race engine design and development firm founded in London in 1958 by development engineer Mike Costin and Keith Duckworth, a mechanical design genius; the word Cosworth came from an amalgamation of their surnames.

Cosworth's initial major project was improvement of the Ford 105E Formula Junior powerplant, which race ace Jim Clark took to victory in 1960. Within a couple of years the company had been involved in its first official Ford production car, the Cortina GT of 1963, in which Cosworth designed the camshaft and introduced Italian carburettor company Weber to the American motor manufacturing giant.

But that was only the start of it. By 1964 Cosworth had moved to a bigger property in Northampton, and the contracts flooded in. Most importantly, in 1965 Ford and Lotus commissioned Cosworth to develop a new Formula One engine, the DFV. It became the most successful engine in the sport's history, scooping a dozen world drivers' championships and ten for constructors – not to mention innumerable victories in Formula 3000 and twice at Le Mans.

The next notable Ford and Cosworth collaboration came in 1969; it was named the BDA. Developed around a regular four-cylinder Ford bottom end, the BDA (which stood for Belt Drive series A) was topped with an innovative Cosworth-designed 16-valve cylinder head. In basic 1.6-litre guise it made an easy 120bhp, being fitted to the Escort RS1600 of 1970; an almost-identical 1.8-litre version followed in the 1975 Escort RS1800. As road cars they were brilliant. But as competition cars they were phenomenal.

BDA-powered Escorts began winning rallies the moment they were launched, and subsequent developments of the engine continued the success, in one form or another, into the present day.

Other motor manufacturers employed Cosworth's engineering services to create competition-derived super saloons – including Opel with its Ascona/Manta 400 and Mercedes-Benz with its 190E 2.3-16 – but none achieved quite the same fame as the BDA/Escort combination.

None, that was, until 1985, when the Cosworth YBB was fitted into Ford's Sierra. Like the BDA, the YBB powerplant was a mixture of humdrum Ford four-cylinder block and

brilliant Cosworth 16-valve cylinder head – only this time it was turbocharged.

The Sierra RS Cosworth was the first production car ever to wear the word Cosworth in its name, and the first to achieve over 100bhp per litre. It was a 1993cc, 204bhp family hatchback, but it was designed and built with one sole goal – to win races.

Ford's marketing experts had long ago subscribed to the 'win on Sunday, sell on Monday' theory. And it was never more true than in the 1980s, when high-profile motorsport victories meant significant showroom appeal among private buyers and fleet managers alike.

Back then, tin-top racing saloons were based on real, recognisable, road-going machines, and homologation rules meant 5000 examples had to be produced in order to qualify for competition. So the special Sierra project was signed off with not just a magnificent engine but also a functional yet head-turning aerodynamic package, including wild rear wing.

The road-going RS Cosworth immediately grabbed public attention, proving to be amazing to look at and dynamically brilliant – better than the majority of contemporary sports cars and faster than many supercars.

Needless to say, race wins came just as quickly. But Ford's intention was never to settle at a mere 300bhp in motorsport trim; the intention was for much, much more. And with a stronger engine, bigger turbo and improved fuelling, it was possible to pretty much double that figure.

The result was the RS500 evolution special of 1987, meaning a further 500 road-going machines were required to enter international competition.

The RS500 wiped the circuit with everything in sight, in turn becoming the most successful racing saloon of all time, winning every championship it was allowed to enter. But it wasn't to last, because the RS500's brightness glowed for a very short time, and it was soon banned by the sport's governing bodies.

Still, Ford was committed to buying 15,000 Cosworth engines, and the solution was even more fruitful: an executive express with the same turbocharged engine but now wearing sedate bodywork and a luxurious cabin.

The Sierra Sapphire Cosworth hit the market in 1988, offering accomplished ability and improved road manners, and selling in greater numbers. Its purpose, of course, wasn't motorsport-based, but that didn't stop Ford from using the Sapphire to develop an entirely new rally winner.

The Sapphire Cosworth 4x4 arrived in 1990, following its rear-wheel-drive predecessor's big-power formula but adding grip at all four corners for improved ability on rough surfaces. For many aficionados it was a revelation.

Yet the four-wheel-drive Sapphire was simply the forerunner to the main act, the Escort RS Cosworth of 1992. Built on a shortened Sapphire floorpan and including many of the same mechanicals, the Cosworth-powered Escort reprised the original Sierra RS's dramatic aerodynamic aids and jaw-

An extension of the brand – the 1987 Sierra Sapphire Cosworth converted the race-based image into a badge for the everyday motoring enthusiast.

dropping looks, with wide wheelarches and extravagant wings.

Again, the Escort achieved instant public recognition, becoming a legend not just in motorsport but among car fans across the board. Driving enthusiasts loved the Cosworth. Tuners and modifiers loved the Cosworth. Young boys loved the Cosworth, as did company directors and well-paid manual workers. Significantly, and unfortunately, car thieves loved the Cosworth too. The badge was soon linked with joyriders; it became interchangeable with the phrase, 'impossible to insure.'

Sales slowed, the market collapsed, and Ford lost interest in its Rallye Sport range.

The RS Cosworth was officially dropped in 1996 but its following among owners never dwindled. They kept the cars alive, often by improving their performance and enhancing the styling. And within a couple of decades these incredible cars had once again become treasured possessions, recognised as much for their place in history as their huge performance.

No wonder, then, that a factory-original Ford RS Cosworth is a truly magnificent machine. Over the years, most examples have been modified, many have been crashed, some stolen, loads broken, and thousands lost to the world. Today, recreating that authentic specification is a tremendous task.

Ford allows no access to contemporaneous records – if such documents exist – and it's fair to say that recording the development of machines made for motorsport was simply not a priority for a major manufacturer.

Indeed, it's only thanks to fans of RS models that their heritage is preserved. As such, pinning down exact production parts and changeover dates is not an exact science; and although this book tries to make an accurate study of factory-original Cosworths, it's inevitable there may be a few mistakes. Which is why, as always, we welcome reader comments and corrections.

This book is not a buying guide, it isn't a restoration manual, and we don't have the space to list the sizes of every nut and bolt involved in the manufacture of a Ford RS Cosworth. Instead, it's a reference – and a tribute – to the engineering excellence and brilliant bits that made up these legendary machines.

SIERRA RS COSWORTH

Moonstone Blue was one of three colours available throughout Sierra RS Cosworth three-door production, the others being Diamond White and Black. This magnificent blue example is owned by Ben Corner, who's its third keeper from new. Never restored or repainted, this 78,000-mile machine looks as fresh and purposeful today as it did when leaving Ford's Genk factory in November 1986.

This was the car that changed a generation. It changed motorsport. It changed public perception of the uninspiring jellymould Sierra. It changed automotive aerodynamics and spawned a culture of imitations. It even changed the way a nation of car enthusiasts think when they hear the word 'cossie'.

Indeed, this was the machine that brought the name Cosworth into our households. Yes, Cosworth – the engineering firm – had been building incredibly successful motorsport powerplants for decades. And yes, Cosworth had been perfecting Ford products since the Mk1 Cortina GT of 1963. But this was the first time the word Cosworth had been used to name a production car. And what an amazing production car it was...

The Sierra RS Cosworth was developed from the outset to be a race winner – a way to return Ford to its rightful position on the podium of tintop championships. Years in the doldrums led blue oval bigwigs Stuart Turner and Walter Hayes to Silverstone, where V6 Capris were being trounced by V8 Rovers. Both agreed a new car was essential for European Group A saloon car racing.

Turner then took American Ford bosses Ed Blanch and Jim Capolongo on a crafty tour of Cosworth's factory, where they managed to stumble across a rather conveniently placed Pinto bottom end wearing an aluminium 16-valve cylinder head. Talk soon turned to turbocharging, and although Cosworth thought the idea was unnecessary, Ford reckoned at least 300bhp in competition guise was essential to guarantee victory.

Motorsport homologation rules meant a minimum of 5000

production cars were required to enter racing and rallying, and drivers insisted on a rear-wheel-drive platform. Ford's then-new Sierra was the obvious solution, and SVE (Special Vehicle Engineering) was assigned to develop a winner.

By autumn 1983 the project was gathering pace, with Cosworth commissioned to build 15,000 engines over the course of three years. The company's creation – codenamed YBB – used a mass-production two-litre Pinto block originally found in the Cortina, kitted out with tougher internals, Cosworth's own twin-cam head, big Garrett T03 turbocharger and intercooler, along with Weber-Marelli fuel injection.

And it wasn't just good. It was incredible.

Ford's brief was for 180bhp in road trim, but detuning to such a measly figure proved to be an unrealistic request; 200bhp was a more sensible goal, and it resulted in the world's first production car boasting more than 100bhp per litre. Yet even the homologated 204bhp was less than most production engines kicked out.

It was all too much for Ford's usual Type 9 five-speed gearbox, so Borg-Warner was called on to provide an alternative. Its American-made T5 transmission was widely used in Ford USA's Mustang, but high-speed testing behind the turbocharged YB engine resulted in bearing seizures due to a lubrication fault; eventually, Borg-Warner set up a unique assembly line for Cosworth-destined gearboxes, causing lengthy delays in getting the sporty new Sierra on sale.

SVE transformed the suspension using a variety of standard stuff, specially-designed components and Granada/Scorpio bits from the parts-bin. Dunlop D40 tyres were chosen to surround 7x15in Rial alloy wheels, while initial reports of twitchiness were countered with revised steering; this was destined to be a 150mph road car, after all.

High-speed stability became integral to the car's design, with positive downforce crucial for circuit racing. Aerodynamicists spent months testing in wind tunnels, grafting countless configurations of spoilers onto an XR4i mule with varying degrees of aesthetic appeal.

Public reaction to the XR's awkward four-pillar bodywork and bi-plane wing meant its shape was already out of favour;

Significantly revised Sierra front end still showed the basic family car beneath aggressive spoilers, splitters, vents and scoops.

Other alterations (92 to the bodywork alone) included cooling vents in the bonnet and an air intake between the headlamps, added after hot-weather trials in Europe. Ghia-level trim was specified, including glass sunroof, tinted windows, plush carpets, posh instruments (with a USA-market Merkur XR4Ti boost gauge) and glorious grey-cloth Recaro front seats.

No options were offered for the UK, besides a choice of three exterior colours: Diamond White, Moonstone Blue and Black. There was also one three-door finished in Rosso Red, factory-built as a special order.

Although Ford's intention was to get the car on sale by the end of 1984, the RS Cosworth wasn't unveiled until the March 1985 Geneva motor show. Over the course of that year, at least ten pre-production Sierras were built, including nine in white and one in black; at least five were left-hand drive. All these cars, it's reckoned, were fitted with T5 gearboxes from the Mustang SVO, rather than Cosworth-specific transmissions.

Assembly of customer cars began at Genk, Belgium in February 1986, on mainstream Sierra lines but with engines from Cosworth in the UK. According to semi-official records, the first production Sierra Cosworth – an LHD machine destined for Germany – left the factory on 12 March 1986.

Figures reported by Ford historians say two British cars were built on 14 April, along with a couple bound for Norway. A Belgian example followed on 30 April, with ten more UK cars in May and 26 in June. It's said that production went into full swing on 17 June 1986, and the majority of Sierra Cosworths were constructed between October and December 1986.

The official launch was 15 July 1986, but most deliveries didn't begin until autumn. In total, there were 5542 three-door RS Cosworths produced, including 2616 for British customers. Other markets included France, Italy, Spain, Austria, Finland, Holland, Portugal and southern Ireland. A few even found their ways to the Canary Islands, America, Australia, New Zealand and Hong Kong.

adding on functional extensions had only made it worse. Yet Ford's stylists turned that ugly duckling into a swan – albeit a swan wearing knuckledusters.

The poverty-spec Sierra three-door bodyshell was instead selected for its simpler lines and lighter weight (the whole finished car was just 1205kg), while new bumpers, wheelarches and side skirts were produced in polyurethane. An enormous whale tail – seen by Ford bosses as a necessary evil – eventually became an iconic symbol of 1980s' extravagance.

Meanwhile, the Cosworth legend grew stronger on racetracks, just as Ford bosses intended. Andy Rouse campaigned a Ford-backed Sierra (Merkur) XR4Ti in the 1985 and '86 rounds of the British Saloon Car Championship; by the time the Cosworth took over, he'd already scooped 14 overall wins and the 1985 crown.

The RS Cosworth was homologated by the start of 1987, and began bagging victories in the (renamed) British Touring Car Championship and World Touring Car Championship. Success was short-lived – because the RS500 took over in August that year. International rally events were also tackled, and a single four-wheel-drive three-door prototype was competed by Ford, registered D373 TAR.

But by 1987 it was all over for the Sierra RS Cosworth production car. Sales continued until summer that year, accompanied by 500 three-doors held back from the initial run of 5542 and converted into RS500s. And that was all Ford needed to maintain motorsport dominance.

Rear view was a revelation from a mainstream manufacturer when the RS Cosworth was launched in 1985. The Sierra turns heads even today.

Engine – Block, Sump and Oil System

It all started with the Pinto – literally. The basis for the magnificent Cosworth YBB powerplant was Ford's ancient boat anchor of an engine, first seen in the Mk3 Cortina and Taunus TC of 1970. The T88-series Pinto featured a thin-wall cast-iron cylinder block and overhead-cam head, and saw service in a variety of mainstream Ford models, most of which were decidedly dull.

That said, the racy Mk1 and Mk2 Escort RS2000s were Pinto-powered, as was the Sierra 2.0iS of 1985, which used a fuel-injected 115bhp version of the T88 two-litre. Now, though, there was a revised cylinder block with a slightly superior, heavier casting, including thicker walls, stronger webbing around the base and improved water galleries.

The digits 205 were generally marked in raised characters on the side of the crankcase – the 20 relating to 2.0 litres and the 5 for 1985, its first year of production. This cylinder block – colloquially known as the 205 block – then became standard fitment in fuel-injected Sierras and Ford Transits, churned out in huge numbers and sold around the world. And it was this common-or-garden 205 block on which the original three-door Sierra RS Cosworth's YBB-designated powerplant was based.

Around 440 YBB engines were built per month at Cosworth's then-new factory at Wellingborough, Northamptonshire. Although pretty much everything else was bespoke, the 205

Pre-production RS Cosworth on test. Note the radio aerial was fitted to the driver's side of this LHD machine but the fuel filler wasn't flipped. A sunroof was standard-fit in the UK but optional in other markets.

Still stunning several decades later, the original RS Cosworth engine bay packed a mighty 204bhp from its YBB powerplant – essentially a turbocharged, 16-valve version of the basic Pinto.

11

Sheer perfection – stunning studio shots of 1985 YBB engine, showing black-painted cast iron Pinto block, alloy 16-valve cylinder head, Garret T03 turbo and alloy fuel rail but lacking the real engine's rear core plug. Please feel free to stop and stare.

YBB powerplants under construction at Cosworth Engineering in 1986. Note the two-bolt thermostat housings, gold-passivated turbo actuators, and orange Fram oil filters.

cylinder block came shipped bare from Ford's foundry and was used without change. The only stipulation laid down by Cosworth was that each block selected to become a YBB had standard bore gradings of 2 or 3. These digits were stamped into the crank case behind the distributor and above the oil filter; each cylinder was represented in sequence (one to four), such as 3223. At Cosworth the area was then sprayed with yellow primer-type paint.

Various casting marks and numbers were found on 205 cylinder blocks, but none were particular to items destined for the Cosworth factory except for the offside lower bellhousing lug, which was stamped with Ford's engine block code N5B (as opposed to NET for a regular two-litre Pinto or NRD for the 2000cc fuel-injected version). The lug was painted in yellow primer.

Usually on Cosworth engines (but not always) the number 205 was cast in raised digits onto the side just below the cylinder head, generally on both sides and in larger characters than the 20 seen on earlier Pinto blocks. It's assumed that such irregularities stemmed from about one in ten blocks being sourced from different foundries and/or at different times from the norm.

The part number (85HM6015BB) was cast in raised characters beneath a small 205 on the exhaust side, which itself sat beneath a machined flat bearing a hand-stamped Ford engine number (positioned just before the offside engine mount) consisting of a two-letter code for the build year and month, followed by a unique five-digit serial number; these

Early YBB engines being built from bare 205 blocks at Cosworth during 1986; the chap in the foreground was brush-painting the blocks in black and spraying yellow primer onto identification codes through a template. Note the core plug at the back of the block, which was removed on late-model Sapphire engines.

seven digits matched the final sequence in the car's VIN number.

The block's date of production was cast into a raised oval on the same side, just behind the engine mount. The first two digits related to the day and week it was made, a letter represented the month (A equalled January, B for February and so on), and the last two digits stood for the year of manufacture (85 meaning 1985). All three-door Sierra Cosworth blocks were built in 1985 or '86 and marked accordingly.

Cosworth also made its own identification marks and serial numbers on each engine. At the front of the crankcase above the water pump was a machined metal flat section, sprayed in yellow primer (through a template) and then stamped by hand with a serial number beginning in YBB and followed by unique digits. Cosworth started numbering from near zero (eg YBB0001), rising into the thousands; the figures did not match Ford's engine number.

The block was brush-painted in satin black (plus bare alloy front cover). Like the Pinto on which it was based, it had a 1993cc capacity. Now, though, there was an 8.0:1 compression ratio, featuring new forged aluminium pistons and rings, designed and manufactured for Cosworth by Mahle. In the crown of each piston was a shallow bowl, with the production date and manufacturer's code marked on top. Only pistons graded 2 or 3 were used; the numbers were stamped beneath the piston crown and corresponding sizes were marked on the cylinder block. Unlike later pistons, the three-door Sierra's had a central (as opposed to offset) gudgeon pin.

Forged and heat-treated steel connecting rods were designed by Cosworth, at 1.5mm longer than the Pinto's. Specific Cosworth bolts secured them to a new forged steel five-bearing crankshaft. Dimensionally identical to the regular Pinto crank, Cosworth's version had hardened and moly-coated bearing journals, nine flywheel bolts, reinforced sprocket gear and oil seals.

Oil jets were directed at the underside of each piston to aid cooling as it reached the bottom of its stroke, in the form of a spray bar brazed onto the oil pickup pipe. It was fed by fluid from a modified Ford oil pump – again based on the Pinto part but featuring a revised cover to connect an additional pipe.

Beneath, a gravity die-cast bare alloy sump (again, a Cosworth design) was connected to the block through a gasket with two cork layers sandwiching one of aluminium. Inside the sump was an internal baffle plate, while externally a gold-passivated tube returned oil from the turbo, linked via a black pipe with grey hose clips on each end.

Oil flow was fed through a Modine oil-to-water heat exchanger, which was coupled to the engine cooling system. It was sandwiched between the block face and oil filter housing – which had a bare, copper-coloured finish and wore a white part-number sticker. An orange Fram disposable oil filter was generally screwed on by Cosworth, although it's possible that white Ford Motorcraft filters were also used; they were certainly fitted by dealers when servicing Sierras.

A gold-passivated oil sender was screwed in towards the rear of the crankcase, which also fed the turbo via a steel braided hose. A yellow-painted, wire-handled, Transit-type dipstick

That's what it was all about – large Garret T03 turbocharger sat alongside Cosworth's remarkable 16-valve cylinder head, topped with textured red cam cover and a couple of legendary logos.

dropped into the sump via a metal tube at the nearside rear.

There was a simple breather system, venting from the side of the crankcase beneath the inlet manifold, into a condensing unit, then through small valves and into the airbox.

At the front of the engine was a large, black, three-groove crank pulley, fastened with a big gold-passivated bolt. It linked belts to the upper (camshaft) pulleys, along with various ancillaries.

The YBB was held in place with engine mounts bolted to a new crossmember. The right-hand-side mount was a unique alloy part with an XR4i rubber insulator, while the left-hand side was Pinto-based. Gold-passivated bolts and black washers held them to the cylinder block, with passivated washers used between insulator and mount. A red paint splash was marked on the black metallic section.

Cylinder head

Cosworth's genius was found in the YBB's 16-valve aluminium alloy cylinder head, which was designed for pure power even in its intended normally-aspirated guise. It had twin belt-driven overhead camshafts, four valves per cylinder and spark plugs mounted centrally in a 50cc pent-roof combustion chamber.

Each head was cast at Cosworth's foundry in Worcester, featuring Ford's 86HF6090AA part number. It was mounted

to the cylinder block with ten bolts, which initially used smaller (21.5mm) washers than the 23mm versions found in later engines. It's reckoned that the first 400 YBBs wore a head with these smaller seats, and all were fitted to early 1986-production three-door Sierras.

Between the head and block was a Pinto-type gasket but with revised openings to match the Cosworth head. When head gasket failure became common in mid-1986, after more than 4000 engines had been produced, a factory recall fitted a revised cylinder head gasket featuring a metal Omega ring, along with a new tapered head bolt.

Inside the head, four valves per cylinder were arranged in a vee, with inlet and exhaust valves opposite each other. Inlet valves had a head diameter of 35-to-35.2mm, while the sodium-cooled exhaust valves had 31-to-31.2mm heads. The valves were operated by their own respective camshafts via hydraulic lifters; both cams had a lift of 8.544mm.

Valve identification was stamped in 5mm characters on the rear end of the cylinder head, indicating oversized valve guides, seats and tappets; oversized tappets were also recorded by an A stamped on the cylinder head adjacent to the tappet bore.

The YBB's twin cams were turned by the crank via a Uniroyal-supplied glassfibre-reinforced toothed rubber belt (wearing white printed lettering) and pulleys sourced from the Escort CVH engine, finished in bare metal and held on with gold-passivated bolts. The belt tensioner was a grey alloy component, also attached with gold-passivated bolts.

The whole mechanism was encased in a unique, textured black plastic timing belt cover, which had a yellow 'check oil daily' sticker on top. It was attached using three black Torx-headed bolts and gold-passivated washers.

Topping the lot was an alloy cam cover, affixed with 20 bolts. It was finished in satin red to give a sand-cast effect as determined by Ford; Cosworth sources said they, "Had to buy paint with lumps in." Once painted, the heads were skimmed to reveal the legendary 'DOHC 16-V TURBO Ford COSWORTH' lettering. The exposed metal was bare alloy – complete with casting marks – and not coated in lacquer. All three-door RS Cosworths were fitted with cam covers designed for a black plastic bayonet-cap-type oil filler.

It's also worth noting that all rear-wheel-drive RS Cosworth cylinder heads (as fitted to YBB engines) were cast with provision for a turbo vibration damper on the exhaust side – a U-shaped extension on the head with two threaded holes. Similarly, the three-door head was cast with two drilled holes for the thermostat housing.

Gold-passivated lifting brackets were mounted onto the cylinder head on the nearside front and offside rear manifold studs. A rubber hose connected to the coolant header tank passed through the eye of the front bracket.

Cooling system

Keeping the Cosworth cool wasn't going to be an easy task, so a whole new system was developed for the turbocharged Sierra. Well, mainly new anyway.

The standard 1985 Sierra 2.0 Pinto water pump was mildly revised, with more vanes; it was finished in black and attached to the engine with gold-passivated bolts. Above the pump was an 88-degree wax thermostat inside a two-bolt alloy housing, complete with outlets for a bleed hose and coolant feed pipe to the turbocharger.

The pump was turned by the crank using a matched pair of belts that also spun the alternator. It circulated coolant through a combination of hard metal pipes and black rubber hoses with white-printed part numbers, attached with Ford-branded Jubilee-type clips. A mixture of new and stock Sierra hoses was used, such as unique heater inlet and outlet pipes that fed a standard matrix assembly; at the cylinder head (behind the inlet manifold) they linked to a stub from a removable coolant temperature sensor housing with two-bolt flange.

A large new radiator featured an aluminium core and black plastic end tanks, and was fitted complete with black plastic shroud that encased a pair of electrically-driven cooling fans (again, black plastic), operated by a thermal switch. A clear/white plastic header tank was mounted on the nearside inner wing, wearing a black plastic pressure cap and black-on-white decal. There were three outlets: at the lower end, the radiator

feed; the top came back from the turbo; in the middle, a coolant level sensor was screwed into place, feeding a warning lamp on the dashboard.

Most notably, the RS Cosworth was equipped with an air-to-air intercooler between the turbo and inlet manifold. It was mounted above the radiator and linked with hoses at each end (black rubber on the cold side, and terracotta silicone to the turbo). The intercooler was fed with air through the front grille (between the headlamps), while a guide plate behind the bumper directed cold air from the lower vents towards the radiator. Warm air then exited through the bonnet vents, which effectively maintained low intake temperatures.

Fuel System

Weber-Marelli multi-point fuel injection and electronic management was selected for the Sierra RS instead of Ford's normal preference for Bosch; this was due to Cosworth founder Keith Duckworth's relationship with the Italian manufacturers (Weber and Magneti-Marelli) in Formula 1.

A 60mm throttle body sat below Cosworth's alloy inlet manifold and plenum chamber; adjustable Weber fuel pressure regulator coupled into the rail on a terracotta-coloured hose.

A new alloy inlet manifold was bolted onto the cylinder head, connected to a bare alloy plenum chamber. Attached were a variety of components, including a 60mm throttle body on a separate elbow, which was supported by a bracket from the engine mounting and fastened with three pairs of dished washers. A throttle position sensor was bolted to the throttle body, and an idle speed control valve was mounted on top.

The plenum was also home to an inlet air temperature sensor, plus vacuum connectors for the MAP sensor, air charge bypass valve, fuel pressure regulator and crankcase ventilation filter.

Affixed to the top was a bright nickel-finished fuel rail feeding four yellow Weber plug-in injectors (one per cylinder), with a bare alloy adjustable Weber fuel pressure regulator on the front end joined with terracotta-coloured rubber connection tube. Gold-passivated brackets linked to a new throttle cable on right-hand-drive cars, while left-hookers used a Pinto 1.3 cable.

Petrol was directed to the fuel rail through steel pipes beneath the car in white plastic clips, with hard plastic in the engine bay and a braided rubber return. The fuel pump – a Bosch 941, which was the same as the part found on contemporary Escort XR3is – was finished in bare metal and mounted within

a satin black-painted bracket alongside a bare-metal fuel filter, connected with braided hoses. Above them, a stock Sierra petrol tank (painted silver) housed an internal swirl pot; the sender was from a standard fuel-injection-engined Sierra.

Inlet air was fed in via a black plastic airbox mounted at the offside front of the engine bay, with lid wearing a yellow sticker and secured by five metal clips. It passed air to the turbo through a large black rubber induction hose, which was printed with white part numbers and secured at each end with a Jubilee-type clip wearing a stamped Ford logo. Inside was a paper air filter element.

The airbox also had two outlets on the side – one for a large rubber hose that linked to the inlet manifold, and the other a black plastic pipe that linked to the air bypass valve.

Exhaust system

Cosworth never intended to fit a turbocharger to the Sierra, but Ford knew forced induction was the way to guarantee motorsport success. It was also clear that only a large turbo would be man enough for the boost pressures that were essential for victory. Let's not forget, the three-door RS Cosworth's

Garrett T3 turbo had 55-trim compressor wheel and 0.48 exhaust housing; it mounted on this two-piece manifold.

reason for existence was motorsport homologation, and the turbo was a huge factor in the scheme.

The unit selected was a water-cooled Garrett AiResearch T03, specced by Cosworth from the T3 range with a 0.48 exhaust housing and 55-trim compressor wheel. It featured an internal wastegate, connected by a rod to an actuator mounted above on a bolted bracket; the actuator had a gold-passivated finish with a 'caution' sticker on the rim; it was coupled up to a hard plastic pipe with a short braided hose and green clip, which in turn connected to an Amal valve (boost control solenoid) atop the intercooler. For road use, boost was set at 8psi (0.55 bar).

Air reached the turbo through a large black rubber hose from the airbox, then out through a terracotta-coloured silicone hose connected to the intercooler. From the cold-air side of the intercooler (the nearside), a black rubber hose linked to the throttle body; all were attached using Ford-stamped Jubilee-type clips.

A black plastic Bosch bypass valve (AKA dump valve) fitted beside the intercooler and connected to the airbox, inlet hose and inlet plenum via black plastic pipes, black hoses with white lettering and Jubilee-type clips.

An oil supply to the turbo was fed from the main oil gallery through a steel-braided hose from the engine's oil pressure warning switch adaptor. An oil return was connected into the sump through a stub pipe. Meanwhile, a (water) coolant feed pipe was routed from the thermostat housing, and a return hard pipe was mounted above the engine, affixed to brackets from the timing belt cover, and connected to the header tank via a rubber hose fed through an engine lifting eye.

The turbo was mounted on a long two-piece heat-resistant nickel-iron exhaust manifold comprising primary and secondary sections. The manifold was fastened to the cylinder head on 8mm studs, while M8 studs were used on the downpipe flange. Towards the end of three-door Sierra production, these weak fittings were swapped for 10mm (M10) versions. A simple coil-sprung turbo vibration damper was unfinished in bare metal, and connected a bracket on the turbo to the cylinder head in the foremost tapped hole. A foil heat shield was attached to the engine bay with three bolts.

Gases were forced from the manifold into a large-bore exhaust system comprising a front downpipe, front silencer, dual pipework into two centre boxes and back into a single rear silencer. The factory-fitted exhaust was a single piece, but Ford service replacements were supplied in four sections. Hanging rubbers were regular Pinto-engined Sierra parts.

Ignition system

Weber-Marelli supplied the Cosworth's electronic ignition and programmed control system, operating through a variety of sensors.

The engine's ECU (electronic control unit) was mounted behind the dashboard, above the passenger glovebox and

Underside of original RS Cosworth, showing alloy sump, bulky T5 gearbox and convoluted route of twin-pipe exhaust system.

accessible through a clipped-in lid. Known as a level one (L1) ECU, it had a metal case with integral mounting flanges, a small, yellow CO adjustment screw on the front face, and part number W45.01. A 35-pin plug connected the ECU to the wiring loom, while a green, a blue and white cable, and a self-test connector were beside it.

Power was fed to the ECU from the battery via a relay in the fuse box, found in the engine bay. The power relay had a brown socket, and there was also a fuel pump relay (with a yellow socket) and the car's ATO standard fuses.

The Cosworth's distributor was a Marelli breakerless unit with automatic advance controlled by the ECU. It was sited under the inlet manifold, and was driven by a skew gear from an auxiliary shaft. Thanks to the distributor's height and position, it used an angled distributor cap (black plastic) with leads pointing backwards; the leads themselves were black silicone with yellow crow's-foot tabs. The leads dipped through the rocker cover onto centrally-located AGPR901C spark plugs. Meanwhile, the king lead connected to a Motorcraft high-output breakerless ignition coil, in a gold-

Ford factory line drawings from 1985 show exactly where everything was meant to be; interestingly, the glass sunroof was omitted from illustrations, so was it a last-minute decision to include the part as standard on UK-destined cars?

passivated finish with large red decal. The coil was encased in a bare metal bracket just in front of the battery tray. A Marelli ignition module was mounted on a bare metal bracket on the inner wing behind the nearside suspension tower.

A mass of sensors fed information back to the ECU, including a red PF01 throttle position sensor (TPS) fitted to the throttle shaft. A black plastic manifold absolute pressure (MAP) sensor lived on a metal bracket on the nearside inner wing and was connected to the plenum chamber by a hose; the bracket was generally a single-piece item but some three-doors were reported to be fitted as standard with the RS500's later two-piece part.

There was an air charge temperature (ACT) sensor screwed into the plenum, an idle speed control valve lived above the throttle body, an engine speed/TDC sensor bolted to the engine beneath the crankshaft pulley, an engine coolant temperature (ECT) sensor screwed into the cylinder head and a boost pressure control solenoid (known as an Amal valve) coupled by hose to the high-pressure side of the turbo and mounted above the intercooler; its white top had a two-pin electrical connector, while the sides had three braided hoses attached into hard black plastic pipes – one to the airbox, one to the inlet and another to the wastegate actuator.

Electrical system

The Cosworth's wiring loom was in two main sections – one part for the engine and another for the body, with a revised fly plug in August 1986. The engine loom was unique to the Cosworth, but the rest was taken from the 2.0i Ghia. It was all wrapped in Ford's usual black loom tape with a mixture of clips, plugs and connectors.

All the other cables were also taken from regular Sierras; the battery leads and battery-to-starter motor cable were the same as V6 models, for example.

The battery itself was a white/clear Motorcraft 60Ah with square terminals and no plastic cover on top. The starter motor was a three-bolt Bosch DW with 1.4Kw output, finished in black.

A bare-aluminium Bosch 90-amp alternator was found at the offside front of the engine, driven by twin belts from the crank pulley. It sat on a substantial black bracket and, at the top, wore a slotted black adjusting plate.

Like normal Sierras, the Cosworth's large black plastic fuse box was found at the rear of the engine bay, beneath the scuttle panel on the driver's side and adjacent to the wiper motor and mechanism. Inside the removable lid was a collection of standard ATO fuses and relays.

Transmission

With all that torque under the bonnet, the Sierra RS Cosworth required a tough transmission. Indeed, despite being sourced from America – where it was well proven in V8-engined machines – the chosen Borg-Warner T5 was initially found lacking when mated to the four-cylinder YBB. A lubrication fault caused bearing seizures during high-speed testing, which delayed RS Cosworth production for several months; in the end it dictated a separate assembly line for suitably-tweaked Cosworth-destined gearboxes.

The Borg-Warner T5 was an all-alloy five-speed gearbox with synchromesh on all gears except reverse. The standard internal ratios were first gear: 2.95:1; second: 1.94:1; third: 1.34:1; fourth: 1:1; overdrive fifth: 0.80:1; reverse: 2.76:1.

First to fourth and reverse gears were found inside the main transmission case, while fifth gear and synchroniser were located in the extension housing on the back of the 'box, operated by an intermediate lever on a pivot pin. Shift forks for first-to-second and third-to-fourth were mounted in the shift cover, which was an assembly extending from the extension housing turret. The shift detent was in the extension housing, consisting of detent plate, selector crank and spring-loaded ball.

The tail of the gearbox was held in place by a unique satin-black steel crossmember attached to the car's floorpan, with a rubber mount connecting it to the T5.

An aluminium bellhousing linked to the cylinder block, covering a new Cosworth-designed steel flywheel, which was balanced with the crankshaft. It was about 25mm larger in diameter than the normal Pinto flywheel, and fitted with nine retaining bolts rather than the previous six.

There was also a heavy-duty clutch assembly, featuring a 9.5in (242mm) diaphragm single-plate clutch with uprated disc, pressure plate and intermediate plate. In left-hand-drive RS Cosworths a regular Sierra 2.0 cable mechanism was used,

but in RHD cars there was a unique cable.

Power was transferred to the rear axle using a two-piece propshaft, painted satin black, attached with blue Torx-headed bolts, and supported in the centre by a ball bearing encased in a rubber insulator that was bolted to the floorpan. It featured three heavy-duty universal joints sourced from the Ford Transit, and a unique reinforced rear section.

The prop turned a Scorpio V6-based 7.5in rear differential assembly (bare alloy) with viscous-coupling LSD (featuring the XR4Ti's 3.64:1 ratio) and rear axle crossmember, which was painted black and had modified mounting points for the Sierra. The differential was fitted to the floorpan with a rubber bush inside a gold-passivated mount.

The driveshafts and stubs were now larger and uprated, at 108mm rather than 100mm. Left bare metal, they wore black rubber gaiters with stainless clips, and mounted to the wheel hubs using blue Torx-headed bolts.

It's worth noting that the T5 had also been used effectively in Ford's turbocharged 2.3-litre Mustang SVO and Merkur XR4Ti (essentially a Stateside version of our Sierra XR4i but with forced induction), which Andy Rouse competed in the British Touring Car Championship until the Cosworth became homologated. This 'box was fitted to the very earliest (1985) Cosworths, complete with different ratios (fifth was 0.63:1) within a Mustang housing, attached on unique mounting lugs.

Suspension and steering

A real mixture of Sierra, Scorpio, specially-designed parts and revised geometry, the first RS Cosworth was a remarkably impressive car to drive, albeit twitchy at speed.

At the front there was the usual independent setup with MacPherson struts (Motorcraft-branded, in black with blue stickers), here incorporating unique Fichtel and Sachs gas-filled twin-tube dampers and lowered 19kg/Nm coil springs (in black with white paint splashes) but with stock Sierra top mounts. At the bottom, the Cosworth struts coupled up to new cast-iron hub carriers and suspension knuckles (left bare), which raised the front roll centre by 92mm to 143mm to meet Group A motorsport requirements; inside, the front wheel bearings, dust seals and caps were taken from the Scorpio.

Revised track control arms (housing larger inner bushes and 12mm rather than 10mm bolts) swung from a new steel crossmember, and at the outer end fastened to the steering knuckles with tapered ball joints and castellated nuts rather than the pinch bolts of later Cosworth models. The arms were also linked by a new 28mm anti-roll bar, which fastened to the Sierra floorpan with Scorpio bushes and attachments, finished in satin black. Yellow paint was dabbed onto the nuts and bolts to confirm they'd been tightened to the correct settings.

Prototypes and 1985 press cars were fitted with solid plastic inner pivot bushes on the track control arms, but they were soon swapped for rubber versions. Criticism of high-speed steering feel then led to the availability of a revised front anti-roll bar for German customers. Likewise, towards the end of three-door Sierra production, the original front anti-roll bar (with H13 stamped beside the track control arm mounting on the offside) was replaced by this reshaped H14 version, which moved the wheels further forwards and increased the castor angle by about one degree; some earlier cars were retrofitted with the H14 but all late-built Sierra Cosworths and subsequent Sapphires received this part at the factory.

The Sierra three-door's steering was closely related to the standard Sierra rack-and-pinion system, being almost identical to other PAS-equipped models but for a revised ratio and minor bearing differences. The Cam Gears rack was now 2.6 turns lock to lock; it had a gold-passivated finish, and had black rubber gaiters clipped onto each end where it adjoined bare-metal track rod ends.

A standard Sierra steering column and lock were fitted to the Cosworth, with GL/Ghia/XR4i horn button switch wire. The power steering pump – a satin black-painted unit as found on standard Sierras and Granadas – was attached to a black bracket with gold-passivated bolts, and mounted on a heavy bracket that was fitted to the cylinder block using a pair of M10 bolts. It was driven by a single belt from the crankshaft pulley. The PAS fluid reservoir was a stock Sierra component, in white/clear plastic with a black screw cap. It was mounted in the nearside front corner of the engine bay alongside the washer fluid reservoir.

At the back of the three-door RS Cosworth was another collection of Sierra, Scorpio and bespoke components. The regular independent rear suspension layout remained, but with modified Scorpio rear beam and rubber bushes; XR4x4 gas-filled single-tube Fichtel and Sachs telescopic dampers; unique lowered 47kg/Nm coil springs (in black, often with yellow and green paint splashes) over white bump-stops; XR4i-type trailing arms but with special uniball joints in place of the usual voided rubber bushes; XR4x4 14mm rear

anti-roll bar and brackets reaching outside the rear arms; rear axle shafts and driveshaft hubs unique to the Cosworth. All except the hubs were finished in black, with the hubs left bare.

Brakes

When it came to stopping its 150mph Sierra, Ford wasn't messing around. The Cosworth's brake setup was far better than anything we'd seen before on a Blue Oval saloon, and in use it was very effective.

At the front, a pair of 283mm x 24.15mm ventilated discs were clamped by Teves four-piston callipers in a gold-zinc finish, complete with Ford Motorcraft pads. The rear was equipped with 273mm x 10.2mm solid discs and Sierra XR4x4-type gold-zinc-finished floating callipers on new carriers; again, Motorcraft pads were used. The black steel splash shields were also unique to the Cosworth but the standard Sierra handbrake lever was coupled to an XR4x4 cable.

The RS Cosworth also benefited from a front/rear split dual-circuit braking system with vacuum servo assistance and the twin-microprocessor Teves Mk2 electronic ABS arrangement as found in Granadas, Scorpios and other ABS-equipped Sierras.

There was a Granada gold-passivated brake booster assembly and alloy single-piston master cylinder attached to the bulkhead in front of the driver, plus black-painted electronic pump. Above the master cylinder was a clear/white plastic brake fluid reservoir, featuring a white plastic screw cap with electrical connections, plus a yellow warning sticker on the body.

The tank was equipped with a yellow warning sticker, and so was the black accumulator, which sat on the right of the reservoir (left when viewed from the front), which also wore a selection of yellow manufacturing stamps.

A gold-passivated actuation assembly was fitted to the nearside inner wing (or the bulkhead on left-hand-drive cars) and connected the brake lines, which were Ford's regular green-coated steel with rubber flexible hoses from the XR4x4. At the engine crossmember, the brake pipe-to-hose connection was screwed and held on with clips, unlike the subsequent Sapphire, which was slotted.

Scorpio-sourced ABS sensors and toothed rotors were at all four wheels, with the rears mounted in the end castings of the suspension arms. The ABS's control unit, relays and fuses were found in the driver's footwell behind the kick panel.

Wheels and tyres

With wide wheelarch extensions designed to take huge racing rims and slick tyres, the road-going RS Cosworth needed some substantial rubber to look the part. Okay, the factory-fitted Dunlop D40 VR15 205/50x15 tyres are tiny by today's standards, but in 1985 they were much bigger than the tyres found on the majority of sports cars.

The contemporary D40s – as fitted to three-door RS

Cosworths – were recognisable by a tread depth indicator running all the way around the central groove of the tyre, which had been deleted by the point of Sapphire production.

Original Sierra RS Cosworth alloy wheels were produced by Rial, sized 7Jx15in with an ET40mm offset. They were finished in Nimbus Grey, with diamond-cut and lacquered spokes. Each had a locking centre cap complete with raised Ford oval logo and one small key for the entire set.

RS Cosworth alloys were cast in the centres with their size,

Ford logo, part number (V86BB-AA) and date of production, which was usually a very similar month to the car's build date. They were held onto the car with a set of alloy wheel nuts incorporating rotating conical washers.

A full-size spare alloy wheel and D40 tyre were installed in the Sierra's luggage compartment, lacking the centre cap. Ford also offered a 5.5x15in steel wheel option for winter tyres, which it's fair to assume was destined for overseas markets and not the UK's annual day or two of snow.

Within the alloy wheels' locking centre caps were the part numbers and date stamps, which invariably pre-dated the car by a month or two.

Original Dunlop D40s had this tread depth indicator running around the centre of the tyre.

Sekurit tinted glass was fitted as standard, wearing date code from several months before the car was built. Here, the 6 represents 1986 and the three dots mean March of that year.

Mesh air intake between headlamps was added during testing to feed the intercooler and aid inlet temperatures..

Body

Iconic. Attention-grabbing. Trendsetting. All words that hold as true for the RS Cosworth today as they did when it was launched in the mid 1980s.

Yet it came from such humble beginnings. The Sierra supercar was based on the bottom-of-the-range three-door hatchback, previously available only in 1.3 and 1.6-litre versions and discontinued in the UK during 1984.

But Ford found the basic three-door body to be lighter and less fussy than the proposed XR4i four-pillar design, and it was finalised for production with few modifications to the shell. Most notable differences were a replacement bulkhead (pressed to accept the ABS-equipped car's brake servo mountings), broader transmission tunnel (which bowed out towards the front footwell) and a straight front towing eye, unlike the standard Sierra's twisted version.

In fact, the whole front lower crossmember was unique to the RS Cosworth, as was the body-coloured polycarbonate

Polycarbonate wheelarch extensions were screwed into pressed slots in the factory bodywork. They easily covered the standard Rial 7x15in alloy wheels.

headlamp surround/grille section, which was based on the Ghia version but incorporated a meshed single-slot intake. It was attached with regular Sierra screws, clips and brackets, wore a standard dark blue Ford oval badge and used the usual 1766mm gasket between itself and the front wings.

Beneath, the front bumper was unique to the original RS Cosworth. It was made from polycarbonate by Phoenix in Hamburg, and incorporated an integral air dam and brake cooling slots. The finish was body-coloured with black insert. A flexible rubber splitter was attached to the bottom.

The RS Cosworth's front wings were almost identical to standard Sierra panels but for small pre-stamped slots around the wheelarches, bunged with square plastic expansion nuts. Body-coloured polycarbonate wheelarch extensions, designed to cover 11in-wide race tyres, were affixed to the wings with double-sided tape and M5 round-headed self-tapping screws into the expansion nuts. Body-coloured plastic caps were fitted over the screw heads, while body-coloured jacking point covers were included behind the front wheels.

Polycarbonate side skirts linked to the front wheelarch extensions, clipped over the Sierra's sill edges and pop-riveted to the inner sill from above. They linked into rear wheelarch extensions, which echoed the fronts – attached with double-sided tape and M5 self-tappers through factory-pressed square slots in the rear quarter panels. Again, there were body-coloured screw caps and jacking covers.

The back bumper looked similar to a standard Sierra part but was totally different, being formed from two pieces and made from smooth polycarbonate, painted body-colour. That said, the upper section was taken from the XR4i, and the bumper attached on regular Sierra brackets. A black insert was included in the bumper, regardless of body colour.

The black insert was repeated within the black plastic

Plastic door handles and door lock surrounds were the same as every other Sierra, and equally easy for thieves to overwhelm.

Twin cooling vents were dropped into a specially-pressed Sierra bonnet, each affixed on four screws from below.

Polycarbonate cooling vents were essential for assisting air temperatures on turbocharged racers running 300bhp-plus, and even proved worthwhile on modified road cars.

Basic three-door Sierra bodyshell was used, but Cosworths were all based on the post-1984 design, which included two-screw striker plate on the B-pillar.

bodyside mouldings, attached to the front wings, doors and rear quarters.

The doors themselves were regular Sierra panels, but it's worth noting that the Cosworth incorporated a different striker pin and reinforcement on the B-pillars from the parts found on base-model UK three-door shells; these bits (with two-screw fitting) were revisions to mainstream Sierras in August 1984, rather than RS-specific.

The door handles were the usual black textured plastic, while the door mirrors were Ghia-spec, electrically-adjustable and heated, with body-coloured housings. As for the door locks, they too were standard minimum-security Ford equipment, with black plastic bezels. Central locking was included (except on motorsport shells and a few foreign cars), operating on the doors and tailgate from flat (pre-Chubb) Ford keys with black handles, one of which was a push-button torch key. All were the same fitting for the doors, tailgate, ignition and petrol cap; Sierra three-doors had a removable, three-pronged filler cap in the offside rear quarter, painted in body colour.

The RS Cosworth's bonnet was modelled on the regular Sierra panel, but was a new pressing with cutouts for the twin polycarbonate cooling vents, which were bolted in from below. There was no insulation applied to the underside of the bonnet.

The normal black plastic slatted scuttle panel cover surrounded a pair of satin black metal windscreen wipers, with a small spoiler on the driver's-side wiper arm, as found on the XR4i. The wipers were controlled by a two-speed switch, with variable intermittent facility. Meanwhile, the electric washers fed nozzles in the plastic scuttle panel from an electric pump mounted on the front of the fluid reservoir.

A laminated bronze-tinted front windscreen was fitted as standard, with no option of heating element seen in the later Sapphire. RS Cosworth side windows were also bronze-tinted;

Original three-eared fuel cap was colour-coded to the bodywork, and operated using the ignition key.

Incredible rear wing was the result of many hours' wind tunnel testing, resulting in positive downforce to deal with 150mph maximum speed – and faster still in race tune.

the door glass was electrically operated using a Sierra Ghia-type five-door motor with regulator mechanism specific to the three-door. That applied to all UK-supplied RS Cosworths, although motorsport machines and several European/left-hand-drive examples were fitted with manual windows. The rear quarter glass was fixed; all the rubbers were standard Sierra parts, with black inserts and covers.

A stock Sierra heated rear window was used, again with bronze-tinted glass. It was cleaned by a single black-coated rear wiper and motor from Bosch, as found in other Sierras; the fluid reservoir was mounted within the passenger-side rear quarter panel, and there was a black plastic nozzle in the top of the tailgate – itself based on a regular Ford Sierra panel but with unique drillings for the rear wing. A silver decal declaring 'Sierra RS Cosworth' was applied to the nearside of the tailgate, with a Ford dark blue oval badge on the offside. Unlike the RS500, there was no pinstripe.

There was a centrally-mounted black boot lock surround and

push-button assembly, as found on other Sierras. The tailgate's gas struts were shared with the XR4i and XR4x4.

Most importantly, of course, the Cosworth was equipped with an enormous single-pole rear wing, finished in body colour except for a satin black lip. It was attached to the tailgate using five M5 retaining screws and two rivets, with seven body-coloured screw covers.

An electrically-operated radio aerial was mounted in the driver's-side rear quarter at the base of the C-pillar. It was controlled by a cable from the back of the stereo head unit.

Road-going Sierra RS Cosworths were fitted with a tilting/sliding tinted-glass sunroof as standard, mounted within a regular Sierra roof panel (all were the same, whether three-door or five-door fitment). That said, a sunroof was a commonly-fitted optional extra in some overseas markets, and a number of left-hand-drive Sierra Cosworths were factory-supplied with plain roofs.

Generally, though, non-sunroof Sierra Cosworth bodyshells were produced for motorsport use. Such shells lacked seam sealer in the usual places but featured all the correct Cosworth brackets and pressings. There was also a batch of lightweight Group A bodies built by Ford in 1989, known as 909 shells due to their 909-prefix part numbers; again, they were purely for motorsport use and lacked sunroofs.

Sierra bodies were dipped in an electronically-impregnated cataphoretic primer, with topcoat paintwork in thermoplastic acrylic for solid colours (Diamond White and Black) or polyester basecoat and clear coat for metallics. Their undersides were left in the cataphoretic primer (similar to Dove Grey or Purbeck Grey), with sealer sprayed or brushed onto high-impact areas and overlap joints. Top coat was wafted under the sills and wheelarches (which also housed black plastic liners), while the spare wheel well and rear towing eye were generally sprayed in satin black, although

Colour-coded Sierra Ghia-spec door mirrors were electrically adjustable and heated.

some original cars were seen with gloss black or primer with traces of topcoat overspray. Inside the car, the floorpan was also finished in grey primer, although Diamond White cars were white everywhere.

Underbonnet

It's hard to notice anything in a Sierra Cosworth's engine bay, other than the magnificent 16-valve, turbocharged powerplant. And that's not really surprising, considering almost everything else was taken from the standard Sierra.

The bulkhead was specific to ABS-equipped cars (such as the 1985-on XR4x4), featuring an inverted-key-shaped cutout for the brake servo with four bolt mounting holes, and an opening for the engine wiring loom to pass into the car. Attached to the bulkhead were a large, black/dark grey insulator pad, hard plastic trim and flexible rubber edge protector from the Sierra 2.0iS. The engine wiring loom ran along the bulkhead in black plastic clips, while in front of the insulator (on the driver's side) was the brake fluid reservoir, along with a foil-backed turbo heat shield attached on a unique bracket with three bolts.

Behind the bulkhead and beneath the scuttle panel were the body-coloured bonnet hinges, bolts and washers, painted while already attached to the car; an earth strap ran from battery to the nearest hinge. There was also a regular Sierra fuse box – a large, black plastic item sitting on the driver's side, next to the wiper motor and mechanism. In the opposite corner – but in front of the bulkhead – was a body-coloured battery tray, containing a square-post white/clear Motorcraft battery.

Standard Sierra inner wings were used, finished in body colour, with round suspension turrets topped with bare metal plates and black plastic caps. In front, on the nearside, was the coolant header tank – a clear/white plastic component wearing a black plastic pressure cap and black-on-white decal on its horizontal surface. Standard Ford clear/white plastic tanks for the power steering fluid and windscreen washer fluid were in the nearside corner of the engine bay, both wearing black plastic caps.

Each outer front wing was date-stamped on the rail where it was welded to the inner wing, a few inches down from the bonnet hinges. The date was stamped by hand when the shell was being constructed, so most three-door RS Cosworths said 86, along with a number for the week of production – generally within a month of the car's build date. There was also a Ford logo stamped into original wings, alongside where they were spot-welded to the bonnet slam panel.

The Cosworth's slam panel was again taken from the standard Sierra, wearing a red asbestos-warning decal, the VIN tag, and a yellow brake system warning sticker on the offside (working from middle out). The black-coated bonnet prop rotated within a clear washer, connecting to a black plastic holder on the bonnet's underside; in the centre was a black-coated bonnet lock and release mechanism, activated by a black plastic-coated cable running along the driver's side inner wing in clips, then through the bulkhead into the cabin.

The slam panel was also stamped with a Ford code, while at each end of the panel was a white plastic stopper, capped with a black rubber insulator. Each front wing rail featured a black rubber insulator pad.

Ghia-spec dual horns were attached to the body crossmember, behind the front bumper and at each side of the lower air intake.

Lighting

Being based on the Sierra Ghia meant the RS Cosworth came equipped with Ford's finest lighting arrangement, including 60/55W halogen H4 headlamps with integral driving lamps. The units were built to Ford requirements by Lucas and Cibie, and both types were fitted to three-door Cosworths on the production line. Carello subsequently took over the contract to make lamp units as official Ford spares.

Beneath the headlamps, a pair of 55W H3 halogen fog lamps were mounted within the front bumper, in clear glass with Ford logo (amber lamps were listed for the German market). The fog lamps were originally seen on the Sierra XR4i.

Beside the fog lamps were the Sierra's 21W indicators, which

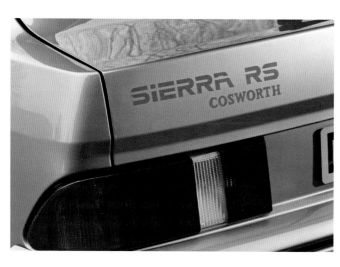

Headlamps, indicators and fog lamps came directly from the Sierra XR4i. The bumper's functional cooling slots were essential for track work.

RS Cosworth rear lights were the same as the lenses on any old Sierra, and equally prone to earthing problems too...

Ghia levels of luxury were chosen for the RS Cosworth, including cut-pile carpets and Raven-coloured velour upholstery.

Early-style RS logo adorned the ECU cover, which clipped out of the passenger side of the Cosworth's dashboard.

wore orange plastic lenses, and were the same parts as those found on the Ghia, mounted on the same fixings. British-bound Cosworths had square 5W orange plastic side repeaters on the front wings, above the rubbing strips behind the front wheels. Repeaters weren't required for some markets – such as Germany – so these cars went without.

Standard Sierra rear lights were used, and again sourced from a variety of manufacturers, including Hella and Lucas; it's probable that Hella was most common on the Cosworth. The rear clusters incorporated fog lamps and reversing lights at each side. A pair of number plate lamps were recessed into the rear bumper.

Inside, the Cosworth's courtesy lamps were again taken from the Ghia, including map lights in an overhead console and a single load compartment lamp.

Interior

Ghia trim level was specified for the RS Cosworth (for the UK, at least), which included such luxuries as electrically-operated front windows and additional soundproofing.

Most importantly, though, the Cosworth added better front seats, in the form of Recaro LS recliners finished in Ford's Roma and Cashmere grey cloth trim. The driver's seat had height adjustment via a wheel under the front, while each seat boasted sliding base extensions, adjustable head rests, silver-

A perfect driving position – the three-spoke leather-rimmed steering wheel looked perfect and gave fabulous feedback too.

High-spec Mk1 Sierra graphic information module and digital clock with stopwatch sat above fancy ECU2 sound system with radio/cassette head unit and separate power amplifier.

on-black Recaro badges, map pockets in the seat backs, and dual black plastic levers to tip the backrests for rear-seat access.

The rear bench was trimmed to match the front seats, in Roma and Cashmere grey cloth. It used an XR4x4 cushion, with 60/40 split backrest.

RS Cosworth door cards were also covered in Roma and Cashmere grey cloth along with Raven vinyl, and included grey carpeted front door bins. The door panels incorporated grey plastic handles, black plastic door release levers and locking mechanisms, attached with black screws; base-spec European cars had window winders too. The driver's door card was also home to the black plastic electric mirror control switch.

Meanwhile, the rear quarter panels received matching Raven vinyl/Roma and Cashmere grey cloth, along with black plastic ashtrays in each side.

The RS Cosworth three-door's dashboard was based on that of lesser Sierras, with one or two alterations. Its easy-split surround was finished in Shadow Grey plastic/vinyl, complete with centrally-mounted grey-plastic speaker grille recessed into a speakerless hole. At the passenger side was a removable cover wearing an old-style black RS logo in a shaped recess; removing the cover allowed access to the car's engine ECU. To the outside of the dashboard was a base/XR4i-spec plain black plastic adjustable heater vent, and above it a smaller rectangular vent for demisting the side window.

Recaro LS recliners were trimmed in Roma and Cashmere grey velour. Each base had sliding leg extensions, and the driver's seat boasted height adjustment too.

Recaro seat badges were the same as the emblems found in several sporty cars of the period, such as the Escort RS Turbo, Capri 2.8i, Vauxhall's Cavalier SRi and Opel's Manta GT/E.

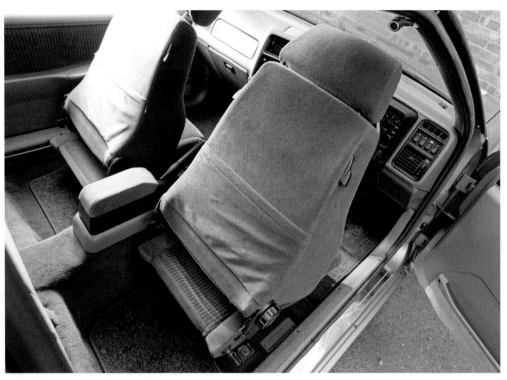

Map pockets were found in the front seat backrests; note the twin levers to tip the Recaros forward.

Split/folding rear seat was upholstered in Roma and Cashmere grey velour to match the Recaro fronts.

The passenger-side lower dashboard was made from a harder plastic than the top section, and incorporated a speaker grille (complete with speaker) alongside the main glovebox – a Shadow Grey plastic enclosure that hinged downwards by pressing its black plastic release button. Inside the glovebox was a grey-carpeted base and small, round light.

The middle of the dashboard was dominated by a pair of upper adjustable heater vents above a strip of warning lights – brake pad wear, low coolant level and low windscreen washer fluid level (all illuminated yellow) on the left, then low fuel (illuminated yellow) and engine management (illuminated red) on the right.

Below the warning lights was a three-button digital solid-state clock with green LEDs, to the right of which sat Ford's funky graphic information module, taken from the Sierra Ghia. Showing an illuminated overhead view of the Sierra, it advised on ice, bulb failures and doors or tailgate being open.

The lower fascia was home to the Sierra L/GL/Ghia's black plastic compartment for its three-speed illuminated heater fan control, ashtray and recessed/illuminated cigarette lighter, along with its audio equipment: Ford's ECU2 electronic sound system including radio/cassette head unit and separate power amplifier was standard in the UK but European examples lacked the amp, having a basic stereo plus four-speaker joystick control in the gap between fan switch and fag lighter.

The RS Cosworth's main instrument cluster was again Ghia-based, albeit with one or two alterations. The standard black plastic housing encased heater control sliders on the left, and a set of dials in front of the driver. A large rev counter featured white digits (0 to 7) and an orange needle; at the top left was a turbo boost gauge taken from the American Merkur XR4Ti. Meanwhile, a large 170mph speedometer was on the right; it was printed with white MPH digits, with smaller yellow KMH digits on the inside (well, that was the spec for UK cars; reverse it for other markets). The speedo also featured an orange needle, plus mileometer and trip recorder, reset by a button in the bottom of the dial. Smaller gauges sat between the rev counter and speedo – to the left a 60-litre fuel gauge with orange needle, and a coolant temperature gauge with orange needle on the right.

Below was a pair of yellow-illuminated ABS failure lamps, which were placed above a strip of warning lights for headlamp main beam, oil pressure, direction indicators, ignition/alternator and handbrake/brake failure.

Beneath the instrument cluster was, on the left, a fascia illumination dimmer control and, on the right, an intermittent speed controller for the windscreen wipers.

A further black plastic panel was situated to the right of the cluster, housing illuminated rocker switches for the rear wash/wipe, heated rear window, rear fog lamps and front fog lamps. Above them was a side-window demisting vent, while below was a base/XR4i-type adjustable heater vent, again in plain black plastic.

A hard grey plastic lower dashboard section housed the right-hand-side front speaker, small storage shelf and, to the driver's left leg, a small drop-down coin holder.

The usual Sierra black-plastic steering column shroud sprouted black stalks for indicators, main beam and headlamp flashers on the left-hand side, with one on the right for headlamps/sidelights and another for windscreen wipers and washers. Atop the shroud was a red push-button for the hazard warning flashers. To the outside was the ignition lock, operated from the same keys as the doors, tailgate and petrol cap. Underneath was an orange plastic lever to release the bonnet.

The RS Cosworth steering wheel was a slightly-dished

The door cards were trimmed to match the seats, in Roma and Cashmere grey cloth, Raven vinyl and carpeted door pockets. The electric mirror controls also resided on the driver's door.

Optimistic speedo? Maybe not – 170mph was easily achievable when a YBB engine was tuned.

Sliding/tilting glass sunroof was standard spec for all road-going Sierra RS Cosworths available in the UK. The Ghia-spec roof console included twin map reading lamps.

XR3i-style three-spoke with leather rim and centre horn push featuring a blue Ford oval badge. A matching black leather-covered gearknob was fitted with a polished black emblem featuring the five-speed shift pattern printed in white. There was a black rubber concertina-type gear lever gaiter, which was unique to the Cosworth; beneath it, there was a stock Sierra inner gaiter.

A black plastic gear lever surround was screwed into a Raven/Shadow Grey plastic centre console. Behind the

The RS Cosworth rear parcel shelf included a storage box, designed to accommodate a Ford first-aid kit for the German market.

gearstick was a pair of black plastic rocker switches for the electrically-operated front windows (standard on UK-bound cars but an optional extra in mainland Europe), which sat on a raised section above an oddments tray. A standard Sierra handbrake lever, incorporating black plastic handle and black push-button, sat inside a lidded storage box at the rear of the console; it was topped with an armrest trimmed in grey cloth, and housed cassette storage tape holders.

The pedal box was based on the regular Pinto 1.6/1.8/2.0-engined Sierra setup, including black levers and pedal rubbers; the only difference was its clip at the clutch cable.

Shadow Grey plastic kick panels were fitted at the side of each footwell, attached with black screws and overlapping unique black door rubbers. They connected to Shadow Grey plastic door scuff plates, which attached with black screws.

A Ghia-spec dark grey (Raven 86) carpet was used in the RS Cosworth, as also found in the XR4x4 (which also used the same transmission tunnel insulator beneath the carpet). There was a ribbed black driver's heel pad, and on the offside sill a Raven plastic flap with a cap covering the car's chassis number.

Seat belt rails ran along the back of the inner sills, with regular Sierra inertia-reel seat belts mounted on each B-pillar. The rear seat featured two lap/diagonal inertia reels and one centre static lap belt, again as found on all other 1986 Sierras.

RS Cosworth A-pillar trims were Shadow Grey plastic, while the B-pillar and C-pillar trims were Steel Grey 83 plastic, leading up to a Dawn Grey 86 Beaumont cloth velour headlining, as found on the XR4i from August 1985 onwards. Three grey grab handles were fitted for passengers; the driver's side received plastic plugs instead.

The standard Sierra black plastic dipping rear-view mirror was bonded to the top of the windscreen, flanked by a pair of black/grey sun visors from the Sierra L, GL, Laser and 2.0iS; the passenger's visor incorporated a vanity mirror.

All right-hand-drive road-going Sierra RS Cosworths were fitted with a glass sunroof, complete with sliding roof blind and winder handle assembly in Dawn Grey; some European cars were factory-fitted with a plain roof, the sunroof being a popular optional extra. A Ghia/XR4x4 overhead console was also fitted, also in Dawn Grey; it housed the courtesy light and individually-switched, swivelling map-reading lights.

Inside boot

Practicality was a happy side-effect of the RS Cosworth's basis being a standard three-door Sierra shell. And this meant the luggage compartment was just as cavernous as the hatchback you'd use for shopping trips. Well, almost.

A mild reduction in boot space was due to the inclusion of a full-size spare wheel – the Cosworth had a 7Jx15in Rial cross-spoke alloy in the well with Dunlop D40 VR15 205/50x15 tyre; it was finished in the same gunmetal grey with diamond-cut and lacquered spokes, lacking only the centre cap of the road wheels. The only difference was a balance weight on the

Just a humble family hatchback – the RS Cosworth was as practical as any run-of-the-mill Sierra, if a little heavier on the fuel consumption and insurance costs.

Insulating pad beneath boot mat raised the luggage compartment floor level to tolerate the ultra-wide 7x15in spare alloy wheel.

Original jack and wheelbrace were strapped into the rear panel with rubber bungees, accessed from inside the boot.

outside, rather than inside, of the rim. It was retained using a black metal eyelet screwed through one of the wheel's bolt holes. A steel wheel option was available for winter use in some markets, but it's doubtful that any UK cars were so equipped.

To accommodate the bulky spare wheel, the RS Cosworth's boot floor was artificially raised using a unique sponge pad, which lifted the boot mat to the same height. The carpet itself was special for the Cosworth, in Shadow Grey 86 with a black plastic handle; there were also matching carpeted rear seat backs visible in the luggage compartment. Plastic fasteners were in Shadow Grey 86.

There was a tilting/removable one-piece parcel shelf, trimmed in Shadow Grey 86 fabric, dangling from the tailgate on black rubber straps; the tailgate itself was assisted by black XR4i-type gas struts. In the corner of the parcel shelf was a dark grey hard plastic storage box, designed to accommodate a red first-aid kit; the kit was included only in certain markets (most notably Germany) but also offered to UK buyers as a Ford accessory. The shelf's side supports were Raven plastic.

Inside the tailgate, a grey plastic panel was clipped into place to cover the wiper mechanism. When closed, the tailgate was clasped by a standard Sierra boot latch. There was also a date stamp, giving the week and year of the shell's production.

Matching Raven 86 plastic trim panels surrounded the inner wheelarches inside the boot, and a similar, separate piece covered the electric aerial mechanism on the driver's side. A black plastic piece ran across the back panel; inside was a wheelbrace and T-shaped jack, fastened in with two rubber bungee cords of differing lengths.

A clear plastic courtesy lamp was clipped into the rear panel towards the nearside centre, and operated when the tailgate was lifted. The base of the passenger-side C-pillar housed a clear plastic cap for the Sierra's rear washer fluid reservoir, surrounded by a black grommet.

Colour schemes and interior trim

Colour	Code	Introduced	Discontinued	Decals	Interior colour
Diamond White	B	Launch	December 1986	Silver	Grey
Black	A	Launch	December 1986	Silver	Grey
Moonstone Blue	K	Launch	December 1986	Silver	Grey

Diamond White

Black

Moonstone Blue

SIERRA RS500 COSWORTH

Well-known and widely loved in the Ford RS world, this Diamond White RS500 was part of Mark Bailey's Bonkers Collection, and passed to a new custodian since the photographs were taken. Fastidiously clean and fantastically desirable, Mark's Sierra is build number 468, and has covered a mere 13,961 miles with full service history. There are very few RS500s in such amazing condition.

Motorsport legend. Somehow, the phrase doesn't sound significant enough for a car of this calibre. The Sierra RS500 Cosworth was the kind of machine that appears only once every generation. The type that redefines its breed. The sort that's talked of in hushed tones for decades to come.

The RS500 was built to win, and winning is what it did best. The RS500 was the most successful tin-top race car of all time, in terms of ratio of events entered to those it won. In Group A touring car racing, it scooped 40 outright victories in succession. It was so good that it was effectively banned by the sport's governing bodies before its development had even reached full swing.

Yet, unlike the majority of purpose-built competition machines that appeared since the Sierra's heyday, the RS500 was based pretty closely on a car the average consumer could stroll up to a showroom and buy – and, using a number of off-the-shelf components, that anyone with a big enough budget could order directly from the manufacturer.

The irony is that none of the motorsport Sierras that give this car its name were in fact official RS500s. The Ford Sierra RS500 Cosworth was always, without exception, a fully-trimmed road car, whereas RS500 racers were built from three-door Ford Motorsport shells, lacking sunroofs, seam sealer and suck like. The RS500 tag was merely the homologation-spec production version of the already-successful

Stock Sierra RS Cosworth bodykit was enhanced for the RS500 with extra tailgate lower spoiler and gurney flap on the rear wing, with RS500 stickers and pinstripe to remind buyers where the extra £4000 was being spent.

Sierra RS Cosworth – but now with added muscles.

When Ford began campaigning the three-door Sierra RS, there was no doubt that a stronger, more powerful version would be required for total racetrack domination. A version that, thanks to forced induction, aerodynamic developments and typical Ford brilliance, would be unbeatable.

Whereas 5000 examples of the original Sierra were required for initial homologation, Group A rules required a further production of 500 evolution models before they were allowed to compete. Each was forced to be equipped with the basic ingredients that were essential to improve the racing equivalent.

Increased performance was top of the list, and Keith Duckworth reckoned 500bhp (in race trim) would do the trick. The original YBB was clearly capable of big figures but Keith knew the ideal enhancements to reach the magical goal.

The Sierra's existing T03 turbocharger ran out of puff at high speeds, so a whopping T4 was specified, along with manifold revisions to increase airflow, and an enormous intercooler. The tuned-up touring car would need to feed on ocean-loads of petrol, so an extra bank of fuel injectors was designed to sit alongside the usual four; homologation rules said nothing about the functionality of factory-fitted parts, so Ford simply left the productionised injectors blanked off. The road-car's ECU wasn't even capable of triggering them.

A strengthened cylinder block was developed to handle sustained boost pressure, based on a stiffer casting of the 205 block, with thicker metal around the cylinder walls and

Even meaner than a regular RS Cosworth, the RS500's additional bumper scoop, wider vents and deeper splitter made a more menacing image in rear-view mirrors.

The same nose-down stance as a standard Sierra Cosworth, now exaggerated with the RS500's deeper front splitter and raised rear wing.

Enlarged RS500 rear wing and additional boot spoiler are obvious from this angle, making even a Sierra Cosworth appear tame in comparison.

smaller core plugs.

Ford manufactured the blocks at its West German foundry, which normally produced run-of-the-mill Pintos. They were then shipped to Cosworth in the UK, where around 650 complete new engines – now codenamed YBD – were built up, the majority between May and June 1987.

Cosworth also made minor alterations to the oil and water systems, tweaked the head (very mildly) to keep FISA (motorsport's governing body) inspectors happy, and adapted the ancillaries to fit around all those new components.

There was no doubt that the YBD would be capable of immense performance and, even though the regular RS Cosworth was equipped with wild aerodynamic aids, Ford now had the makings of a family saloon with the potential to outrun single-seat racers. Anything that could help high-speed stability would be a bonus.

So, in addition to the three-door's jaw-dropping bodykit, the RS500 gained an even wilder package, which was again produced by Phoenix in Hamburg. The whale-tail rear wing was modified to include a 30mm gurney flap, complemented by a rubber Sierra 2.0iS-style boot spoiler. At the front, the existing RS bumper was reworked with enlarged lower air intakes and an extra slat beneath the grille to feed the big intercooler, and a pair of vents were found in place of the usual fog lamps. There was also a deeper rubber splitter, which wrapped around the bumper's edges.

The standard car's drag coefficient was raised from 0.34 to an official figure of 0.345 (unofficially around 0.36) but there was now much greater downforce, increased by 20kg up front and 105kg at the back.

Experience on circuits also dictated substantial changes to the race car's rear suspension geometry, yet Ford found a cheap way to cheat the system – a pair of pretend brackets tacked onto the standard rear axle to suggest a suitable spot for attaching new trailing arms. The fact that they'd never work in practice meant nothing to achieving FISA's approval.

Would it have hurt Ford to equip the road-going RS500 with loads more power and fully-functioning trick bits to justify its price tag of £4000 above the regular RS Cosworth? Probably not. But then again, more additions would have meant an increase in the production schedule for the RS500, and time was already in short supply.

In part, that was due to the practicalities of a massive mainstream manufacturer assembling a low-volume model. The answer was to build 500 extra Sierra RS Cosworths on the Genk production line, and convert them to evolution spec sometime afterwards.

Genk couldn't cope with such a specialised service, while Karmann (which held a long car-building relationship with Ford) would have taken too long. Instead, Ford appointed Aston Martin Tickford in Bedworth, Warwickshire, which had a proven track record of constructing officially-backed

Five hundred standard Sierra RS Cosworths were plucked from the production lines and returned to the UK for conversion into RS500s. Here's around half the allocation lined up at Ford's storage area at Frog Island, Essex.

Ford wanted all RS500s to be factory Black, but by that point all three-door RS Cosworths had already been built. When Ford established there weren't enough cars available for conversion, Diamond White and Moonstone Blue were offered too.

All finished and ready for delivery – a transporter-load of RS500s leaving Tickford before being sent to Ford RS dealers.

RS500s under construction in Tickford's dedicated assembly area. This was hand-building, not high-tech.

Tickford Capris. The contract for RS500 production was awarded in March 1987, with assembly scheduled to run for six weeks from June.

Ford's intention was for every RS500 to be finished in black, but Ford's internal order for 500 regular Cosworths was delayed so much that, by December 1986, three-door production had already ended. There weren't enough black cars available for allocation, so 56 had to be Diamond White and 52 were Moonstone Blue; the remaining 392 were factory Black. All were right-hand drive, all were fitted with a glass

sunroof, and all were intended for sale in the UK.

The entire batch had been built in sequence, with VIN numbers starting at WFOEXXGBBEGG38600 and ending with WFOEXXGBBEGG39099. All 500 were then transferred from Genk into a storage yard in Dagenham, where each car had its body coated in wax, its clutch pedal held open and its exhaust blocked, in an attempt at preservation.

From there, the cars were drip-fed to Aston Martin Tickford. Four white examples were built as prototypes (numbers GG38721, 38750, 38759 and 38794) in December 1986, followed by three Sierras to train the workforce, beginning with build number five on 9 April 1987. Three more came in April for motoring press assessment, three were for validation and one was used for promotional photography.

Full production began soon afterwards, and the last RS500 was completed on 30 July 1987, which coincided with the on-sale date for the first customer car. As many as 29 RS500s were being turned out each day from Aston Martin Tickford's small-scale assembly lines, comprising 12 teams of workers.

Each car was selected at random (VIN had no relationship to build number) and taken through a conversion process, beginning with removal of the hardened storage wax and rectification of rough treatment received during transportation. The original YBB engines were winched out and returned to Cosworth, where they were tidied up (their water pumps had corroded while idle) and sent to Genk for use in the forthcoming Sapphire. Each RS500 was instead fitted with a YBD (again chosen at random), along with revised ancillaries.

The rear suspension had its brackets tacked on, the new spoilers were added, and RS500 stickers applied. The front splitter was placed in the boot for fitting by the receiving dealership; similarly, the original fog lamps were bunged in a box, in case the owner preferred them to the RS500 grilles.

All 500 cars were then stored in a yard, where they were counted by FISA inspectors.

That figure included the prototypes and press cars, individually numbered by Cosworth (1 to 500) in order of assembly; it's worth noting that the Sierras were taken from storage at random, rather in a sequence corresponding with their Ford chassis numbers; likewise, the YBD engines were renumbered by Cosworth – YBD0015 to YBD0537 – but the engines weren't used in any logical order, and each RS500's VIN plate still wore the number of its ousted YBB engine instead.

Despite its high cost, lack of optional extras and unremarkable performance (with 224bhp and lots of turbo lag it was barely better than the regular car) the RS500 became a hit, shaded only by the success of its motorsport counterparts.

The Group A machine was homologated in August 1987, started winning straight away (Group A Cosworths were by that point unofficially running in RS500 spec), scooped the 1987 World Touring Car Championship, blitzed the 1988 European Touring Car Championship, and was outlawed soon afterwards. But such is the price of success.

Beefed-up YBD powerplant developed just 224bhp from standard but was capable of more than double that figure without any internal modifications. This was a two-litre production car from a mainstream manufacturer, remember, and it was way back in 1987.

Engine – Block, Sump and Oil System

If there was one thing special about the Sierra RS500 Cosworth, it was the YBD powerplant — a reworked version of the original RS Cosworth's YBB engine, sharing the same 1993cc capacity and 8.0:1 compression ratio.

Now, though, instead of the YBB's production-spec Pinto cylinder block, an uprated version was developed to cope with the strains of big boost and endurance racing. Still made from iron, and still wearing a 205 casting number (in raised digits adjacent to piston number two on each side of the crankcase), around 1000 to 1500 YBD blocks were produced at Ford's West German foundry, where regular Pintos were cast day-to-day. It was reinforced with thicker metal around the cylinder walls, stronger top and bottom decks, smaller core plugs (25mm diameter, rather than the regular block's 38mm), and other minor differences, such as a threaded casting above the rear core plug. It's reckoned that YBD blocks were cast in two separate batches, which created two distinctly different blocks – those (found in road cars, with extra webbing) and later types without.

As an all-new iron casting, the YBD didn't wear the typical Ford two-letter/five-number serial; instead, the block was (usually) stamped with a GG-prefix number on the flat plate on the side of the block behind the alternator, along with

Cosworth's own identification code at the front on a bare metal flat above the water pump, sprayed with yellow primer. Fitted into RS500s, the codes began at YBD0015 and rose to YBD0537 but engines weren't fitted in sequence – for example, the very last RS500 was reportedly equipped with YBD0516. An additional number of YBDs (perhaps 130 extras) were fully built up as crate engines for Ford's spares department.

As usual, the block had a smaller raised 205 cast into the lower section of the crankcase just in front of the offside engine mount. There was also an additional series of cast digits, including the casting's part number (H88HM6015BA) plus a raised Ford logo. Behind the engine mount, the block's production date was cast into a raised oval – two digits represented the day and week of manufacture (14), the next letter related to the month (E for May) and the final two digits being the year (87 meaning 1987).

The exterior or the block was brush-painted satin black. Inside, the YBB components were more than adequate for the YBD – it used the same bowled pistons (Mahle forged aluminium) and rings, the same forged and heat-treated steel connecting rods, and the same forged-steel five-bearing crankshaft with hardened moly-coated bearing journals, nine flywheel bolts, reinforced sprocket gear and oil seals.

The regular YBB gravity die-cast bare alloy sump was

Ford promotional pic of the RS500. Even with the bonnet removed this is a busy engine bay.

feed for increased flow.

As usual, a Modine oil-to-water heat exchanger was linked to the engine's cooling system, and placed between the cylinder block and bare copper-coloured oil filter housing. The housing wore a white sticker with its part number; the oil filter was an orange Fram disposable item when screwed-on by Cosworth, or a Motorcraft filter when worked on by Ford.

At the back of the crankcase was a gold-passivated oil sender, which screwed into the block and also fed oil to the turbocharger through a steel braided hose; the return, on the turbo side, was through a gold-passivated pipe, connected using a black hose with grey clips at each end.

The YBB's breather system was carried over to the RS500, vented from the crankcase below the inlet manifold via a condensing unit and valves, and into the airbox. The same went for the pulley arrangement, which included the existing big black three-groove crank pulley with gold-passivated bolt.

Likewise, the original Sierra Cosworth's front crossmember was retained, along with the alloy engine mounts and rubber insulators derived from a mixture of Pinto and XR4i components. Again, the mounts were attached using gold-passivated bolts and black washers to the cylinder block, with passivated washers between insulators and mounts.

Cylinder Head

Much was made of the RS500's reworked cylinder head, which was essential for feeding 550bhp touring car engines with fuel and air. To achieve such demands, the road car's head had to be homologated with matching enlarged inlet and exhaust ports. Well, sort of.

In fact, the YBD head was barely any different from that of a regular Cosworth YBB. Homologation rules mentioned only entry diameters of the ports, so there was no need for Ford to spend hours finely honing each cylinder head to competition standards when a quick enlargement would suffice. And in the RS500's case, that meant opening the ports to rally homologation-spec 24.5mm/24mm inlet/exhaust dimensions just part-way inside – cheap, quick and easy.

The other alteration was a set of extra dowels on the intake side of the head, to attach the RS500's new inlet manifold.

The casting continued the YBB's provision for a turbo vibration damper, in the form of a flat U-shaped extension on the exhaust side with two drilled holes. The YBD's head was also made with threaded holes for a three-bolt thermostat housing, which were used for the first time on the RS500.

Otherwise, the YBD's cylinder head was pretty much a standard YBB component, in early 86HF6090AA guise. That meant an aluminium 16-valve double overhead cam design, with spark plugs mounted centrally in a 50cc pent-roof combustion chamber. As before, the head was attached to the cylinder block using ten tapered bolts and larger (23mm) late-spec washers, along with a revised head gasket incorporating a metal Omega ring.

retained for the YBD, complete with internal baffle plate and the same gasket of two cork layers sandwiching a slice of aluminium. A dipstick with yellow-painted wire handle reached into the sump, connected to the nearside rear of the engine in a metal tube.

Inside the sump, each piston was cooled by oil jets directed from underneath by a spray bar brazed onto the oil pickup pipe. Now, though, the pickup pipe was revised, and was supplied with fluid from a larger-capacity oil pump; it used the same rotor but inside a new housing to provide double

Oil pump had enlarged capacity and pickup pipe was revised.

Surprisingly, the valves remained standard size, at 35-to-35.2mm inlet head diameter and 31-to-31.2mm for the sodium-cooled exhaust valves. There were four per cylinder, arranged in a vee formation and operated by their own hydraulic lifters and respective camshafts; again, the cams were standard RS Cosworth parts, with 8.544mm lift.

The cams ran on bare metal Escort CVH pulleys, attached with gold-passivated bolts and rotated by a Uniroyal glassfibre-reinforced toothed rubber belt, featuring white printed lettering. There was a grey alloy belt tensioner, also held on with gold-passivated bolts. The belts and pulleys were situated behind the usual YBB textured black plastic timing belt cover, complete with yellow 'check oil daily' decal, three black Torx-headed bolts and gold-passivated washers.

Atop the head was the regular alloy cam cover, retained by 20 bolts and wearing a black plastic bayonet-cap oil filler. The RS500's cover was painted sand-cast-effect satin red with raised sections that were skimmed to declare, 'DOHC 16-V TURBO Ford COSWORTH'. The upper section was left with a plain alloy finish, bearing casting marks and no lacquer.

The cylinder head was equipped with gold-passivated lifting brackets mounted on the offside rear and nearside front manifold studs, with a black rubber hose from the coolant header tank fed through the eye of the front bracket.

Cooling System

Much of the RS500's cooling system differed from the standard RS Cosworth – due to re-routing for the bigger turbo and intercooler – while the rest remained unaltered.

At the front of the car was a normal Sierra Cosworth radiator with aluminium core and black plastic end tanks, along with the usual twin black plastic electrically-driven cooling fans within a black plastic shroud, and triggered by a thermal switch. On the RS500, though, the radiator had special

Huge intercooler was RS500-specific and built by Lingerer & Reich, complete with manufacturer-name casting and silver decal.

Water pump was all-new, with special casting and forward-facing return outlet.

brackets to mount it to a unique intercooler – now an enormous (73.5cm x 42cm) satin-black component produced by Lingerer & Reich, complete with manufacturer casting and silver decal. There was also a revised plastic cowling underneath, which functioned as a cold-air guide plate.

The YBD's water pump was upgraded with more vanes, and looked externally similar to the later 4x4 part but shallower in depth. Above it was the regular 88-degree wax thermostat, now inside a new housing, which was attached with three retaining bolts instead of the original car's two. A similar setup was carried over to the 4x4, although the RS500 had a special casting with a differently-shaped front bolt-on section; the return pipe faced forwards whereas the 4x4's looked backwards and had just the one bleed bolt; the RS500 had a gasket between the head and housing, while the 4x4 used a rubber O-ring.

As for the coolant header tank, that was a standard Sierra Cosworth unit, in clear/white plastic, mounted on the nearside inner wing, topped with a black plastic pressure cap and equipped with a black-on-white decal.

The RS500's coolant hoses were a mixture of unique and standard Sierra Cosworth; the oil cooler pipes were stock, while others were reshaped. The radiator top and bottom hoses were angled differently; the header tank's lower hose was completely different, as it returned into the thermostat housing rather than the previous version, which dropped down into a metal pipe that ran along the bottom of the radiator and joined the bottom hose from the water pump.

The RS500's bulkhead-to-water pump hoses were also altered – the small black heater matrix pipe pointed downwards instead of the standard three-door's hose, which had two 45-degree kinks. The RS500's hose then dropped

down to meet a revised metal heater matrix-to-water pump tube, which was positioned much lower in order to clear the T4 turbo (the standard Sierra Cosworth's ran between the turbo and manifold); this tube was kinked to wrap around assorted RS500 components; a rubber fitting on the right of the tube also bent down before turning to fit the water pump.

Fuel System

A con? Not quite. But anyone buying an RS500 expecting it to be glugging petrol through twice as many injectors was sadly mistaken. Yes, the homologation-spec Sierra doubled up on fuel rails, but it was all for show – and wouldn't even operate unless several major components (such as the engine ECU) were replaced.

Nevertheless, most of the impressive competition-type kit was included under the bonnet – and, to this day, few other production cars have been equipped with two injectors per cylinder. The RS500 featured a new alloy inlet manifold with provision for eight injectors, plus an enlarged elbow that housed an idle speed control valve (unlike the regular YBB, where the idle valve was fitted onto the top of the throttle body). Speaking of which, the YBD's alloy throttle body was considerably larger, measuring 76mm as opposed to the standard RS Cosworth's 60mm diameter.

An octuplet of standard yellow Weber plug-in injectors were clipped into a bright-nickel double-decker fuel rail, complete with upper take-off to supply the lower section – which was blanked from the factory with a piece of aluminium dowel. Each of the new bank of injectors had its own clip, looped into a dummy wiring loom with a multi-plug that connected to nothing else; instead it was simply tucked out of sight behind the car's battery.

Eight injectors but only four plumbed-in – the RS500's fuel rail in position on the inlet manifold.

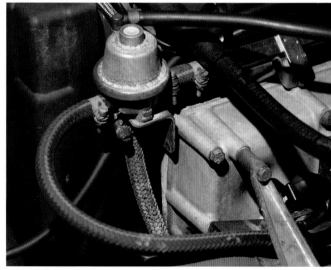

RS500's fuel pressure regulator had an extra outlet to supply petrol to the special car's additional fuel rail.

It was a similar story for the RS500's fuel pressure regulator – a bare alloy adjustable Weber item as before but now boasting an extra outlet to supply petrol to the impotent second rail; needless to say, this hole was blanked off, using aluminium dowel.

The previous YBB fittings were still attached to the YBD's plenum chamber, including vacuum connectors for the MAP sensor, air charge bypass valve, fuel pressure regulator, crankcase ventilation filter and inlet air temperature sensor.

A standard Sierra Cosworth throttle cable was used for the RS500, although its (gold-passivated) bracket was reworked to make room for that extra fuel rail. The fuel lines, too, were taken from the regular machine; steel pipes ran underneath the car, and hard plastic pipes entered the engine bay, along with a braided rubber return.

The RS500's fuel tank was unchanged from its predecessor – a run-of-the-mill silver-painted Sierra component, including an internal swirl pot. There was a standard fuel injection-model-Sierra sender and a bare metal-finished Bosch 941 fuel pump mounted within a satin black-painted bracket, which was attached beneath the spare wheel well. Beside it was a bare-metal fuel filter, connected with braided hoses.

The other major improvement over the standard three-door Sierra Cosworth was the RS500's air intake system, which was enlarged from 56mm to 65mm bore, including bigger airbox base, revised airbox lid and three meatier induction hoses, now made from blue silicone and wrapped in terracotta-coloured outer material. A similar terracotta-coloured hose fed air into the throttle body via the intercooler. One black rubber hose led from the airbox to the inlet manifold, while a small-bore black hose with yellow stripe linked it to the air bypass valve. The RS500's airbox base was also connected to

Throttle cable bracket was reworked to fit around the RS500's extra fuel rail.

Special MAP sensor bracket was needed to clear the RS500's throttle body; some standard Sierra RS Cosworths also wore this Ford part.

RS500 airbox had bigger base, revised lid and larger outlet diameter.

Enormous Garrett T4 turbo was essential for big power; it required equally huge air intake pipework.

Garrett T4 turbo – it's what all the fuss was about.

Gigantic T4 turbo took up some serious space under the Sierra's bonnet, requiring reworking of many components to make it fit.

a completely reworked cold air intake snorkel from above the intercooler. As before, the airbox used stainless steel clips and a paper air filter element.

Exhaust System

If you could name one component that differentiated the RS500 from its more commonplace Cosworth counterpart, the huge T4 turbocharger – or Garrett AiResearch T31/T04 to give it Ford's official name – was what made all the impact.

Quite simply, Ford wanted to annihilate everything else on the track, and a bigger turbo was essential for making enough power (over 550bhp in full-blown form). So when rival teams noticed Sierra touring cars were already bending the rules by using massive turbos, it merely hurried the RS500's arrival.

As before, homologation rules said all 500 production cars should have the motorsport machine's turbo, and the fact that the T4 was far too large for a detuned road car was mostly irrelevant. Indeed, despite the RS500's increase in factory-standard output to an unremarkable 224bhp, its performance out of the box was no better than the normal Sierra RS Cosworth – thanks primarily to loads of turbo lag. But the potential for improvement was immense.

The T4 was physically bigger than before, and sat closer to the engine on the existing two-piece nickel-iron exhaust manifold, which connected to the cylinder head and downpipes on M10 studs. The exhaust system was standard Sierra RS Cosworth, with the only difference being an added restrictor in the downpipe to prevent the turbo from overboosting. As before, the mild steel system ran from the downpipe into a front silencer, followed by twin pipes, two centre boxes and a single rear silencer, and all held up on standard Sierra rubbers. The entire system was fitted in one piece during production,

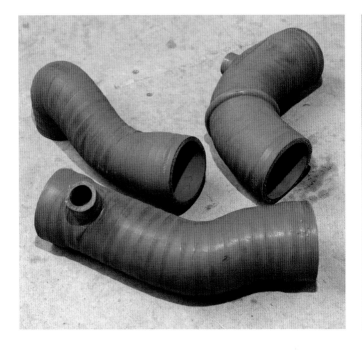

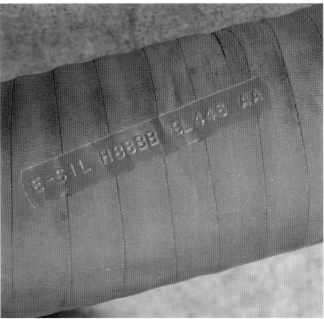

but Ford service replacements were made in four sections.

Like the original turbo, the T4 featured an internal wastegate, which was linked by a rod to a gold-passivated actuator that was bolted to the turbo housing on a bracket. A black hose with red stripe and green (or red) metal clip linked to the air bypass valve, as did a black hose with yellow stripe and red (or green) clip; the other end attached to the side of the airbox. The valve was the same Bosch black plastic part as before, but now moved to run through the intake's cold side using a small pink hose that clipped onto a pipe parallel to the bonnet slam panel and into a terracotta-coloured silicone hose, which in turn fitted onto the throttle body.

On the front of the turbo was a large-diameter terracotta-coloured silicone inlet hose, wrapped over blue silicone and

Horse shoe-shaped turbo damper was an official Ford RS500 upgrade in February 1989.

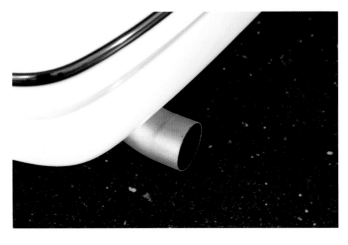

Original RS500 exhaust was the same as a standard three-door Cosworth's, including subtle silver-coloured tailpipe.

Small pink hose was used to extend dump valve pipework to the cold air side of the engine.

printed with its Ford part number. It was attached at the other end to the RS500's unique airbox using Ford-branded Jubilee-type hose clamps.

The T4 took the same feed from the main oil gallery through a steel-braided hose from the oil pressure warning switch adaptor at the nearside rear of the cylinder block, with an oil return to the sump via a stub pipe. The turbo's water coolant feed came from a unique thermostat housing, and its return to the header tank was in a reshaped hard pipe that followed the YBB's route of across the top of the engine, through a lifting eye and affixed with brackets and Torx-headed bolts onto the timing belt cover.

A new heat shield was attached to the engine bay above the turbo on three gold-passivated brackets; the shield was made from fibreglass and painted black on top, silver underneath.

There was also a turbo vibration damper, which is often cited as a different part from the regular RS Cosworth. In fact, that was only partly true. RS500s left the Tickford factory wearing the usual sprung damper, but a series of cracked cylinder heads led to an official Ford upgrade in February 1989, which replaced the damper during any routine service for the horse shoe-shaped part now found on almost all RS500s.

Ignition System

The RS500's ignition system was closely based on the regular three-door RS Cosworth's, using most of the same Weber-Marelli electronics and sensors.

At its heart was a revised L1 (level one) ECU (electronic control unit), located as before behind a clipped-in lid in the dashboard above the passenger-side glovebox. The ECU was essentially the same part – featuring metal case with integral mounting flange, yellow CO adjustment screw on the front and part number W45.01 – but now with a software map suitable for the T4 turbo and four yellow fuel injectors. Incidentally, this ECU was not capable of controlling all eight of the RS500's injectors.

As before, the ECU was connected to the Sierra's wiring loom on a 35-pin plug, with a green, a blue and white cable, and a self-test connector beside it. Power came from the battery through a fuse box-mounted relay with a brown socket; beside it in the fuse box (mounted in the engine bay) was a fuel pump relay (plugged into a yellow socket) and the usual ATO standard fuses.

Most of the electronic sensors that talked to the ECU were taken directly from the original Sierra RS Cosworth, although several were found in new places – such as the PF01 throttle position sensor (black or red), idle speed control valve (moved further back), boost pressure control solenoid (relocated on a special bracket and requiring a new hose due to the RS500's larger intercooler) and black plastic manifold absolute pressure (MAP) sensor, which was moved to make room for the larger throttle body and idle speed control valve. It was fitted to the inner wing on a two-piece metal bracket rather than the regular RS Cosworth's single-piece item.

Other sensors were carried over for the RS500, including the plenum-mounted air charge temperature (ACT) sensor, the engine coolant temperature (ECT) sensor screwed into the cylinder head, and the engine speed/TDC sensor bolted to the engine beneath the crankshaft pulley.

The RS500 used the regular RS Cosworth's Marelli breakerless distributor with automatic advance, which was driven by a skew gear from an auxiliary shaft and positioned beneath the inlet manifold. The same black plastic backwards-angled cap was fitted, along with black silicone leads wearing yellow crow's-foot tabs. They were attached to AGPR901C spark plugs centrally-located in the cylinder head, along with a Motorcraft high-output breakerless ignition coil wrapped in a bare metal bracket on the inner wing behind the nearside suspension tower, and a Marelli ignition module.

Electrical System

Like the regular RS Cosworth, the RS500 was half bespoke and half run-of-the-mill Sierra.

The boring bits were from the 2.0i Ghia (and three-door RS

Minute mocked-up section of wiring loom was installed for the non-functioning extra injectors.

Alternator adjusting bar was made smaller to make room in the engine bay for the RS500's T4 turbo.

Cosworth, naturally), such as the body wiring loom, which included cables for twin horns and front fog lamps, and was wrapped in Ford's usual black loom tape. The donor Sierra Cosworth's engine loom was used in its entirety, albeit with the addition of a small additional dummy loom and connectors at the RS500's extra row of fuel injectors.

Again, the fuse box was standard Sierra – a large black plastic unit housing normal ATO fuses and relays, and placed at the back of the engine bay beneath the driver's-side scuttle panel. There was a white/clear Motorcraft 60Ah battery (with no cover) and leads from the Sierra V6. The starter motor was a black-painted three-bolt Bosch DW with 1.4Kw output, as found in a variety of other Ford cars and vans.

The usual RS Cosworth bare-aluminium Bosch 90-amp alternator was fitted to the YBD engine, but repositioned lower down to make room for the big T4 turbo using a dropped mounting plate and shorter adjuster bar made by Tickford. The alternator's heat shield was also a revised component.

Transmission

Proof that the original RS Cosworth's Borg-Warner T5 gearbox was capable of handling huge power, it remained completely unaltered in the RS500, despite the potential for transmission-tearing torque.

The T5 five-speed featured an aluminium casing and synchromesh on all gears except reverse. The ratios were the same too, with first gear: 2.95:1; second: 1.94:1; third: 1.34:1; fourth: 1:1; fifth: 0.80:1; reverse: 2.76:1.

The gearbox was connected to the cylinder block with an aluminium bellhousing, which contained the stock Cosworth balanced-steel nine-bolt flywheel. Drive was through the standard heavy-duty clutch assembly, including a 9.5in (240mm) diaphragm single-plate clutch featuring an uprated disc, pressure plate and intermediate plate. The RS500 used the previous RS Cosworth-specific cable and clutch mechanism.

The T5's main transmission case contained first to fourth and reverse gears, with fifth and synchroniser found at the back of the gearbox in an extension housing, operated by a pivot pin and intermediate lever.

Protruding from the extension housing turret was a shift cover assembly, where shift forks for first-to-second and third-to-fourth were found. Meanwhile, the extension housing contained the shift detent, comprising detent plate, selector crank and spring-loaded ball.

The usual RS satin-black steel crossmember and rubber mount assembly attached the T5's tail to the floorpan. From there, the gearbox was linked to a two-piece satin black propshaft with blue-headed bolts, and was supported in the middle with a ball bearing in a rubber insulator, bolted to the floorpan. It featured the Sierra three-door's heavy-duty universal joints (originally found on the Ford Transit) and a reinforced rear section.

Power was taken through the prop to a Scorpio V6 7.5in differential in a bare alloy casing, with viscous-coupling LSD (the donor Cosworth's 3.64:1 ratio was retained); it was supported by a rubber bush inside a gold-passivated mount, which connected to the floorpan on four bolts.

The differential turned a pair of 108mm Cosworth-specific driveshafts and stubs – again left in a bare metal finish, with unpainted ends and black rubber gaiters with stainless clips. The outer ends were attached to the rear wheel hubs on blue Torx-headed bolts.

Suspension and steering

As an evolution model designed for racing, you'd reasonably expect the RS500's suspension to radically differ from the regular RS Cosworth on which it was based. Yet, in reality, Ford used its time-served knack for rule-bending and cost-cutting to escape with adding the fewest modifications possible.

The RS500's front end was pure three-door Sierra Cosworth, unchanged from the original December 1986-built machine.

That meant the same Motorcraft-branded MacPherson struts, finished in black, featuring Fichtel and Sachs gas-filled twin-tube dampers, lowered coil springs (black-coated, with

Homologation rules meant adding puny additional trailing arm brackets to the rear axle beam.

white paint splashes) and standard Sierra top mounts.

The struts were dropped into Cosworth-specific cast-iron hub carriers and suspension knuckles, all unpainted. The front wheel bearings, dust seals and caps were Ford Scorpio kit. The Sierra three-door's black-finished track control arms (with 12mm bolts) and crossmember remained, complete with tapered ball joints and castellated nuts at the knuckle ends. So, too, did the satin black 28mm anti-roll bar, Scorpio bushes and brackets, along with yellow paint dabs on the nuts and bolts. Because all RS500s were constructed towards the end of three-door production (December 1986), all had the later H14-type anti-roll bar, which moved the front wheels further forwards than the previous H13 part.

The existing RS steering system was retained, including standard Sierra-based PAS Cam Gears rack and pinion setup, with revised ratio of 2.6 turns lock to lock. The steering rack was black-painted, with bare-metal track rod ends and black rubber gaiters clipped on. Similarly, the steering column and lock were standard Sierra components, complete with GL/Ghia/XR4i horn button switch wire.

A satin black-finished power steering hydraulic pump was attached to a black bracket with gold-passivated bolts, as before, and positioned on a cylinder block-mounted bracket with a pair of M10 bolts at the induction side. The pump was driven by the crankshaft pulley via a single vee belt, while the regular Ford Sierra PAS fluid reservoir was also used.

Homologation laws meant the RS500 road car required suspension mounting points in the same places as it would run in competition spec, which was where Ford's trickery came in handy. No one said the road-going RS500 had to be fitted with fully-functioning components (as we'd already seen with the blanked-off eight-injector fuel rail), so Ford pretty-much mocked the rules rather than investing in a massive re-engineering project.

Circuit-racing Sierras featured revised mounting points for adjustable rear suspension trailing arms, and Ford's cheap solution was to add a pair of extra brackets to the existing Sierra Cosworth's rear beam in order to replicate the new positioning – in practice, that meant Tickford staff tack-welding useless U-shaped brackets (one at each side) onto every car. Meanwhile, each RS500 retained the donor car's mountings and rubber bushes – essentially a modified Scorpio rear beam (finished in satin black), XR4i-type trailing arms (with special uniball joints), XR4x4 gas-filled single-tube Fichtel and Sachs telescopic dampers, lowered coil springs (in black, with yellow and green paint splashes), XR4x4 14mm rear anti-roll bar and brackets reaching outside the rear arms, and regular RS rear axle shafts and driveshaft hubs.

And that was it. There was nothing else remarkable about the RS500's underpinnings.

Had motorsport governing bodies not cancelled virtually every championship in which the RS500 was dominant, it's probable that further development of the Sierra's running gear would have taken place. As it was, the RS500 was mind-blowingly good before Ford's work was finished. But that's another story.

Brakes

It might be common for today's high-performance saloons and to boast enormous racetrack-derived braking systems, but for 1987 Ford there was none of that frippery. Instead, the standard Sierra RS Cosworth's entire braking system was retained, deemed worthy of hauling up 224bhp.

And that was fair enough – at the front, the braking system comprised a pair of 283mm x 24.15mm ventilated discs and gold-passivated Teves four-piston callipers containing Ford Motorcraft pads. At the back was a pair of 273mm x 10.2mm solid discs and Sierra XR4x4-type gold-passivated floating callipers with Motorcraft pads, on Cosworth-specific carriers. Black steel splash shields sat between discs and hubs, while an XR4x4 handbrake cable was operated by a regular Sierra handbrake lever.

The same Ford Granada/Scorpio/Sierra Teves Mk2 electronic ABS setup was used on the RS500, complete with Scorpio ABS sensors and toothed rotors mounted at each wheel, with the rears fitted into the suspension arm end castings.

A Granada gold-passivated brake booster assembly and alloy single-piston master cylinder sat on the bulkhead in front of the driver, complete with black-painted electronic pump. A clear/white plastic brake fluid reservoir was above the cylinder, topped with a white plastic screw cap and white electrical connections. The reservoir body was equipped with a yellow warning sticker, as was the black accumulator, which sat on the right of the reservoir (left when viewed from the front of the car), which also wore a selection of yellow stamps.

Like the original Sierra Cosworth, the RS500 had an alloy and gold-passivated actuation assembly mounted on the nearside inner wing. The RS500's brake lines were also untouched – just the usual with XR4x4-type rubber flexible hoses and green-coated steel pipes. The brake pipe-to-hose connection was screwed on at the engine crossmember, and retained with clips.

The standard RS Cosworth's ABS ECU, relays and fuses remained in place on the RS500, in the driver's footwell, behind the kick panel.

Wheels and tyres

Motorsport rules allowed massive wheels and tyres without specific requirements for the road car, so the RS500 kept the donor Sierra's Rial 7Jx15in alloys, with the usual ET40mm offset. The size, Ford logo, part number (V86BB-AA) and date of production (usually October to December 1986) were cast in the wheel centres beneath a locking centre cap with raised Ford oval logo; one small key was provided for all four alloys.

As before, the same shiny finish was used, with Nimbus Grey inners, and diamond-cut and lacquered spokes. Each wheel was attached to the RS500 with a set of alloy wheel nuts incorporating rotating conical washers.

Dunlop D40 VR15 205/50x15 tyres were retained, again with the earlier design including a tread depth indicator running all the way around the central groove of the tyre. The same type of tyre was wrapped over the RS500's full-size spare alloy wheel in the well beneath the boot floor; this wheel wore no centre cap.

Dunlop SP Sport D40 rubber wrapped around 7x15in alloy wheels – all the same as the standard Sierra RS Cosworth. The inner wheelarches wore black plastic liners.

Gunmetal grey centre caps covered Rial-produced RS Cosworth 7x15in alloy wheels, complete with locks and matching keys.

Wire grilles were added to the front bumper in place of original fog lamps, which were boxed up in the boot for future fitment.

Body

Wild wings were key to the original Sierra RS Cosworth's head-turning appearance, and for the RS500 Ford opted to make them even wilder.

Thanks to the race car's need for high-speed downforce (Sierra touring cars were reputedly recorded at 187mph on track) and increased cooling, the road-going RS500 was homologated with revised front and rear spoilers produced by Phoenix in Hamburg.

At the front, the original three-door Cosworth's polycarbonate bumper was reworked to incorporate an additional air scoop across the top (beneath the radiator grille) and a narrower number plate recess above a pair of enlarged lower intakes (3in wider at each side), all of which were intended to feed the massive intercooler and reduce air intake temperatures. As before, a straight body-coloured towing eye protruded from the right-hand-side upper slot.

The original fog lamps were removed by Tickford and transferred to a cardboard box, which was plonked into the luggage compartment in case the owner wanted to fit them later. In their place was a pair of black metal grilles designed to divert air to the front brakes, and – on white or blue cars – the bumper was sprayed satin black within each recess. A black bumper insert was included regardless of body colour.

Beneath the bumper, the original rubber splitter was replaced by a deeper two-piece plastic version, which wrapped around the corners and sides of the bumper. Fitting was done by the

Biplane rear wing arrangement included remanufactured upper wing with 30mm gurney flap extension plus lower rear spoiler, which was based on a Ford accessory but with cutout for the wing's central pylon.

Large vertical gurney flap made an impressive edge to the standard Sierra RS Cosworth rear wing. Note the positioning of the central pylon within the rubber lower spoiler.

Rubber RS500 lower spoiler was a special part, complete with shaped central cutout and unique part number, featuring a large C after Type: 0195.

supplying dealership; until then, the splitter was stored in the car's boot for transportation. Meanwhile, a new plastic radiator cowling was fitted behind the front bumper – again to direct air towards the big intercooler.

At the back, the Sierra three-door's rear wing was removed (and returned to Ford for keeping in stock as a spare part) and replaced with an even larger version. Although the main moulding was identical, the RS500 whale-tail was equipped with a 30mm gurney flap extension in satin black. Naturally, it used the same mounting points – five M5 retaining screws and two rivets, topped with seven body-coloured screw covers.

Below the wing was an additional lower spoiler, made from flexible black rubber. Broadly similar in style to a Sierra 2.0iS part, the RS500's differed by virtue of a central vee-shaped cutout (produced in the moulding) around the wing's central pylon, it was shaped more acutely at the corners (where it wrapped around onto the rear quarters – unlike the 2.0iS part, which was the same width as the tailgate) and also lacked a vertical overlap onto the boot lid. An official Ford accessory spoiler was almost identical to the RS500's, lacking only the central cutout; this spoiler was moulded with a part number of 0195 on the underside, whereas the RS500's read 0195C.

The rear lower spoiler was clamped to the edges of the tailgate lid from underneath, and there were clear stickers on the rear wings to stop the spoiler from rubbing against the car's paintwork. Many RS500s were also applied with anti-rust solution where the brackets attached.

These modifications raised the standard car's drag factor (from 0.34 to something like 0.36) but, most importantly, increased downforce by 20kg up front and 105kg on the rear.

Almost everything else was standard Sierra RS Cosworth. That meant a base-model three-door Sierra bodyshell with subtle differences, including a bulkhead pressing to take the ABS-equipped brake booster mountings and broad transmission tunnel, along with unique front crossmember. Because all road-going RS500s were converted into Tickford trim from right-hand-drive Sierra Cosworths, all were fitted with a tilting/sliding tinted-glass sunroof.

The usual Cosworth body-coloured polycarbonate headlamp surround/grille was fitted, complete with meshed single-slot air intake. A standard mid-blue Ford oval badge was slapped in the middle, and the fittings were regular Sierra stuff – screws, clips and brackets, and a 1766mm gasket between the front wings.

The wings themselves remained untouched, being standard Sierra panels except for small pre-stamped slots around the wheelarches, filled with square plastic expansion nuts. Polycarbonate wheelarch extensions in body colour were attached to the wings with M5 round-headed self-tapping screws and double-sided tape. Body-coloured plastic caps covered the screw heads, and there were body-coloured jacking point covers behind the front wheels.

The front wheelarch extensions were connected at their

An extra mouth was added to the RS500 front bumper beneath the standard Sierra Cosworth's meshed front air intake.

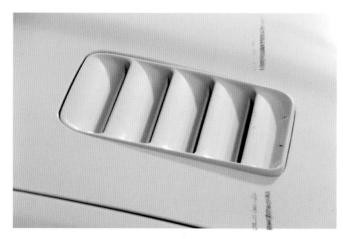

trailing edges to body-coloured polycarbonate side skirts, which clipped over the sills and were pop-riveted to the inner sills from above. At the skirts' trailing edges they were linked to rear wheelarch extensions – again, in body-coloured polycarbonate – attached with double-sided tape and M5 self-tapping screws into square slots in the rear quarter panels. Body-coloured jacking covers and screw caps were fitted.

The stock Sierra RS Cosworth rear bumper was retained, made from smooth polycarbonate in two pieces and finished in body-coloured paint; it was mounted on normal Sierra brackets. The bumper featured a black insert, which was echoed in black bodyside mouldings on the front wings, doors and rear quarters.

The stock Cosworth bonnet remained untouched, complete with pressed cut-outs for twin polycarbonate cooling vents, bolted on from below. Underneath, though, there was a section of thick silver foil insulation applied to the underside of the bonnet, hand-cut and stuck on by Tickford to deal with heat from the enormous turbo.

A standard Sierra black plastic slatted scuttle panel cover was mounted at the base of the RS500's laminated bronze-tinted front windscreen. It housed a pair of satin black metal wipers, including a small spoiler on the driver's-side arm. Washer nozzles in the plastic scuttle panel were fed by an electric pump mounted on the front of the fluid reservoir.

RS500 doors were, again, the usual three-door Sierra parts, complete with late-spec striker pin and reinforcement on the B-pillars. The doors wore standard black textured plastic handles above regular Ford door locks with black bezels; they were operated by flat keys with black plastic handles (one with push-button torch), which had the same pattern for the doors, tailgate, ignition and petrol cap (a removable three-pronged body-coloured filler cap in the offside rear quarter).

Plastic side rubbing strips were the same as a regular three-door RS Cosworth's, as were the body-coloured wheelarch screw caps.

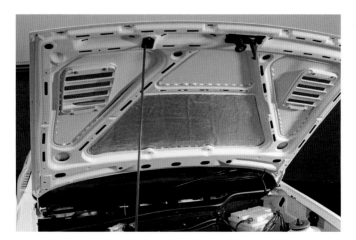

Sierra RS Cosworth's vented bonnet was retained for the RS500, albeit with the addition of thick silver foil insulation for the huge T4 turbo.

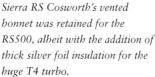

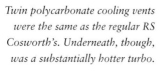

Twin polycarbonate cooling vents were the same as the regular RS Cosworth's. Underneath, though, was a substantially hotter turbo.

Black plastic door handle and lock cover were basic Ford Sierra kit. The pinstripe was RS500-only.

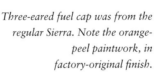

Three-eared fuel cap was from the regular Sierra. Note the orange-peel paintwork, in factory-original finish.

The door mirrors were electrically-adjustable and heated, with body-coloured housings on black plastic cases. Black frames and rubbers surrounded bronze-tinted side glass, with those in the doors electrically operated using a specific Sierra three-door regulator mechanism. All RS500s had fixed rear quarter windows.

At the back there was a standard Sierra heated rear window in bronze-tinted glass, complete with black-coated rear wiper powered by a Bosch motor. It was fitted into a Cosworth-specific tailgate, with unique drillings for the whale tail. As usual, the RS500 featured a black plastic washer nozzle in the top of the tailgate, fed by a fluid reservoir within the nearside rear quarter panel. Likewise, the centrally-mounted black boot lock surround and push-button assembly was the same as the part on other Sierras, and the tailgate's gas lifting struts were taken from the XR4i and XR4x4.

Like the regular RS Cosworth, the RS500 was equipped with an electrically-operated radio aerial, mounted in the driver's-side rear quarter at the base of the C-pillar. Now, though, there was a safety switch that retracted the aerial when the tailgate was lifted, which stopped the lower spoiler from snapping it off. It was operated by a relay that cut power to the aerial when the boot was released.

As before, just three exterior paint colours were offered for the RS500 – Diamond White or Black (thermoplastic acrylics) or Moonstone Blue (polyester basecoat and clear coat), with build quantities of 56, 392 and 52 respectively. All were finished the same underneath – cataphoretic primer, with sealer sprayed or brushed onto high-impact areas and overlaps. The top coat was wafted underneath the sills and wheelarches (which received black plastic liners afterwards), while the spare wheel well and rear towing eye were generally sprayed in satin black.

Meanwhile, the inside of the bodyshell – beneath the carpets and insulation – was finished in grey primer on Black and Moonstone Blue cars, and white on Diamond White examples.

All RS500s wore the same silver decals, which read 'Sierra RS500 Cosworth' on the nearside of the tailgate, reflected with a mid-blue oval Ford badge on the offside. The RS500 was also adorned with pinstripes along each side (six metres of silver tape per car), including an RS500 logo on each front wing. The Tickford badges often seen on RS500s today were added later by owners, and never fitted during production.

A minor addition but it meant so much – RS500 sticker was added to the regular Sierra Cosworth decals.

Silver-coloured RS500 decals and six meters of silver tape were applied to every RS500.

Underbonnet

Beneath the bonnet of an RS500 most of the obvious modifications were applied to the new YBD powerplant. But there were still one or two subtle differences to differentiate the homologation special from its regular RS Cosworth base.

The bulkhead was unchanged – it was a specific panel for ABS-equipped cars, featuring an inverted-key-shaped cutout for the brake servo, four mounting bolt holes, and an aperture for the engine wiring loom to go into the cabin. The three-door Cosworth's standard black/dark grey insulator pad was affixed to the bulkhead, complete with hard plastic trim and flexible rubber edge protector that were originally seen on the Sierra 2.0iS.

Black plastic clips pinned the engine wiring loom to the bulkhead, while a unique dummy section of loom ran from the blanked-off extra row of injectors to the battery, where it was tucked away out of sight. That battery – a square-post white/clear Motorcraft 60Ah component – lived on the nearside, just in front of the bulkhead, on a body-coloured metal tray. The difference with the RS500 was that Tickford hacked the corner off the tray to make room for the car's eight-injector setup; the roughly sawn-off steel was left unpainted.

At the driver's side of the bulkhead was the brake fluid reservoir and a turbo heat shield that was unique to the RS500, made from fibreglass and painted black on one side, silver on the other.

As always, the regular Sierra body-coloured bonnet hinges, bolts and washers were fitted, and the standard Sierra inner wings remained, painted body colour. The round suspension turrets were fitted with bare metal plates and black plastic caps.

At the nearside front was the clear/white plastic coolant header tank, with black-on-white decal on its horizontal surface and topped with a black plastic pressure cap. The nearside corner of the engine bay also housed stock Ford clear/white plastic tanks for the windscreen washer fluid and power steering fluid.

Across the front of the RS500 was the usual Sierra bonnet slam panel, complete with VIN tag, red asbestos warning

decal and yellow brake system warning sticker on the offside. A black-coated bonnet prop was housed within a clear plastic washer and mated to a black plastic holder on the underside of the bonnet. The regular black-coated bonnet release mechanism sat in the middle, while at each side was a white plastic stopper topped with a black rubber insulator. The front wing rails housed black rubber insulator pads.

As always, the slam panel was stamped with a part/batch number, as were the front wings where they overlapped; in the RS500's case, all were produced in 1986.

Special fibreglass RS500 turbo heat shield was black on top, silver underneath. It was attached on three brackets.

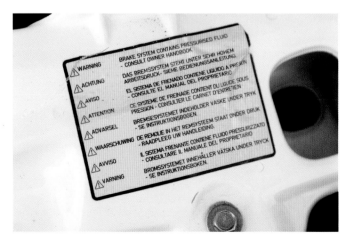

Brake fluid warning sticker was found on the slam panel, just in front of the bonnet prop.

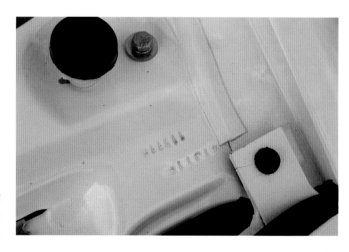

Original factory slam panel stamps, as found on even regular Ford Sierras.

Headlamps and indicators were from the original RS Cosworth but the fog lamp grilles were new, as was the black plastic lower splitter, which wrapped around the bumper corners.

Simple, standard Sierra rear lights and original blue oval Ford badge.

Lighting

When the standard Sierra RS Cosworth was converted into an RS500 there was a solitary change to its lighting setup – the removal of the 55W H3 halogen fog lamps from the front bumper and into a box in the boot. Instead, Tickford added a pair of brake cooling duct grilles, leaving it up to the eventual owner to install the fog lamps if preferred; the wiring was left in place behind the bumper, and several RS500 buyers did indeed retrofit the lamps.

Everything else was identical. That meant 60/55W halogen H4 headlamps with integral driving lamps, as originally found in the Sierra Ghia; Cibie or Lucas were genuine fitments.

Ghia-spec 21W indicators with orange plastic lenses sat beside the new fog lamp grilles, and the usual Ford square orange plastic 5W side repeaters were fitted to the front wings just behind the wheelarches.

At the back, the standard Sierra light clusters were made by Hella or Lucas, although in the Cosworth's case they were most likely Hella. Each unit included reversing lights and fog lamps. Beneath the number plate, recessed into the back bumper, was a pair of small lamps.

The RS500's interior courtesy lamp was as before – Ghia-type with map lights in an overhead console. In the boot was a single luggage compartment lamp.

Nothing new, but why change a great thing? The RS500's cabin was pure Sierra RS Cosworth, complete with Recaro front seats and three-spoke steering wheel.

Interior

Tickford didn't touch the RS500's interior. Every component was carried over from the Sierra Cosworth and not a single piece was added.

But what about the individually-numbered Tickford plaque on the centre console? Despite popular assumptions, these black build plates – often found between the cars' electric window switches – were produced by the RS Owners' Club for the RS500's tenth anniversary, and were not fitted from new.

Indeed, what the RS500 buyer received was internally a regular RS Cosworth. The specification was centred around a pair of reclining Recaro front seats trimmed in Ford's Roma and Cashmere grey velour, complete with folding rear bench (and 60/40 split back rest) covered in the same material. At the front, each seat incorporated adjustable headrests, sliding base extensions, silver-on-black Recaro badges, and map pockets in the seat backs. Each Recaro could have its backrest tipped forward using one of two black plastic levers, while the driver's seat could be adjusted for height using a hand-wheel under the front.

RS500 door cards were trimmed in Roma and Cashmere grey velour plus Raven vinyl and grey-carpeted front door bins. Grey plastic handles sat alongside black plastic door release levers and locking mechanisms, held on with black screws. On the driver's door card was a black plastic electric mirror control switch. Similarly, the rear quarter panels wore Raven vinyl/Roma and Cashmere grey cloth, plus black plastic ashtrays at each side.

A Shadow Grey vinyl/plastic dashboard was fitted, with centrally-mounted grey-plastic speaker grille and no speaker beneath – instead there was a pair of speakers, one at each side of the lower dashboard.

Special build-number plaque is an aftermarket item found on the majority of surviving RS500s, not fitted by the Tickford factory.

Unbeatable driving position and three-spoke leather-rimmed steering wheel were carried over from the RS500's Sierra Cosworth basis.

Regular Sierra RS Cosworth front seats in Roma and Cashmere grey velour were equally perfect in the RS500.

Split/folding Roma and Cashmere grey velour rear seat was retained from the original three-door RS Cosworth.

The RS500's instrument cluster was contained within a standard black plastic surround, which featured heater control sliders on the left and a host of dials. Included was a large rev counter with an orange needle and white digits reading from 0 to 7, and a turbo boost gauge in the top left. At the right-hand side of the cluster was a large 170mph speedometer with an orange needle and white-printed MPH digits, plus smaller yellow numbering for KMH; within the dial were a mileometer and trip recorder, reset by a button at the bottom. Between the rev counter and speedo were smaller gauges: a coolant temperature gauge with orange needle on the right, and a 60-litre fuel gauge with orange needle on the left.

A pair of yellow-illuminated ABS failure warning lamps were beneath the smaller instruments, along with a strip of warning lights for headlamp main beam, oil pressure, direction indicators, ignition/alternator and handbrake/brake failure.

Below the dials were a fascia illumination dimmer control on the left, and an intermittent speed controller for the windscreen wipers to the right. Meanwhile, at the right-hand side of the cluster was a separate black plastic panel that housed illuminated rocker switches for the rear wash/wipe, heated rear window, rear fog lamps and front fog lamps. A side-window demisting vent was above, with a base/XR4i-type adjustable heater vent below, also made from plain black plastic (lacking the silver outline of Ghia-type Sierras).

In front of the driver's legs was a hard grey plastic lower dashboard section, which was home to the right-hand-side front speaker, a small storage shelf and a small, hinged coin holder with black velour-type lining.

A stock black plastic Sierra steering column shroud protruded from the lower dash, complete with the usual black stalks for indicators, main beam and headlamp flashers on the left, a single stalk on the right to control headlamps/sidelights, and one more for the windscreen wipers and washers. A red push-button for the car's hazard warning flashers sat on top of the shroud, while the ignition lock sprouted from the outside. Beneath the column was an orange plastic bonnet release lever.

As before, the RS500's steering wheel was a slightly-dished three-spoke item with leather rim and centre horn push, topped with a blue Ford oval logo.

On the passenger-side fascia, in pride of place, was a removable ECU cover with black RS logo. Beside it was a plain black plastic adjustable heater vent, with a smaller rectangular vent for demisting the side window above.

The lower dashboard was made from a harder plastic than the top section, and housed the main glovebox, which was a Shadow Grey plastic enclosure with black plastic release button. Inside the glovebox there was a grey-carpeted base and a small round lamp.

At the centre of the RS500's dashboard was a pair of adjustable heater vents, which sat above a strip of warning lights for brake pad wear, low coolant level, low windscreen washer fluid level and low fuel (all illuminated yellow), and engine management (illuminated red).

A three-button solid-state digital clock with green LEDs was below, and the Sierra Ghia's graphic information module was to the right, which displayed an overhead view of the car to warn of ice, bulb failures, and open doors or tailgate.

Lower down was the higher-spec-Sierra black plastic compartment that contained a Ford ECU2 electronic sound system incorporating radio/cassette head unit and separate power amplifier, three-speed illuminated heater fan control, ashtray and illuminated cigar lighter.

Beneath was a Raven/Shadow Grey plastic centre console, which included a black plastic gear lever surround, black rubber concertina-type gear lever gaiter and black gearstick topped with a black leather-covered gearknob; it was crowned with a polished black emblem showing a white-printed five-speed shift pattern.

A pair of black plastic rocker switches for the electrically-operated front windows was placed behind the gearstick surround, just above an oddments tray. The usual Sierra handbrake lever (featuring a black plastic handle and black push-button) emerged from a lidded storage box, topped with a grey cloth armrest; inside there was storage for audio cassette tapes.

The RS500's carpet was Ghia-type cut-pile velour in dark grey (Raven 86), complete with ribbed black driver's heel pad, and a Raven 86 plastic flap with a cap on the offside sill, which lifted to reveal the car's chassis number.

At the side of each front footwell was a hard Shadow Grey plastic kick panel, affixed with black screws. In the driver's footwell was a regular Pinto-engined Sierra pedal box, featuring black levers and pedal rubbers, plus RS Cosworth-specific clutch cable clip.

The kick panel trailing edges overlapped black door rubbers, which sat beside Shadow Grey plastic door scuff plates attached with black screws. Black seat belt rails ran along the inner sills, with regular Sierra inertia-reel seat belts mounted on each B-pillar. In the back were two lap/diagonal inertia reels and one centre static lap belt, again as found on all other 1986 Sierras.

All RS500s were fitted with a glass sunroof, Dawn Grey sliding roof blind and winder handle assembly, along with Dawn Grey overhead console that was home to the courtesy light and swivelling individually-switched map-reading lights. There was also a Dawn Grey 86 Beaumont cloth headlining plus Shadow Grey plastic A-pillar trims and Steel Grey 83 plastic covers over the B- and C-pillars. Three grey grab handles were supplied for the safety of screaming passengers, while the driver's side instead wore plastic plugs.

A pair of black/grey sun visors (the passenger's incorporating a vanity mirror) flanked a stock Sierra black dipping rear-view mirror, which was bonded to the top of the windscreen.

RS500 door cars were unchanged, again in Roma and Cashmere grey velour with Raven vinyl.

Sierra Cosworth instruments with 170mph speedo and Merkur XR4Ti boost gauge.

Inside Boot

A motorsport legend, maybe, but that didn't stop the RS500 from doubling up as a practical shopping car.

Like the regular three-door RS Cosworth, the RS500's luggage compartment was very much standard Sierra, albeit housing a raised boot floor by means of a grey sponge pad, which served to lift the boot mat to the same height as the Cosworth's full-sized spare wheel; a 7Jx15in Rial cross-spoke

Carpeted parcel shelf included plastic storage box for first aid kit (not included).

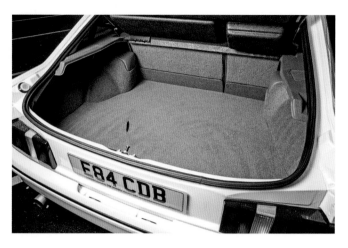

As practical as it was powerful, the RS500's stock Sierra luggage compartment made it a perfect machine for high-speed shopping.

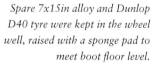

Spare 7x15in alloy and Dunlop D40 tyre were kept in the wheel well, raised with a sponge pad to meet boot floor level.

alloy sat in the well, wearing the normal Dunlop D40 VR15 205/50x15 tyre. The wheel was finished identically to the four road wheels (in gunmetal grey with diamond-cut spokes) but without a centre cap. It also had balance weights attached on the outside face, rather than the invisibly-mounted weights of the other rims. The wheel was held in place using a black metal eyelet screwed through one of the wheel's bolt holes.

Above the wheel was the unique RS Cosworth carpet in Shadow Grey 86, complete with black plastic handle. A matching carpet was applied to the rear seat backs, along with Shadow Grey 86 plastic fasteners.

The same shade – Shadow Grey 86 – was used on the RS500's tilting/removable one-piece parcel shelf, which included a dark grey plastic storage box that was intended to house Ford's red-packaged first-aid kit. The parcel shelf hung from the tailgate on black rubber straps alongside black XR4i-type gas struts, which held the heavy lid in the air.

When lifted, a clear plastic courtesy lamp would be lit; it was clipped into the rear panel near the middle. Meanwhile, there was a regular Sierra rear washer fluid reservoir with clear cap, surrounded by a black grommet, at the base of the nearside C-pillar.

On the inside of the tailgate was a grey plastic panel, which clipped into position over the rear wiper motor. Below was a regular Sierra hatchback boot latch.

The parcel shelf's side supports were Raven 86 plastic, as were the inner wheelarch trims and electric aerial cover. Across the back panel was a black plastic trim, which covered a standard Ford wheelbrace and T-shaped jack, both held in place using black rubber bungees of differing sizes.

The only difference from the regular RS Cosworth? That was a pair of standard-issue fog lamps in a box, removed from the front bumper by Tickford and included for the eventual owner to fit if desired. Most did not.

Colour schemes and interior trim

Colour	Code	Introduced	Discontinued	Decals	Interior colour
Diamond White	B	June 1987	July 1987	Silver	Grey
Black	A	June 1987	July 1987	Silver	Grey
Moonstone Blue	K	June 1987	July 1987	Silver	Grey

Diamond White

Black

Moonstone Blue

RS500 Production Numbers

Build no.	Colour	Build no.	Colour	Build no.	Colour	Build no.	Colour	Build no.	Colour	Build no.	Colour	Build no.	Colour	Build no.	Colour
1	Diamond White	64	Black	127	Black	190	Black	253	Black	316	Black	379	Black	442	Diamond White
2	Diamond White	65	Black	128	Black	191	Diamond White	254	Black	317	Black	380	Black	443	Diamond White
3	Diamond White	66	Black	129	Black	192	Diamond White	255	Black	318	Black	381	Black	444	Diamond White
4	Diamond White	67	Black	130	Black	193	Black	256	Black	319	Black	382	Black	445	Diamond White
5	Black	68	Black	131	Black	194	Black	257	Black	320	Black	383	Black	446	Diamond White
6	Black	69	Black	132	Black	195	Black	258	Black	321	Black	384	Black	447	Diamond White
7	Black	70	Black	133	Black	196	Black	259	Black	322	Black	385	Black	448	Diamond White
8	Black	71	Black	134	Black	197	Black	260	Black	323	Black	386	Black	449	Diamond White
9	Black	72	Black	135	Black	198	Black	261	Black	324	Black	387	Black	450	Diamond White
10	Black	73	Black	136	Black	199	Black	262	Black	325	Black	388	Black	451	Diamond White
11	Black	74	Black	137	Black	200	Black	263	Black	326	Black	389	Black	452	Diamond White
12	Black	75	Black	138	Black	201	Black	264	Black	327	Black	390	Black	453	Diamond White
13	Black	76	Black	139	Black	202	Black	265	Black	328	Black	391	Black	454	Diamond White
14	Black	77	Black	140	Black	203	Black	266	Black	329	Black	392	Black	455	Diamond White
15	Black	78	Black	141	Black	204	Black	267	Black	330	Black	393	Black	456	Diamond White
16	Black	79	Black	142	Black	205	Black	268	Black	331	Black	394	Black	457	Diamond White
17	Black	80	Black	143	Black	206	Black	269	Black	332	Black	395	Black	458	Diamond White
18	Black	81	Black	144	Black	207	Black	270	Black	333	Black	396	Black	459	Moonstone Blue
19	Black	82	Black	145	Black	208	Black	271	Black	334	Black	397	Diamond White	460	Moonstone Blue
20	Black	83	Black	146	Black	209	Black	272	Black	335	Black	398	Diamond White	461	Moonstone Blue
21	Black	84	Black	147	Black	210	Black	273	Black	336	Black	399	Diamond White	462	Moonstone Blue
22	Black	85	Black	148	Black	211	Black	274	Black	337	Black	400	Diamond White	463	Moonstone Blue
23	Black	86	Black	149	Black	212	Black	275	Black	338	Black	401	Black	464	Moonstone Blue
24	Black	87	Black	150	Black	213	Black	276	Black	339	Black	402	Diamond White	465	Moonstone Blue
25	Black	88	Black	151	Black	214	Black	277	Black	340	Black	403	Moonstone Blue	466	Moonstone Blue
26	Black	89	Black	152	Black	215	Black	278	Black	341	Black	404	Moonstone Blue	467	Moonstone Blue
27	Black	90	Black	153	Black	216	Black	279	Black	342	Black	405	Moonstone Blue	468	Diamond White
28	Black	91	Black	154	Black	217	Black	280	Black	343	Black	406	Moonstone Blue	469	Moonstone Blue
29	Black	92	Black	155	Black	218	Black	281	Black	344	Black	407	Moonstone Blue	470	Moonstone Blue
30	Black	93	Black	156	Black	219	Black	282	Black	345	Black	408	Moonstone Blue	471	Moonstone Blue
31	Black	94	Black	157	Black	220	Black	283	Black	346	Black	409	Moonstone Blue	472	Moonstone Blue
32	Black	95	Black	158	Black	221	Black	284	Black	347	Black	410	Moonstone Blue	473	Moonstone Blue
33	Black	96	Black	159	Black	222	Black	285	Black	348	Black	411	Moonstone Blue	474	Moonstone Blue
34	Black	97	Black	160	Black	223	Black	286	Black	349	Black	412	Moonstone Blue	475	Moonstone Blue
35	Black	98	Black	161	Black	224	Black	287	Black	350	Black	413	Moonstone Blue	476	Diamond White
36	Black	99	Black	162	Black	225	Black	288	Black	351	Black	414	Moonstone Blue	477	Diamond White
37	Black	100	Black	163	Black	226	Black	289	Black	352	Black	415	Moonstone Blue	478	Diamond White
38	Black	101	Black	164	Black	227	Black	290	Black	353	Black	416	Moonstone Blue	479	Diamond White
39	Black	102	Black	165	Black	228	Black	291	Black	354	Black	417	Diamond White	480	Moonstone Blue
40	Black	103	Black	166	Black	229	Black	292	Black	355	Black	418	Black	481	Moonstone Blue
41	Black	104	Black	167	Black	230	Black	293	Black	356	Black	419	Diamond White	482	Diamond White
42	Black	105	Black	168	Black	231	Black	294	Black	357	Black	420	Diamond White	483	Diamond White
43	Black	106	Black	169	Black	232	Black	295	Black	358	Black	421	Diamond White	484	Moonstone Blue
44	Black	107	Black	170	Black	233	Black	296	Black	359	Black	422	Diamond White	485	Moonstone Blue
45	Black	108	Black	171	Black	234	Black	297	Black	360	Black	423	Diamond White	486	Moonstone Blue
46	Black	109	Black	172	Black	235	Black	298	Black	361	Black	424	Diamond White	487	Moonstone Blue
47	Black	110	Black	173	Black	236	Black	299	Black	362	Black	425	Diamond White	488	Moonstone Blue
48	Black	111	Black	174	Black	237	Black	300	Black	363	Black	426	Diamond White	489	Moonstone Blue
49	Black	112	Black	175	Black	238	Black	301	Black	364	Black	427	Diamond White	490	Moonstone Blue
50	Black	113	Black	176	Black	239	Black	302	Black	365	Black	428	Moonstone Blue	491	Moonstone Blue
51	Black	114	Black	177	Black	240	Black	303	Black	366	Black	429	Moonstone Blue	492	Moonstone Blue
52	Black	115	Black	178	Black	241	Black	304	Black	367	Black	430	Diamond White	493	Moonstone Blue
53	Black	116	Black	179	Black	242	Black	305	Black	368	Black	431	Diamond White	494	Moonstone Blue
54	Black	117	Black	180	Black	243	Black	306	Black	369	Black	432	Diamond White	495	Moonstone Blue
55	Black	118	Black	181	Black	244	Black	307	Black	370	Black	433	Diamond White	496	Moonstone Blue
56	Black	119	Black	182	Black	245	Black	308	Black	371	Black	434	Diamond White	497	Moonstone Blue
57	Black	120	Black	183	Black	246	Black	309	Black	372	Black	435	Diamond White	498	Moonstone Blue
58	Black	121	Black	184	Black	247	Black	310	Black	373	Black	436	Diamond White	499	Moonstone Blue
59	Black	122	Black	185	Black	248	Black	311	Black	374	Black	437	Diamond White	500	Moonstone Blue
60	Black	123	Black	186	Black	249	Black	312	Black	375	Black	438	Diamond White		
61	Black	124	Black	187	Black	250	Black	313	Black	376	Black	439	Diamond White		
62	Black	125	Black	188	Black	251	Black	314	Black	377	Black	440	Diamond White		
63	Black	126	Black	189	Black	252	Black	315	Black	378	Black	441	Diamond White		

SIERRA SAPPHIRE RS COSWORTH

Surely the finest Sapphire Cosworth in existence, Marc McCubbin's June 1989 machine left the factory in Magenta with Raven leather upholstery. A one-owner weekend car until 2003, Marc acquired the Sapphire after it had covered around 40,000 miles. He stripped the underside of wax, photographed and measured each sticker and paint splash, then restored it all to factory specification. In contrast, the bodywork is mostly original, with only the bonnet, bumpers, skirts and one wing having been resprayed. To date, Marc's Sapphire is still unbeaten on the concourse Ford scene.

The wild styling was long gone. A competition career was unnecessary, and limited production was a thing of the past. By 1987, the Sierra RS Cosworth had become mainstream. And it was a greater success than ever.

The four-door Cosworth outsold its predecessor in vast quantities. It was a more accomplished road car, and it kept the fires burning for further motorsport success. It truly deserves its place in history.

Ford had already conceived a second-generation Sierra Cosworth before the original version had been seen in public. As far back as 1984, the Sierra Mk2 was scheduled to arrive in 1987 alongside a new four-door saloon variant. Talk of transferring the go-faster goodies into a restyled three-door body went quiet when it was realised such a machine simply wasn't needed; the bewinged competition-spec Sierra had been built in sufficient numbers for motorsport homologation, and the RS500 would annihilate the competition. Job done.

Yet Ford was committed to buying a further 10,000 engines from Cosworth. And, besides, Blue Oval bosses saw potential in a new market sector – the executive express arena normally occupied by the likes of BMW.

A brief fling with a YB-engined Scorpio (complete with

automatic transmission) was thankfully discarded, and the incoming four-door mid-sized saloon (tagged Sierra Sapphire in the UK but simply Sierra everywhere else) was deemed more suitable. Ghia trim was specified for a refined, high-end feel.

The project was approved on 8 April 1986, and Ford's Special Vehicle Engineering (SVE) department began work on a suitable shell, stuffing the three-door's complete mechanicals beneath the subtle saloon bodywork. The lack of motorsport ambition meant SVE could engineer a machine for taking company directors to meetings without looking like boy-racers; the whale-tail was binned, the wide wheelarches were ditched, and the bonnet vents had been cast aside (they were thought to be useless unless fitted to a 300bhp racer).

The first prototype even went without a rear spoiler, although a restrained wrap-around wing was added after sessions in Ford's German wind tunnel proved why downforce is needed in a high-speed machine.

A happy coincidence of choosing the four-door body was its significantly stiffer shell than the hatchback variant, which worked well alongside Ford's revisions for the mainstream Sierra Mk2. The chassis side rails and seat crossmembers were said to be uprated, an acoustic polystyrene filled the front windscreen pillars, the Mk1's raised rain gutters were swapped for a flush drip rail, and aerodynamic stakes were used on the rear pillars to aid crosswind stability.

In practice, this meant the original RS Cosworth's running gear took on a more civilised feeling, despite only minor alterations: softer dampers, harder springs, a chunkier rear

anti-roll bar and tamer geometry. Again, 7x15in alloy wheels were used, albeit now in a new lattice design. The handling was instantly recognised as less nervous than its predecessor's – better suited to everyday use yet equally capable of high-speed work.

Eight prototypes were constructed in 1986 and 1987, in left-

One of three initial launch colours – the others being Diamond White and Mercury Grey – this Crystal Blue Sapphire RS Cosworth left the factory in July 1988 complete with cloth interior, at the time the only option. Currently owned by Damon Sargent, this original 60,000-mile machine has been treated to minor cosmetic attention and some underbonnet modifications but otherwise remains as Ford intended.

The last right-hand-drive Sapphire Cosworth to leave the Genk production line (alongside a left-hand-drive Pacifica Blue example, the very final car and kept in Ford's hands), this November 1992-built 4x4 was painted in one-off Mallard Green and UK-registered from new on 2 March 1993. Still showing a mere 19,632 miles, this Sapphire was at the time of photography driven occasionally and formed part of the renowned Bonkers Collection owned by Mark Bailey. It has since been sold to another Ford fan.

Still a slightly nose-down stance, the Sapphire's suspension was tweaked by Ford to be more comfortable and less twitchy than the Sierra, with no detriment to the Cosworth's handling ability.

on UK cars' back doors weren't used in any other market.

As for that all-conquering Cosworth YBB powerplant, it remained almost unchanged from its days in the three-door version. Indeed, 500 early Sapphires were equipped with engines that were initially fitted to November 1986-built Sierras and subsequently shipped to Tickford for conversion into RS500s; when these cars had meatier YBD engines added, the old YBBs were sent back to Cosworth, freshened up with new water pumps and returned to Genk.

The powerplant was still force-fed by a Garrett T03B turbo and intercooler, still based on an iron 205 (Pinto) block, and still running Weber-Marelli management, albeit with an updated ECU. The tough but tractor-like T5 transmission remained in place, along with the usual 7.5in limited-slip differential. As before, Teves supplied the four-pot front brake callipers and ABS.

True to its executive aspirations, the Sapphire's cabin was sprinkled with upmarket equipment, including velour Recaro seats, leather steering wheel and gearknob, heated windscreen and electric windows (all-round on British cars; just the fronts in Europe). The three-door's boost gauge was now absent from beside the rev counter and 170mph speedometer; Ford bosses reckoned the average businessman wouldn't be concerned with such frivolities.

But why not? With 204bhp (minimum) and a superior drag coefficient (0.33 compared with the three-door's 0.34), the Sapphire Cosworth was capable of 150mph and hitting 60mph from standstill in just 6.1 seconds.

Sales began in January 1988, distributed among the UK, southern Ireland, West Germany, Spain, France, Finland, Denmark, Belgium, Holland, Portugal, Norway, Hong Kong, Singapore, Canary Islands, Macao and South Africa; it's reckoned around half of the rear-wheel-drive Sapphire

and right-hand-drive. A further 70 pre-production cars were assembled at Genk in September 1987, with full production supposed to begin soon after. In practice, construction of the Sapphire Cosworth probably began during January 1988.

All were then built on mainstream Belgian assembly lines alongside run-of-the-mill models. Based on Ghia bodies (complete with glass sunroofs and a complement of electrical luxuries), the initial batch of cars came in a choice of three colours: Diamond White, Mercury Grey or Crystal Blue. They wore bumpers, functional skirts and rear spoilers supplied by Marley, and a Sierra RS Cosworth badge on the bootlid. Well, British-bound cars did, anyway; for the rest of Europe it was simply a Sierra Cosworth. Similarly, the tiny Sapphire badges

Restrained by Cosworth standards, the Sapphire incarnation was nevertheless purposeful from the front, with deep front bumper, wide air scoops and rubber lower diffuser. The rear-wheel-drive model went without bonnet vents.

Gone was the wild rear wing, but the Sapphire's back end was still unmistakable to car enthusiasts. Maybe it was the small aerofoil, maybe it was the large-bore exhaust pipe, or perhaps it was the Cosworth badge on the boot.

Cosworth's 13,839 production run came to Great Britain, with the last delivered in 1990.

A few alterations appeared along the way, including constant evolution of the YBB engine, small specification changes, an option of leather upholstery from 1989 and new colours: Crystal Blue and Mercury Grey were ousted in favour of Moonstone Blue, Flint Grey, Black and Magenta.

But all that stuff was trivial compared with the revisions for January 1990: the Sierra Sapphire Cosworth 4x4 was in many ways a new model, with a heavily-reworked engine (Ford said 80 per cent of the parts were updated, including a stronger cylinder block and larger intercooler); power was increased to 220bhp, the brakes were replaced all-round, and – most importantly – the entire transmission was swapped for a modified version of the Sierra XR4x4 setup.

Even during the three-door's reign on racetracks, Ford had chosen to use the V6-powered, four-wheel-drive, five-door Sierra for rallying alongside its rear-drive counterpart; a close-ratio MT75 gearbox had been homologated for the XR4x4, and it was obvious even in 1987 that a mixture of the two machines would be ideal for loose-surface work.

While Ford's motorsport crew built one or two four-wheel-drive three-door Cosworths, SVE began work on the four-door version during 1988; two prototypes were followed by a series of pre-production cars put together on the regular assembly line.

Ford's proven Ferguson-type system was used, with viscous-coupling limited-slip differentials and a torque split of 34 per cent to the front wheels and 66 at the rear. To accommodate the front driveshafts, the Sapphire's bodyshell was suitably reworked with cutouts in the front chassis rails, and there was a unique engine sump. The whole system added a 50kg weight penalty (or thereabouts), dulling performance only slightly – it still reached 150mph but rest-to-60mph took 6.6 seconds.

Blue Oval bosses dictated there should be no visual changes from the existing four-door Cosworth, turning down the motorsport department's requests for wide wheelarches but accepting the cooling requirement for bonnet louvres. Tinted rear lamp lenses and small 4x4 badges on the front wings were the other big giveaways.

More paintwork options were added, including Nouveau Red, Moondust Silver and Smokestone Blue.

UK cars were initially equipped with Cosworth's new YBJ engine, which wore the traditional red rocker cover, but swapped to the catalytic converter-equipped YBG in August 1991, complete with green cam cover. Power output and performance were unchanged.

Alongside the cats, the revised RS Cosworth gained shark-tooth 15in alloys, modernised dashboard and electric sunroof. Air conditioning became an optional extra. Late models came with a fully colour-coded rear spoiler and four-spoke steering wheel, and the final pair were finished in ultra-rare colours – a Mallard Green right-hand drive car and a left-hooker in

Pacifica Blue. The four-wheel-drive Sapphire ceased production in November/December 1992 and was officially discontinued in April 1993, after around 12,250 examples had been built.

By then, of course, the Sapphire Cosworth 4x4 had proved itself an accomplished all-rounder. Testers raved about its roadholding, and the car made a reasonable impact in world rallying (motorsport homologation had been achieved in August 1990, after 5000 road cars were completed).

Yet its achievements were rapidly overlooked when the Escort RS Cosworth appeared in 1992, based on a shortened Sapphire Cosworth 4x4 floorpan. And, although motorsport dominance and extrovert styling are what make headlines, the supercar-slaying Sapphire certainly left its mark.

The Sapphire was arguably better to drive than any Cosworth road car before or since, and it dramatically outsold the others. It was an amazing success.

Sapphire 4x4 was the only Cosworth to sit level, rather than nose-down. This car's late-spec shark-tooth alloy wheels and Mallard Green paintwork updated the ageing model's looks in line with its 1992 production.

Line drawing of original Sapphire Cosworth shows the mechanical layout was pretty much unchanged from its three-door predecessor.

Engine – Block, Sump and Oil system (RWD)

Motorsport homologation meant Ford had to build 5000 Sierra Cosworth road cars, yet the firm committed itself to buying 15,000 YBB engines from Cosworth. Thanks to such an oversight, the remaining two-thirds of production found homes in the Sapphire; in fact, 500 early cars received engines removed from the November 1986-built three-door Sierras that were converted into RS500s by Tickford in July 1987; other than a freshen-up and new water pump, it all remained the same. So, what was the specification of that YBB powerplant?

Like the original Sierra Cosworth, the cylinder block was an iron 205 Pinto, complete with this casting's revised water galleries, thicker walls and stronger webbing around the base. As before, cylinder blocks were taken from the same batches as those destined for mainstream fuel-injected Sierras and Ford Transits; because they were produced in such massive quantities, there was a fair bit of variation between castings.

Usually, the numbers 205 were found in large, raised digits on both sides of the crankcase just below the cylinder head (which explains why it's commonly referred to as a 205 block); the 20 meant 2.0 litres and the 5 represented 1985, the block's first year of production.

Ford selected the blocks specifically for Cosworth, but

there was nothing really special about them – simply that the standard bore gradings had to be 2 or 3. These numbers were stamped into the crank case above the oil filter, behind the distributor; each cylinder was listed sequentially from one to four, such as 2323. Once the blocks had been shipped from Ford's foundry to Cosworth's Wellingborough factory, the stamped part of the cylinder block was sprayed with yellow primer. The rest of the block was brush-painted in satin black (although the front cover was bare alloy).

The offside lower bellhousing lug was also sprayed in yellow primer where it was stamped with Ford's engine block code of N5B. In contrast, a standard two-litre Pinto was NET, and the 2000cc fuel-injected version was NRD.

Other, less important, casting marks were found on each cylinder block, which were normal for all 205s. There was the part number – 85HM6015BB – in raised characters on the exhaust side, just beneath a small 205. Above, and just in front the offside engine mount, was a machined flat section with an engine number hand-stamped by Ford; the engine number comprised two letters for the build year and month, followed by a five-digit serial number. As usual, this code matched the car's VIN number.

On the same side was a raised oval, where the block's production date was cast. Its first pair of digits represented

YBB engine production at Cosworth in 1989. By this point, the red-painted screw-cap cam cover was in use.

the day and week of manufacture, the next letter relating to the month (A for January, B for February etc) and the final two digits being the year (87 meaning 1987, for example).

Minor revisions were made during production, and later-built (1988-to-90) 205 blocks had mildly stiffer castings and slightly larger bosses. That said, it would take a keen eye (and maybe a micrometer) to spot them. It's also worth noting that rear-wheel-drive Sapphires tended to have 1987 or 1988-made cylinder blocks; '89 and '90 blocks were generally produced for the Ford spares department rather than fitment

into factory-built cars.

Further serial numbers and identification marks were made on each block by Cosworth. Above the water pump, at the front of the engine, was a machined flat section, sprayed in yellow primer (using a masking template) by Cosworth and hand-stamped with a number, which began with YBB and was followed by a series of unique digits. YBB numbering began in three figures (such as 001) and rose into the thousands; of course, Sapphire engines were usually four or five figures. It's worth mentioning that these digits did not relate to Ford's

Wonderful YBB engine continued into the rear-wheel-drive Sapphire Cosworth with only minor revisions.

Creating the legend – Cosworth factory workers constructing Sapphire-destined YBB engines in 1989.

unique engine number.

As before, the Sapphire's YBB was 1993cc, with an 8.0:1 compression ratio. It contained the same Cosworth-designed, Mahle-made forged aluminium pistons and rings, which featured a crown with a shallow bowl; the manufacturer's code and production date were marked on top. Gradings of 2 or 3 were selected for pistons, stamped beneath each piston crown with corresponding sizes marked on the cylinder block.

Contrary to popular belief, piston revisions occurred around halfway into Sapphire production, with the early-type centre-pin pistons being replaced by a 1mm offset gudgeon pin. This design was carried forward into the Sapphire Cosworth 4x4, albeit with a 4cc larger piston bowl in the later car.

The Sapphire's Cosworth-designed connecting rods were the same throughout production (other than minor casting differences), made from forged heat-treated steel. They attached to the Cosworth five-bearing forged-steel crankshaft, as before; it featured hardened/moly-coated bearing journals, nine flywheel bolts, reinforced sprocket gear and oil seals.

Each piston was cooled as it reached the bottom of its stroke, using a spray bar brazed onto the oil pickup pipe. A modified Ford Pinto oil pump connected to the extra pipe, complete with a revised cover.

The oil pan was the previous car's gravity die-cast bare alloy sump, with internal baffle plate. It attached to the cylinder block via a multi-layered gasket (aluminium between two layers of cork). Oil was returned to the sump from the turbo through a gold-passivated tube, attached at the top with two bolts and linked via a black rubber pipe with grey hose clips on each end. Meanwhile, a dipstick tube reached into the back of the sump at the nearside, complete with yellow-painted, wire-looped dipstick.

A Modine oil-to-water heat exchanger was fitted into the oil feed system between the cylinder block face and oil filter housing, which wore a white sticker (displaying the part number) on its bare copper-coloured surface. Cosworth favoured orange Fram disposable oil filters, although there's a fair chance that white Ford Motorcraft filters were also used at some point during vehicle production.

At the nearside rear of the block was a threaded gold-passivated oil sender, which also fed oil to the turbo through a steel braided hose that took a path around the back of the engine. The usual crankcase breather system ran from the block beneath the inlet manifold, through a condensing unit and into the intake airbox.

A black three-slotted crank pulley was found at the front of the engine, held on with a large gold-passivated bolt. It turned belts of the camshaft pulleys and engine ancillaries.

The Sierra Cosworth three-door's engine mounts were fitted between the Sapphire's crossmember and cylinder block. At the right-hand side was a mixture of XR4i insulator and special alloy casting, while the left-hand side was from the regular Pinto powerplant, complete with red paint splash. They were attached using gold-passivated bolts and black or passivated washers.

Engine - block, sump and oil system (4x4)

By 1989 Ford had honoured its commitment to purchasing 15,000 YB engines from Cosworth. Indeed, historians suggest 18,990 YBBs were built before Ford switched from rear-wheel-drive to the Sapphire Cosworth 4x4.

So in came the YBJ and YBG, reckoned by Ford to be all-new in four-fifths of their components but essentially the same as one another. The difference between YBJ and YBG was that

Cosworth YBG engine came to the UK in February 1992, complete with catalytic converters and lambda sensors. The green cam cover was an easy identifier. Note this car's air conditioning pipework just in front of the battery and nearside inner wing.

the latter was designed to run with twin catalytic converters, although all were fine for use with unleaded petrol – because the mechanical bits were identical. Indeed, the only variances were the added cats, revised ECU settings and different-coloured cam covers. But more of that later.

Both units were developed together and began production in autumn 1989, ready for the Sapphire 4x4's launch at the beginning of 1990. British cars, until August 1991, were equipped with the YBJ; the YBG was used thereafter.

Crucially, the YBJ and YBG were built around a new reinforced cylinder block to cope with the additional stresses of a four-wheel-drive transmission system. Although at direct glance it looked the same as its predecessor, it was stiffened around the base, with extra thickness in the cast iron to halfway up the crankcase. There were also internal differences in the casting around the cylinder head bolt drillings, along with provision around the water jackets for long studs.

This cylinder block was known as a 200 block due to the large raised digits cast into each side of the crankcase just below the cylinder head, adjacent to cylinder number two. In this case the 20 stood for 2.0 litres and the 0 represented 1990 – the new model year for the 4x4 block's autumn 1989 introduction.

The raised 200 was repeated in smaller digits just in front of the offside engine mount, alongside a Ford oval and over

the part number V90HM6015AA. Above was a machined flat surface wearing the hand-stamped Ford engine number, composed of two letters for the build year and month, followed by a five-digit serial number, which corresponded with the car's chassis number.

True to form, Cosworth employees stamped the firm's own unique engine number into the front of the cylinder block, just above the water pump. The YB code was followed by a J or G (depending on application) and a unique series of four or five digits. This engine number did not match the Ford number found on the side of the block.

The engine block's production date was also cast on the exhaust side of the crankcase, as always in a raised oval. It featured two digits to represent the day and week of manufacture, a letter relating to the month (A for January, B for February etc) and another two digits being the year (89 meaning 1989 and so on).

The 200 block was cast specifically for Cosworth, and factory-fitted only into four-wheel-drive Sierras and Escorts. As such, there were fewer casting differences than found on 205 blocks. But that's not to say all 200 blocks were created equal. Quite the opposite, in fact...

Early 200 blocks – built during 1989 and fitted to the first Sapphire Cosworth 4x4s (unless rumours of a few early 4x4s with 205 blocks are true) – used a relatively poor casting, and

YBB's red cam cover was altered in July 1988 to take screw-thread oil filler instead of earlier bayonet cap.

were known to crack during use; it's likely that many were replaced under warranty when reasonably new.

These 1989-manufactured blocks differed from later castings in several ways. Most notably, there was a core plug in the rear (gearbox end) of the block of all Pinto family engines, which was deleted from 1992 onwards; the 200 block was now cast as the 90HM6015AB. As found on all 205 blocks, there was also provision for a Pinto's mechanical fuel pump drive on the 200, complete with boss and drillings on the inlet side, towards the front of the engine. Although the casting remained, the drillings were deleted in August 1990 for the 1991 model year; earlier cars blanked off the fuel pump recess

YBB engine receiving its cylinder head at Cosworth in 1989.

with an extra section on their PAS pump mounting bracket, which was deleted at the same time.

There were no further revisions to the cylinder block during Sierra Sapphire production.

Internally, there were more differences between the content of 205 and 200 blocks. The 4x4 (200 engine) had a revised crankshaft; still a five-bearing forged-steel crank with nine flywheel bolts, it now had a longer nose and interference-fit front pulley, which was pressed on (as opposed to the 205's, which slid into place and was notorious for coming loose). The 200's crank was not as well-balanced as its predecessor's.

The YBB's forged steel connecting rods were carried over (with minor casting revisions as time went on) and the pistons were a similar design to the later-type YBB's, with a 1mm offset gudgeon pin. However, 4x4 pistons featured a 4cc larger bowl than before, which worked with a new cylinder head (including 46cc combustion chamber rather than the earlier head's 50cc) and retained the original 8:1 compression ratio.

An under-piston oil spray bar was retained for the 4x4, brazed onto the oil pickup pipe and directing oil out of jets pointed up the cylinder bores. The oil pump was replaced, though: the YBB pump had a bearing on only one side of the rotor shaft, which was found to wear internally; instead, the 200-based engine had a supporting spigot on the upper side to hold it square in the housing; externally, a raised noggin was visible in the centre of what looked like the top of the oil pump, along with five bolt fixings.

An all-new sump was cast for the 4x4, still in bare alloy but now featuring tunnels for the front driveshafts to pass through. The baffle plate was revised but the sump gasket was carried over from before, being aluminium sandwiched between two layers of cork.

A new dipstick and tube was now in use, albeit in the same position at the nearside rear of the engine. The dipstick now featured a metal rod with yellow plastic handle, and the tube benefited from a wider opening at the top.

Again, a Modine oil cooler/heat exchanger was placed between the cylinder block face and the oil filter housing, but now it was a chunkier unit with offset inlet/outlets. There was also a new, larger oil filter.

The 200's breather system was revised, featuring a condensing unit with two outlets rather than the YBB's single. It still sat beneath the inlet manifold and ran pipework to the intake airbox. The previous engine's gold-passivated oil sender assembly remained in the same position at the nearside rear of the cylinder block.

Several crank pulleys were used on the Sapphire Cosworth, as previously mentioned. Early cars wore a three-vee pulley, while later cars (from August 1990) had a single poly-vee version. There was also another type – the twin poly-vee – used from October 1991 on air-conditioning-equipped Sapphires.

Needless to say, the 4x4 Sapphire required new engine mounts to mate to its alloy engine crossmember, which was also found on the 2.0 twin-cam 4x4. The new mounts featured circular rubbers (from the 2.0 4x4) inside oval alloy plates, which then bolted into the crossmember using long studs, mildy raising the engine in the process.

Cylinder head

Sapphire cylinder heads were cast in aluminium alloy by Cosworth at its foundry in Worcester. Although the original 16-valve, twin-overhead camshaft design remained the same, Cosworth cylinder heads progressed through a constant development process, with each incarnation gradually becoming better than the last.

The changes were reflected in Ford's traditional part numbering system, which can be roughly deciphered in the following way.

The first Sapphire Cosworths were equipped with the Sierra three-door's cylinder head (in late-1986-spec with 23mm head washers), which had the part number 86HF6090AA. The 86 related to the part's design year, 6090 meant cylinder head and the suffix (AA) was the version. Generally, the first of these two letters indicated a major casting/mould version and the second was a less significant revision.

In early-to-mid 1988 the 86HF6090BA head arrived, which followed the RS500's pattern of including a casting with threaded holes for a three-bolt thermostat housing (not fitted) rather than the earlier two found on the first Sapphires. It also featured long oil galleries and eight NPT bungs screwed into the voids at each end. BA head drillings were bigger than before, being beefed up to stop the casting from splitting at the front and rear of the head (with successful results).

Soon after the BA head came the 86HF6090CA, which featured only internal changes; the majority of rear-wheel-drive Sapphires wore this cylinder head. In 1989 it was replaced with the 86HF6090CB, which benefited from 4x4-type cooling jackets, with a closed deck on both sides instead of open slots around the exhaust ports. The turbo damper mounting remained in place.

The CB didn't last long, though, because the YBB was replaced with the YBJ and YBG in the Sapphire 4x4. The first 4x4 head (and the only part found on the four-wheel-drive Sapphire) was the 89HF6090AA, which differed from the rear-wheel-drive cylinder head by including a 46cc combustion chamber volume rather than the YBB's 50cc. The casting now lacked provision for a turbo damper, and the head bolt pillars were altered inside. The water galleries were the closed-deck versions found on CB heads.

As before, all Sapphire Cosworth cylinder heads had 23mm ports and standard valve sizes – 35-to-35.2mm inlet head diameters, and 31-to-31.2mm sodium-cooled exhaust valves. There were four valves per cylinder, arranged in a vee, with inlet and exhaust valves on opposite sides. They were opened by hydraulic lifters and a pair of camshafts, each with 8.544mm lift. It was all standard RS Cosworth stuff, along

with the revised head gasket, as introduced in mid-1986. The only difference came with the 4x4 head, which had larger exhaust manifold gasket faces.

The valve sizes were stamped on the back of the cylinder head in 5mm digits, which described any oversized valve guides, seats and tappets. If the tappets were oversized, a letter A would be stamped onto the cylinder head adjacent to the tappet bore.

A Uniroyal glassfibre-reinforced toothed rubber timing belt, with printed white lettering, turned the cams using a pair of Escort CVH pulleys, which were left bare and attached with gold-passivated bolts. The grey alloy belt tensioner was also attached using gold-passivated bolts.

On the front of the YBB engine was a textured black plastic timing belt cover, which wore a yellow 'check oil daily' sticker on top and – on early cars – a white 'refer to manual' decal on

Green cam cover was new for the environmentally-conscious YBG engine.

New timing belt cover was manufactured for the 4x4, with rounded top and bold logos.

the upper front face. The cover was held onto the engine with three black Torx-headed bolts and gold-passivated washers. For the YBG and YBJ there was a new, rounded cover – again in textured black plastic but now emblazoned with Ford and Cosworth logos across the front. Three black Torx-headed bolts and washers attached the cover to the engine.

Three different cam covers were found on the Sapphire Cosworth. Until July 1988 there was the original three-door Sierra-type cam cover (V86HF6582AA part number), finished in textured red 'sand-cast' paint, skimmed to reveal bare alloy sections with embossed and still-painted DOHC 16-V TURBO and Ford COSWORTH logos. The exposed metal was left rough and uncoated. This cam cover featured a bayonet-cap oil filler, made from black plastic.

From July 1988 came the V86HF6582AB cam cover, which was identical to the earlier part but designed to accommodate a screw-threaded filler cap (with ENGINE OIL and oil can diagram in raised characters inside a yellow circle); it was still painted red. Finally, the YBG engine's green cam cover was added in February 1992 – the same but for the colour, and now featuring a V89HF6582AA part number in the casting. The filler cap changed with the introduction of the 4x4, sacrificing its raised lettering in favour of the same yellow characters now flush with the surface of the cap.

All YBB cylinder heads were cast with a turbo damper mounting on the exhaust side, but this was omitted from YBG and YBJ heads. The usual gold-passivated lifting brackets were mounted onto the cylinder head on the nearside front and offside rear manifold studs no matter which engine, but the 4x4 lost the hose brackets across the top of the cam cover thanks to this model's revised cooling system.

Cooling System

Three different cooling systems were found on Sapphire Cosworths, depending on year of build and specification.

Rear-wheel-drive cars were fitted with a similar setup to the three-door Sierra RS. A revised Sierra 2.0 Pinto water pump (featuring more vanes) was painted black and fitted to the front of the engine on gold-passivated bolts. Above it was a two-bolt alloy thermostat housing containing an 88-degree wax thermostat. There were outlets for a bleed hose and coolant feed pipe to the turbo.

A pair of matched belts from the crank pulley were used to rotate the water pump, along with the alternator. The pump pushed coolant around a series of hard metal pipes and black rubber hoses with white-printed part numbers, fastened on using Ford-branded Jubilee-type clips. These were the same hoses found on the three-door Cosworth, sourced from regular Sierras plus unique inlet and outlet pipes. A removable two-bolt coolant sensor housing was fitted on a stub at the rear of the cylinder head, under the inlet manifold, along with a blue sensor.

A clear/white plastic header tank was mounted on the nearside inner wing, with an upper inlet from the turbocharger and lower stub to feed the radiator. One difference from the Sierra three-door was that the central outlet – which previously connected to a coolant level sensor – was now blanked off. The tank was topped with a black plastic pressure cap and black-on-white antifreeze sticker. The cap was replaced with a yellow version in 1989, when Ford made a universal change towards highlighting service items.

In front of the engine was the three-door Cosworth's radiator, which had an aluminium core and black plastic end tanks. Attached to it was a black plastic shroud enclosing a pair of electrically-driven black plastic cooling fans, which were operated by a thermal switch.

As before, the Sierra Cosworth's air-to-air intercooler was used between the turbo and inlet manifold, mounted above the radiator complete with guide plate to direct cold air; it was a different shape for the Sapphire due to the new car's redesigned nose. The intercooler was linked with hoses at each end – black rubber on the cold air side, and terracotta silicone to the turbo.

For the Sapphire Cosworth 4x4, Ford revised the cooling system, based on lessons learned from the RS500. Although it was the same in principle, most of the components were replaced.

There was a new, more effective water pump, which had larger impeller and deeper body. The thermostat housing was now bigger too, having a three-bolt fitting rather than the previous two. The new design allowed coolant to circulate around the cylinder head prior to the thermostat opening, so the housing also featured a return pipe inlet, as well as the rear-wheel-drive Sapphire's single outlet. Although the casting looked similar to the RS500's, the 4x4's return pipe faced backwards (the RS500's pointed forwards) and was fitted using a rubber O-ring rather than a gasket between the cylinder head and thermostat housing.

The 4x4's pipework routing was substantially altered, using new coolant hoses that wrapped neatly around the front of the engine bay rather than across the top of the engine. They were connected to a new plastic header tank, which had two outlets at the bottom about an inch apart; the upper hose (the return from the turbo) was now a much bigger bore than before.

Most importantly, the 4x4 boasted a substantially larger intercooler (wider and deeper) than its predecessor, now claimed to have 78 per cent improved efficiency. It sat on new mounting brackets, with a different fan shroud and revised radiator, and connected into the cooling system with shorter hoses. A new fan and motor assembly appeared in January 1991.

As for the third cooling system, it arrived around August 1991 with the air-conditioning option in the UK (although it was listed for European cars from October 1990). The system used additional components sourced from other Fords, including a compressor and clutch assembly from the 2.0DOHC 4x4, along with heater/blower assembly, pump, new pipework, new wiring loom, different upper bulkhead, and dashboard switch with warning lamp. The official engine designations for air conditioning-equipped Sapphire Cosworths were YBG (AIR) and YBJ (AIR) depending on whether or not catalytic converters were present.

Fuel System

Providing petrol to the Sapphire Cosworth (usually in great quantities) was a job for Weber-Marelli multi-point fuel injection and electronic management. In the first four-door incarnation, the whole lot was lifted almost entirely from the three-door Sierra RS Cosworth.

At the cylinder head was an alloy inlet manifold, with an alloy plenum chamber bolted into place. A 60mm throttle body was fitted on a separate elbow, fastened with three pairs of dished washers and supported by a bracket from the nearside engine mounting. There was a throttle position sensor bolted to the throttle body, and an idle speed control valve was mounted above.

An inlet air temperature sensor was also connected to the plenum chamber, along with vacuum connectors for the fuel pressure regulator, MAP sensor, air charge bypass valve and crankcase ventilation filter.

A bright nickel-finished fuel rail was mounted on top, complete with four yellow Weber plug-in injectors (one for each cylinder). At the front of the rail was a bare alloy adjustable Weber fuel pressure regulator, connected through a short black rubber hose. The throttle cable came directly from the Sierra RS Cosworth, although left-hand-drive examples used a regular Pinto 1.3-litre part. The cable was mounted though a gold-passivated bracket, and (on UK cars) wrapped around the slam panel, up the offside inner wing and through the bulkhead at the driver's side.

Fuel was fed to the rail along steel pipes attached to the underside of the car's floorpan using white plastic clips. In the engine bay the pipes switched to hard black plastic and a braided rubber fuel return.

Like the Sierra, the Sapphire was equipped with a Bosch 941 electric fuel pump, which had a bare metal finish, and was fitted inside a standard-Sierra satin black support bracket along with a bare-metal fuel filter, coupled up via braided hoses. Again, the fuel tank and sender were stock Sierra 2.0i/V6 components. The tank was painted silver, and housed an internal swirl pot in white plastic; the original tank featured a circular pressing near to the differential casing, rather than a rectangular shape seen on some aftermarket tanks.

A black plastic airbox was mounted at the front of the offside inner wing, again the same as the three-door Sierra component and including an identical paper element. The airbox lid was held on with five wire clips, and featured a

Wonderful YBB engine continued into the rear-wheel-drive Sapphire Cosworth with yellow fuel injectors and separate fuel pressure regulator at the front of the rail.

series of outlets – the turbo was fed with air through a large black rubber induction hose, which attached with a Ford-branded Jubilee-type clip and wore its part numbers printed in white. A tee from this hose connected it to a dump valve between the turbo and intercooler.

There were also two smaller outlets from the airbox lid, which linked to the inlet manifold and air bypass valve through a large rubber hose and a mixture of black plastic pipe and braided hose. A square inlet scoop fed cold air into the base of the airbox.

Rear-wheel-drive Sapphire Cosworth had the same exhaust system as its three-door predecessor. Body-colour paintwork was wafted onto the spare wheel well when the car was sprayed from above.

Garrett T03 turbo and actuator were the same as the parts found on the RS Cosworth three-door; the turbo damper was dropped from the following 4x4.

Bosch dump valve lived in the right-hand-side front corner of the engine bay above the intercooler.

min versus the earlier 311cc/min). Meanwhile, the throttle body was revised, having a recessed adjuster screw rather than the YBB's protruding part.

At the front of the engine, the air cleaner assembly stayed mostly the same, but a revised inlet hose was needed for the 4x4's new turbo. Its elbow to reach the dump valve was now on the corner of the hose, rather than teeing off from beside the airbox. A narrower intake scoop was connected to the airbox base to make room for the 4x4's larger intercooler.

The other, less notable alteration for the 4x4 was a new fuel filler pipe, which linked to the updated external flap assembly.

Exhaust System

It looked substantially longer than the Sierra hatchback, but the Sapphire's saloon body had very similar proportions – which meant a new exhaust was not required.

So the rear-wheel-drive Sapphire Cosworth received its three-door predecessor's entire system from tip to tail.

At the engine, the water-cooled T3 turbo remained in place. Officially a Garrett AiResearch T03, this Cosworth-spec T3 featured a 0.48 exhaust housing and 55-trim compressor wheel. An internal wastegate was controlled by a gold-passivated actuator attached above the turbo on a bracket. A silver 'caution' decal was stuck to the rim of the actuator, while a braided hose and hard black plastic pipe linked it to an Amal valve. As before, the Sapphire's standard boost pressure was 8psi (0.55 bar).

A bracket between compressor and exhaust housings was used to connect a bare metal turbo vibration damper with single-coil spring mechanism, which was bolted to the cylinder head in the foremost tapped hole. Behind the turbo, a foil heat shield was attached to the engine bay with three bolts; again, these parts were carried over from the three-door RS Cosworth.

The turbo was supplied with air from the airbox through a big, black rubber hose, and exited to the intercooler via a terracotta-coloured silicone hose connected to the intercooler. Air then travelled through the intercooler to the throttle body on another black rubber hose. A black rubber hose was also fitted between the intercooler and a black plastic Bosch bypass valve, which was teed off from the main air inlet hose. Ford-stamped Jubilee-type clips were used throughout.

The turbo had an oil feed through a steel-braided hose from the engine's oil pressure warning switch adaptor, while an oil return pipe was connected to the sump with a black rubber hose and a pair of clips. Water cooling was through a feed pipe from the thermostat housing, which in turn went back to the header tank via a hard pipe mounted on top of the cam cover using brackets from the timing belt cover; a rubber hose helped to route it through the foremost engine lifting eye.

On a rear-wheel-drive Sapphire the turbo was mounted on a long two-piece manifold made from heat-resistant nickel-iron and composed of primary and secondary sections. It fastened

Several alterations were made for the Sapphire 4x4. The inlet manifold remained the same (despite being referred to by Ford as 'stiffened') but the plenum chamber was broader to increase volume, and it was now cast in one piece with its elbow. The fuel rail was changed too, now matt-finished and incorporating an integral fuel pressure regulator; unlike the subsequent Escort, the Sapphire's regulator was adjustable. A revised fuel return pipe was required, but the remaining fuel lines were the same as the previous Sapphire Cosworth's.

Most notably, the yellow Weber injectors were swapped to dark blue versions, which were mildly higher-flowing (328cc/

to the cylinder head and downpipe flange on M10 studs.

The back of the turbo's exhaust housing connected to a large-bore downpipe, which in turn fed the exhaust system. After the downpipe there was a front silencer that split into two pipes, followed by a single box, another pipe, a pair of centre boxes and finally back into a single pipe and rear silencer – very restrictive. The hanging rubbers were simply regular Ford parts from any old Pinto-engined Sierra.

It's worth noting that the factory system was constructed in a single piece, but Ford service replacement exhausts came in four sections. All just the same as the three-door RS Cosworth, and all applied with small, blue part number stickers.

In contrast, few components were carried over to the Sapphire 4x4. The turbo was still a T3 (okay, it was now referred to as T03B) but this time there was a 0.48 exhaust housing with 60-trim compressor wheel and larger internals to accept it, along with a lead seal and profile changes within the housing. And whereas the rear-wheel-drive car's actuator was mounted on a separate bracket above the turbo, the 4x4's was bolted onto the front of the compressor housing in a nine o'clock position.

The turbo manifold was altered, being a one-piece component designed for improved throttle response rather than outright power, while the coolant inlet and outlet tubes changed for the new turbo position; the coolant return hose ran along the bonnet slam panel towards the header tank, rather than over the top of the engine.

Most noticeably, the turbo heat shield was now a large black piece that sat horizontally over the turbo rather than vertically behind it, and attached with one bolt and two clips; a different shield was fitted to cars equipped with air conditioning, available from 1991.

The turbo damper was also deleted now, too, because Ford felt the new engine wouldn't be required to produce 500bhp.

Needless to say, the exhaust system was also revised. The first 4x4 Sapphire Cosworths (with YBJ engine) had a downpipe that crossed under the gearbox in parallel with the front anti-roll bar and added an extra silencer into the first pair of pipes (now making a total of five boxes); the rear silencer was a single aluminiumised box. The system was made in two pieces for production, or three as a service item.

The YBG-engined version added a pair of catalytic converters too, which were fitted in the exhaust system before the centre silencers, in place of the previous boxes. Each cat looked like a small silencer, and required additional underbody heat shields to cope with ultra-high temperatures, along with special insulators made from high-temperature-resistant natural rubber. YBG-engined Sapphires also had a small pre-cat in the downpipe, plus a carbon canister assembly mounted behind the turbo and heat shield.

All of which went to prove, if ever it was needed, that Ford deliberately stifled the Cosworth not just for emissions but noise and power too.

Garrett's T3 turbo continued into the 4x4, now mildly modified to make the T03B. The heat shield was a completely new design.

Early Ford development 4x4, displaying exhaust and rear axle layout.

Ignition System

Much of the original Sapphire Cosworth's Weber-Marelli ignition system was lifted straight from its predecessor, but there were one or two updates to the electronics.

Most importantly, the previous level one ECU (electronic control unit) was swapped for a level six (L6) version. The part number was now W45.06 (stamped into the cover on an identity plate), there was a large white CO adjustment screw on the front face, and clipped-down (rather than screwed-in) transistors. It looked otherwise the same as the L1, having a metal case with integral mounting flanges, and a 35-pin wiring loom plug. A green cable, a blue and white cable, and a self-diagnostic port sat alongside the ECU, which remained in position behind the passenger-side dashboard, above the glovebox and accessed through a clipped-in lid (which now lacked an RS logo); the ABS computer was mounted on top.

The ECU was powered from the battery via a brown relay found in the fuse box in the engine bay, where there was a yellow relay for the fuel pump, along with the car's other ATO standard fuses.

The ECU controlled the Sapphire's distributor, which was the same Marelli breakerless unit that was found in the original RS Cosworth. It featured an automatic advance, and was driven by a skew gear from an auxiliary shaft. Situated beneath the inlet manifold, the distributor was fitted with an angled distributor cap made from black plastic, with black silicone plug leads reaching backwards horizontally. Each lead was numbered with a yellow crow's-foot tab, and fed through the rocker cover down onto AGPR901C spark plugs mounted centrally in the cylinder head. The king lead reached over to a Ford Motorcraft high-output breakerless ignition coil, which was painted black and wore a red label. It was mounted in a bare metal bracket on the inner wing in front of the coolant header tank, along with a Marelli ignition module attached

Twin belts turned the alternator from the crankshaft pulley.

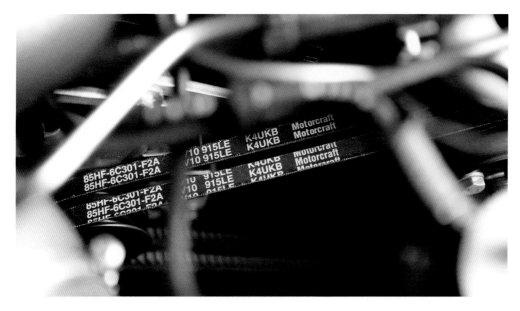

to the inner wing behind the nearside front suspension turret.

A collection of sensors sent information to the ECU. There was a black plastic manifold absolute pressure (MAP) sensor mounted on a single-piece bare metal bracket attached to the inner wing below the header tank, which linked by a hose to the plenum chamber.

The plenum was home to an air charge temperature (ACT) sensor, there was an idle speed control valve above the throttle body, an engine coolant temperature (ECT) sensor was screwed into the cylinder head, and a red PF01 throttle position sensor (TPS) was fitted to the throttle shaft.

Meanwhile, an engine speed/TDC sensor bolted to the engine beneath the crankshaft pulley, and a boost pressure control solenoid (commonly referred to as an Amal valve) was mounted above the intercooler and connected by a hose to the high-pressure side of the turbo. It featured a white top with a two-pin electrical connector, while the sides had three braided hoses attached into hard black plastic pipes to the airbox, inlet manifold and the wastegate actuator.

The 4x4's ignition system was essentially similar but with several vital alterations. Its brain was now a Weber-Marelli level eight (L8) ECU, which was a development of the L6, adding more controllability. It was now found behind (rather than above) the passenger glovebox. There was still a white mixture screw, but now the mounting flange was gone from the case. Internally there was more circuitry too.

YBJ- and YBG-engined cars' ECUs differed in that the catalytic-converter-equipped model's ECU (also an L8) added lambda control. The YBJ ECU had a red CO adjustment screw, red label and WD48.08/L3E.31 or WD48.08/L3H.34 part number, while the YBG featured a bunged adjustment hole, green sticker and WD48.08/L3H.93 part number.

The 4x4 was equipped with a PF09 throttle position sensor, which on early cars was red, later switching to black plastic. Functionally, they were identical. Its distributor was now revised (and again for catalytic-converter cars), and from February 1990 became shorter overall, allowing for a conventional distributor cap rather than the earlier model's angled part. The HT leads were naturally changed for length, while the 4x4 benefited from Ford Motorcraft's first platinum-tipped spark plugs, the AGPR902P (or AGPR12PP11 for the YBG engine).

The ignition coil, MAP sensor and so on remained the same.

Electrical System

For the first Sapphire Cosworths, Ford mixed the body's 2.0i Ghia wiring loom with what was essentially the three-door RS Cosworth's engine loom, joined by a fly plug and wrapped in typical Ford black loom tape, attached using a selection of regular plugs, clips and connectors.

In 1989 the loom was revised to fit in with Ford's international 'clean hands' strategy of colour-coding all the bits you'd need to regularly undo for checking and servicing.

That meant the loom connectors becoming yellow to match the dipstick, header tank cap and so on. Quite why the fuel injector plugs were also yellow is anyone's guess... At this point, the connectors also received push-down springs for quick removal and replacement.

The 4x4 Cosworth's loom looked similar to the late-model rear-wheel-drive car's wiring but was changed where it met the body loom, now featuring three large connectors for all wires to pass through, allowing the ECU to remain in situ if removing the engine (previously, the ECU had to be removed with the rest of the engine loom). These looms also had wiring and plugs for lambda sensors, the sensors themselves being fitted only to YBG-engined cars. There were detail loom changes too, such as a reduction in wiring length in some lighting circuits.

As before, the standard Sierra fuse box was included on the bulkhead panel, just in front of the driver, alongside the wiper motor and mechanism. Beneath its black plastic lid was the usual selection of relays and standard ATO fuses.

At the opposite side of the engine bay, again beneath the scuttle panel, was a regular white/clear Motorcraft 60Ah battery with square terminals. It was left open, with no plastic cover on top.

The rear-wheel-drive Sapphire Cosworth's starter motor was the previous three-bolt Bosch DW with 1.4Kw output, finished in black, whereas the 4x4's starter motor was a Magnetti Marelli M78R. The alternator was a bare-aluminium Bosch NI-70A 70-amp unit on European-market rear-wheel-drive cars, but swapped to a Bosch NI-90A 90-amp version for the UK and 4x4, which looked identical other than a blue sticker rather than the previous red. It was fitted on a heavy black bracket at the offside front of the engine, along with a slotted black adjusting plate. Alternator drive was by twin belts from the crankshaft pulley.

There were revisions to the Sapphire's body loom during production, with new internal door wiring in August 1991. Thanks to the Cosworth's desirability with car thieves and getaway drivers, a factory alarm system was added as standard in 1990; an 'alarm-activated' light also appeared on the dashboard.

Transmission – Rear-wheel-drive

Tough, purposeful and race-proven – if a little heavy – the three-door Sierra RS Cosworth's transmission was carried over to the Sapphire Cosworth, almost unaltered. Why change what works so well?

The gearbox was an all-aluminium Borg-Warner T5 five-speed manual, with synchromesh on all gears apart from reverse. Its ratios were as follows: first gear: 2.95:1; second: 1.94:1; third: 1.34:1; fourth: 1:1; overdrive fifth: 0.80:1; reverse: 2.76:1.

Inside the main transmission case were first to fourth and reverse gears, with fifth and synchroniser found in an

RS Cosworth's 7.5in differential originated in the Ford Granada/ Scorpio but was beefed up with broader driveshafts.

extension housing on the back of the gearbox, operated by an intermediate lever on a pivot pin. The shift detent was also found in the extension housing, comprising detent plate, selector crank and spring-loaded ball. Meanwhile, an assembly extending from the extension housing turret contained shift forks for first-to-second and third-to-fourth.

For the Sapphire, Ford fitted a speedometer worm drive ball and Circlip (instead of retaining clip), and a caged needle roller bearing on the input shaft rather than the 15 loose needle rollers used before.

Ford also kept the Sierra's heavy-duty clutch assembly, consisting of a 9.5in (242mm) diaphragm single-plate clutch with uprated disc, pressure plate and intermediate plate. The same unique-to-Cosworths clutch cable mechanism was used on right-hand-drive Sapphires, while left-hookers had a standard Sierra 2.0 cable.

Likewise, the three-door's Cosworth-designed billet steel flywheel was unchanged, balanced with the crankshaft and fitted on nine retaining bolts. It was found inside an aluminium bellhousing, which in turn connected to the cylinder block.

To hold the gearbox in the tunnel, its tail was bolted to a rubber mount in a satin-black steel crossmember attached to the floorpan. It turned the previous car's two-piece propshaft, finished in satin black and attached with blue Torx-headed bolts. A central support comprised a ball bearing encased in a rubber insulator, which was bolted to the floorpan. The propshaft included three Ford Transit heavy-duty universal joints and a reinforced rear section.

The prop fed power to the Cosworth's Scorpio V6-based 7.5in rear differential assembly, left in a bare alloy finish. There

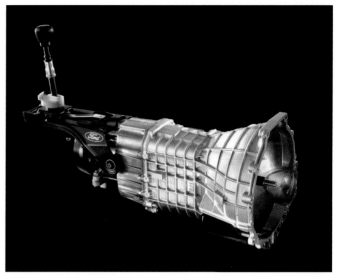

MT75 gearbox in all its glory – not as tough as the T5 but it allowed the Cosworth to continue as an all-wheel-drive rally contender.

Four-wheel drive meant a new alloy sump and crossmember.

Detailed line drawing of Sapphire Cosworth 4x4, cleverly revealing the four-wheel-drive transmission layout.

was the same viscous-coupling LSD with 3.64:1 ratio and black-painted rear axle crossmember. A large gold-passivated mount containing a rubber bush was used to attach the diff to the floorpan.

Again, the Sierra's beefy (31mm diameter) driveshafts and 108mm stubs were used, left bare. They featured black rubber gaiters with stainless clips, and were connected to the wheel hubs using blue Torx-headed bolts.

It's often rumoured that Ford produced Sapphire Cosworths with automatic gearboxes but, although it was discussed before production, it was never a factory option. There were, though, aftermarket conversions completed by automatic transmission specialist Somar Transtec and Oxford Ford dealer Hartford Motors, which could be ordered from new and retained the manufacturer's warranty.

The conversion used parts-bin components from the Pinto 2.0-engined Sierra auto, including A4LD gearbox, pedal box, gearshift assembly, torque converter and propshaft. Naturally, it dulled the Cosworth experience and sold only in double figures, mainly to disabled motorists.

Transmission – 4x4

When Ford decided to send the Sierra rallying, a combination of Cosworth power and four-wheel drive was the obvious solution. With the V6 Sierra XR4x4 already adequate on the rough stuff, using its transmission system behind the turbocharged YB powerplant made perfect sense. And, despite suggestions of seriously strengthening the running gear, the Sapphire Cosworth 4x4 used nothing more than a mildly uprated version of the existing system found in contemporary four-wheel-drive Fords.

At its heart was an MT75 five-speed gearbox – MT standing for manual transmission and 75 being the distance in millimetres between the main and layshaft centres. The MT75 was introduced in late 1988 on regular Sierra, Granada/Scorpio and Transit models to replace the ageing Type 9, being stronger, lighter and shorter.

Constructed in aluminium alloy with a ribbed casing, the MT75 featured synchromesh on all forward and reverse gears. It was essentially the same 'box found in the Sierra XR4x4 2.9, with identical gear ratios: first was 3.61:1; second was 2.08:1; third was 1.36:1; fourth was 1:1; fifth was 0.83:1.

The only alterations were the input shaft, the bellhousing connection between transmission, engine and sump (which had two longer flange bolts), plus a vent hole for the double-lipped radial oil seal in the transfer box, which, if oil dripped out, would indicate any damage to the seals. Crucially, the Cosworth's clutch release lever and aperture were on the opposite side to the V6 position.

The exact-same unit was subsequently carried over to the Escort Cosworth, although by that point (late in Sapphire production, probably during 1991) the 'box had been revised with a slightly longer output shaft and a new rubber propshaft coupling.

It's worth noting that the Cosworth-type MT75 was found in the Sierra 2.0 XR4x4 (also released in February 1990), being physically identical but for a different clutch release lever and third gear ratio, of 1.44:1.

Inside the MT75's ribbed alloy bellhousing was the rear-wheel-drive Cosworth's 242mm clutch assembly but on a heavier flywheel, intended to decrease the risk of stalling. Side by side, the 4x4's flywheel was visibly quite different from its predecessor, having a virtually flat rear face rather than the rear-wheel-drive car's machined, hollowed-out steel.

The clutch cable on right-hand-drive Sapphire Cosworth 4x4s was shared with the Sierra 2.0 XR4x4, while the left-hand-drive machine used the rear-wheel-drive car's cable.

The back of the gearbox was supported on a ribbed aluminium bracket with inset rubber insulator from the 2.0 XR4x4, which in turn attached to the floorpan.

Behind the gearbox (in place of the usual rear-wheel-drive MT75's extension housing) was a chain-driven aluminium alloy transfer box. Here, the torque was split between 34 per cent to the front wheels and 66 per cent to the rear via an epicyclic centre differential with viscous coupling to limit slip.

This setup was identical to the original Sierra XR4x4, encompassing Ford's proven take on the Ferguson four-wheel-drive system, which was developed by Ford SVE using viscous coupling limited-slip differentials manufactured by the GKN-ZF partnership at Viscodrive.

Power was taken from the centre differential by Hi-Vo transfer chain (with 31-tooth chain wheels) and a short propshaft, along the right-hand-side of the engine, towards the front wheels. Here, bolted to the right of the sump, was a 6.5in diameter spiral-bevel final drive open differential in an aluminium case. An extension shaft in a support bearing ran through the sump (below the crank) and mated to equal-length driveshafts based on those of the 2.9-litre XR4x4 but shorter, and fitted with constant velocity joints at each end.

The rear wheels were driven by a two-piece propshaft from the transfer casing towards the rear differential; late-model Sapphires gained a revised prop with different centre bearing and circular insulator. The tail of the propshaft slid into a 7in viscous coupling limited-slip diff taken directly from the Sierra XR4x4 V6, complete with 3.62:1 final drive ratio and 47 crownwheel teeth to its 13 pinion teeth. It was contained within a bare alloy casing.

As before, the diff was supported from the floorpan by a big gold-passivated mount with rubber bush, as found in the

Most of the Sapphire Cosworth's front suspension was taken from the previous Sierra in late-spec guise with H14 anti-roll bar, although the track control arms and steering knuckles had different fittings.

regular Sierra. It distributed power to the rear wheels through a pair of bare driveshafts (Granada-sourced, in 28mm diameter with 100mm flanges) with black rubber gaiters and stainless steel clips, which were connected to the hubs on blue Torx-headed bolts.

Suspension and steering

Stiffer in the bodyshell than its three-door predecessor and less nervous on the road, the rear-drive Sapphire RS is today considered to be the sweetest handling of all Cosworth

Steering rack came straight from the original Sierra RS Cosworth, with 2.6 turns from lock to lock. Note the yellow spray-paint, applied on the production line after assembly.

Sapphire rear suspension setup was Sierra Cosworth-based, and mostly painted black. Springs were colour-splashed to denote fitment, while driveshafts were left uncoated. Note the bar-code sticker on the trailing arm.

which differed from the three-door's in an attempt to return the roll centre to something resembling a standard Sierra setting. Instead of the original Cosworth's steering knuckle setup – where tapered ball joints and castellated nuts attached the track control arms – Sapphires were fitted with pinch bolts. The inner ends of the track control arms slotted into the Sierra's steel satin-black-painted engine crossmember. The main change here was a slot at each side for the brake hose connections, as opposed to the Sierra's screwed fittings; both types were held on with clips.

The late-spec Sierra three-door H14 anti-roll bar was retained for the Sapphire, in 28mm diameter with increased castor angle. As before, it was attached to the chassis using Scorpio fittings and bushes, and finished in satin black. Dabs of yellow paint were used to confirm the nuts and bolts had been correctly tightened.

Like the Sierra, the Sapphire was equipped with a rack and pinion steering system, similar to other PAS-equipped models but for a revised ratio and different bearings. Produced by Cam Gears, the rack took 2.6 turns from lock to lock. It had a passivated finish, and featured black rubber gaiters clipped onto each end, with bare-metal track rod ends. An orange paper tag was wrapped around the rack and yellow paint sprayed onto the rack after production, presumably for fluid/ tightening checks.

models. Yet, fundamentally, it was unchanged from the car that went before.

The Sapphire's front end wore the three-door's MacPherson struts, painted black along with colour splashes to denote fitment. The Fichtel and Sachs gas-filled twin-tube dampers ran softer settings, while the lowered coil springs featured increased rates (now 21kg/Nm rather than the previous 19kg/Nm). Again, the coils were finished in black, with red/orange/ blue/green paint splashes. The suspension top mounts were standard Sierra stuff.

The Sapphire's struts were seated into cast-iron hub carriers,

The stock Sierra steering column and lock were kept for the Cosworth, as was the PAS fluid reservoir, which was clear plastic with a black screw cap. It remained mounted at the nearside front corner of the engine bay, gaining a yellow cap from May 1989. Likewise, the power steering pump was carried over from other Sierras and Granadas, being painted satin black and affixed to a black bracket using gold-passivated bolts; it was then attached to the cylinder block on a heavy bracket with a pair of M10 bolts. The mounting bracket also included an extra section to blank off the redundant fuel pump hole intended for Pinto applications. Again, it was spun by a single belt from the crank pulley.

The rear end of the Sapphire Cosworth kept the same independent suspension as its predecessor, albeit with some tweaks. The Fichtel and Sachs gas-filled single-tube telescopic dampers (black-painted) were softer, while the lowered coil springs were harder, at 51kg/Nm rather than the previous 47kg/Nm; they were finished in black, with blue/ green/orange paint splashes. The upper rubbers were standard Sierra kit.

As before, there was a modified Scorpio rear beam (painted black) and black rubber bushes. Applied to the beam were paper bar-code stickers plus an orange square for part identification. The rear trailing arms were XR4i-type but incorporated the three-door Cosworth's uniball joints in place of the usual rubber bushes. The rear axle shafts and driveshaft hubs were three-door Cosworth kit, but the anti-roll bar was wider and had increased in diameter to 16mm, along with

Rear suspension layout on the 4x4 was very similar to the RWD Sierra Cosworth. This photo shows a Ford pre-production prototype

suitable new brackets, which were now mounted inboard of the trailing arms (rather than outside on the three-door).

Some of the running gear continued onto the Sapphire 4x4, although there were several crucial differences.

At the front, there was an all-new aluminium-alloy crossmember in place of the rear-wheel-drive car's steel component, and a reshaped front anti-roll bar altered the steering geometry, although still measuring 28mm diameter.

The front hubs were within new cast iron knuckles, which housed forged steel wheel spindles fitted with 94-tooth rotors for the ABS sensors. Revised, thicker MacPherson struts were needed to slide into the wider-diameter cups, while the track control arms remained the same. The steering rack and geometry were changed too, exhibiting positive camber angles on the 4x4. Meanwhile, the steering column became adjustable from inside the car, and was now a unique component for four-wheel-drive Sierras.

At the back, the beam was mildly revised for the smaller diff, there were XR4x4 telescopic dampers (which had larger lower mounting points) and the anti-roll bar diameter was increased to 18mm. The rear hubs and bearings were carried over from the rear-wheel-drive Sapphire, as were the trailing arms. The springs had similar rates, but now slightly revised, accompanied by blue/orange paint splashes.

For 1991, the same PAS pump was moved to the turbo side of the engine. A new mounting bracket was produced – now no longer required to fill the Pinto engine's redundant fuel pump hole – and a different bolt-on pulley from the 2.0 DOHC Sierra, along with new PAS hoses for the new location. The reservoir and cap remained the same.

Brakes

Why change a good thing? The three-door Cosworth's braking system was more than adequate for Ford's new executive express, so it was carried over in its entirety to the 150mph rear-wheel-drive Sapphire.

The front stoppers were Teves four-piston callipers, plated in a gold zinc, with Ford pads and 283mm x 24.15mm ventilated discs. The rears were Sierra XR4x4-type gold-zinc-coated floating callipers on Cosworth-specific carriers, along with Ford pads and 273mm x 10.2mm solid discs. Behind them were black steel splash shields; the handbrake mechanism comprised an XR4x4 cable and standard Sierra handle.

Sadly, the 4x4's front callipers were down-specced in typical Ford cost-cutting fashion. Now, 278mm x 24mm vented discs were clamped by floating callipers from the Granada 2.9, albeit with uprated pads and running on new carrier brackets.

The back of the 4x4, though, was slightly improved, benefiting from similar (broader) callipers and ventilated discs, the same diameter as before but 20mm thick. The previous pads were retained but there were reshaped splash guards behind the discs.

Front brakes and suspension knuckles of Ford's development 4x4, still wearing the stock Sapphire Cosworth's Dunlop D40 tyres.

The standard front/rear split dual-circuit braking system with Teves Mk2 electronic ABS was carried over from regular ABS-equipped Sierras, Granadas and Scorpios. The system was almost the same as the three-door setup but for minor alterations, including repositioning of the ABS computer and relays to the top of the main engine ECU, which lived behind the car's glovebox.

The ABS ECU was updated in spring 1989 but visually

Factory Ford brake callipers were supplied in gold-passivated finish.

Lattice-design alloy wheels were fitted to all rear-wheel-drive Sapphire Cosworths and early 4x4 machines. The RWD cars wore these Dunlop D40 205/50x15 tyres.

A Granada-type gold-passivated brake booster assembly and alloy single-piston master cylinder were attached to the bulkhead in front of the driver, along with a black-pained ABS pump and accumulator. On top of the master cylinder was the brake fluid reservoir, made from clear/white plastic with a white screw cap and black electrical connectors, which became yellow on later cars, from 1989. A yellow sticker sat on the reservoir, complete with warning triangle and handbook icons.

On the nearside inner wing was a gold-passivated actuation assembly, which connected the brake lines; left-hand-drive cars had the actuator on the bulkhead. A revised actuator was fitted to the 4x4, the accumulator swapped position from the engine side of the fluid reservoir to the other, and the pipe connections were in different positions.

The Sapphire's brake lines were all Ford's usual green-coated steel with rubber flexible hoses, as found on the three-door Cosworth (in the case of the rear-wheel-drive Sapphire) or the standard Sierra (for the 4x4). The brake pipe-to-hose connection was slotted at the crossmember, rather than the screwed on type of the earlier Sierra.

Wheels and tyres

Same size, different style. The original RS Cosworth's alloy wheel dimensions of 7Jx15in and ET40mm offset were kept for the Sapphire, despite there being no wheelarch extensions to hide them underneath. They fitted just fine anyway, wrapped in Dunlop D40 VR15 205/50x15 rubber.

Unlike earlier D40s, the Dunlops fitted to Sapphires lacked a

Shark-tooth alloys were added to the facelifted Cosworth 4x4 of August 1991, wrapped from new in Bridgestone ER90 205/50 ZR15 rubber.

remained the same. The 4x4 also had a different ABS ECU (now wearing a 4x4 sticker), along with new wiring and different front wheel sensors. In fact, the ABS wiring was updated frequently, with minor changes in August 1988, February 1989 and January 1990.

Scorpio sensors and toothed rotors were fitted at all four wheels; the rears were mounted in the end castings of the suspension arms, with integral wiring.

By the time of Sapphire production, factory-fitted Dunlop D40 tyres had lost the central wear indicator seen on rubber bound for the three-door Sierra Cosworth.

tread depth indicator around the central groove of the tyre. The tread pattern, though, was otherwise identical.

The alloy wheels themselves were a lattice design, finished in Strato Silver paint. Each wheel was cast with its part number on one spoke, its size on another and a Ford oval on the opposite spoke. Casting dates were absent from their faces.

In the middle of each wheel was a small silver-painted centre cap, which wore a Ford logo. The wheels were held on with regular Ford alloy wheel nuts, complete with the usual rotating conical washers.

The same wheels continued into Cosworth 4x4 production, now wearing Bridgestone ER90 205/50 ZR15 tyres.

But from August 1991 there was a new wheel, known as the shark-tooth thanks to its multi-spoke design. All casting marks were now gone from the wheel faces, instead moved to be beneath the large, plastic centre caps. The finish stayed in Strato Silver paintwork.

Bodywork

The four-door Sierra Cosworth saloon was based on a run-of-the-mill Sapphire Ghia bodyshell, with no changes under the skin. Even the front towing eye was now the same on mainstream Sierras, being horizontal rather than vertical.

That was just one of many changes that came with the swap to a Mk2 bodyshell for the start of Sapphire production. Ford had heavily reworked the original Sierra shell to improve body strength and aerodynamics, which resulted in increased stiffness and better safety.

The body side rails and seat crossmember were redesigned, there was polystyrene acoustic filling in the front windscreen pillars, the side windows were 15mm taller, the roof's rain gutters were deleted in favour of hidden drip rails, and chunky strakes were worked into the C-pillars for better crosswind stability. Most obviously, of course, there was a longer bonnet and sleeker, broader headlamps.

It's worth noting that, whereas the first-generation Sierra Cosworth's transmission tunnel was broader than the base model, by the time of rear-wheel-drive Sapphire production all Sierra tunnels were wider, which meant the T5 gearbox slotted straight into place.

But what about that outer skin? What made the Cosworth more special than any other Sapphire?

At the front was a polycarbonate front bumper, manufactured by Marley (provider of parts for the Escort RS Turbo) and filled with plastic foam to resist low-speed impacts. An air intake beneath the number plate recess featured a removable cover to gain better access to a satin-black-painted towing eye, while a broader lower scoop stretched across the width of the car, with brake cooling ducts at each side. Attached to the lower edge was a rubber-and-aluminium air splitter (known as a stone deflector in Ford terms).

The bumper featured a pair of fog lamps, which were fitted into painted recesses (finished in anthracite/dark silver on the

early car and silver on the 4x4). Around the bumper's upper edge was a unique black insert.

Above was a body-coloured plastic strip, which bridged the gap between bumper, headlamps and grille. All Sierras equipped with headlamp wipers had the same section (and all Sapphire Cosworths had the same headlamp wipers with electric washers).

The grille itself looked similar to a regular Sapphire part but with a black plastic mesh-type section rather than the normal slats. As usual, it was attached with two screws, and there was a regular-sized blue oval Ford badge in the centre.

Similarly, the Cosworth's bonnet was the same as any other Sierra's, despite inclusion of Escort RS Turbo vents on the first pre-production prototype; Ford decided they weren't necessary for road cars running less than 300bhp, although paint blistering (around the turbo area) experienced by subsequent owners (often rectified under warranty) would

Cosworth-specific grille remained throughout production, necessitating special headlamps.

Removable section in the front bumper gave access to a satin black-painted towing eye.

Officially still a Sierra RS Cosworth for the UK market, the four-door version was just a Sierra Cosworth in every other country.

Sapphire badges were fitted only to the UK car, even though in Ford terms it was officially the Sierra RS Cosworth four-door.

say otherwise. The problem was addressed on the Sapphire Cosworth 4x4, which gained a pair of new body-coloured vents recessed into a specially-pressed bonnet. Along with all Sierras, the profile of the bonnet was also changed at this point, including a revised shape where it met the windscreen/ scuttle panel; the bonnet corners now swept down towards the wings, rather than upwards as before.

Two rubber seals were attached to the leading edge of the bonnet, where it met the headlamps.

The front wings, doors and rear quarters (which included plastic inner-wheelarch liners front and rear) were completely standard Sapphire stuff, albeit wearing unique side rubbing strip mouldings, in dark grey/black with black inserts. Body-coloured side skirt extensions – again produced by Marley – were attached to the Cosworth's sills with rivets (four 4.4x14.5s and four 3.2x9.5s) and plastic clips. Each side skirt was in two pieces (joined below the front door) and had its own jacking point cover complete with securing strap; the rear cover was slightly shorter than the front.

The front doors wore the usual electrically-operated, heated door mirrors, with body colour-painted covers and black plastic edges as found on the Mk1 Sierra. Later Sapphire

mirrors were essentially identical, although their mounting plates were plastic rather than black-painted metal.

Along with all Sierras, the Cosworth's doors (and door skins) were revised during production (in January 1990 and August 1991) with the most noticeable difference coming in May 1991, when the check straps swapped from a simple fastening on the door pillar to a stronger U-shaped part.

All four doors were opened using textured black plastic handles, and each front door was equipped with a new-type 'high-security' lock with rotating disc plates, rather than spring-loaded tumblers. Motorised electric central locking was standard on the doors and boot lid; new motors and lock assemblies came in January 1990.

A black plastic surround encased a shiny lock aperture, into which a Chubb key could be inserted; the master key was a Ford torch key (including a light that worked from a button on the black plastic handle), and the same key was used for doors, ignition, boot and petrol cap locks. The fuel filler was always located on the left-hand-side of the car (regardless of destination country or where the steering wheel was positioned); on early cars it was covered by a body-coloured flap with thumb handle whereas 4x4s (from January 1990)

European-market four-door Sierra Cosworths dropped the RS badge and made no reference to Sapphire.

All Cosworths were fitted with Sekurit tinted glass, which had a date code using numbers and dots, generally made a few months before the car was built. Here the single dot is for January and the 9 means 1989.

Aerodynamic strakes were used on all Sapphire rear pillars, and not just Cosworths. The standard colour was satin black.

Windscreen wipers were fitted with small aerofoils to keep them glued to the screen at high speed.

had an entirely flush-fitting cap with remote cable release from inside the car.

The Sapphire Cosworth had a colour-coded rear bumper (shared only with the later Sapphire 2000E), housing a black insert. Across the lower edge was a removable towing-eye cover, again body-coloured. The towing eye itself was welded to the spare wheel well underneath, and sprayed satin black.

Compared to its bewinged predecessor, the Sapphire Cosworth wore a discreet (yet effective) wrap-around rear aerofoil, now made by Marley. This wing was a single-piece item, with three integral legs to lift it clear of the boot lid; its design also included a horizontal groove, which divided the wing to give the appearance of a separate aerodynamic section across the rear edge. This piece was painted satin black on most cars, although the final run of 4x4s (reckoned to be the last 200-or-so cars) were equipped with a fully-colour-coded wing; it's not known whether or not this was a cost-cutting exercise by Ford, the well-known penny-pinching expert…

The boot lid looked the same as a normal Sapphire's, including an aerodynamic lip moulded into the design. But it was actually unique to the Cosworth, having drillings for the rear wing/aerofoil, along with an uprated boot lock reinforcer that sat beneath the wing's central support. The boot lid springs were also meatier to cope with the additional weight, and the right-hand-side spring made tougher in February 1989. As with all Sapphires, there was a date stamp on the underside of the boot lid, giving the week and year of build; it was found on the central underside support.

A regular Sapphire lock sat in the middle of the boot lid, featuring a black lifting handle and stainless steel barrel, which pushed in to open the boot. In contrast, the 4x4 had an internal release mechanism, and the external button was now a flush-fitted lock instead (the key could still be used to open the boot). A rubber gasket sat between handle and boot lid of all cars, but the 4x4 gained a new boot lock striker to suit the remote release cable. The boot lock assembly was updated in March 1989, and again in January 1990 for the 4x4.

At the right-hand side of the boot lid was a traditional Ford mid-blue oval badge, while the left-hand side was home to a few rather more important badges. UK-market machines featured a black plastic badge (with brushed-steel-effect highlights) declaring 'SIERRA RS' above a separate COSWORTH emblem, while their European counterparts wore no reference to the Rallye Sport brand, so came with a different badge – simply saying SIERRA – across the top.

Talking of which, UK cars were also equipped with small SAPPHIRE emblems on their back door window trims, but the reference was absent from all other markets. Indeed, the colloquially-named Sapphire Cosworth was simply the Sierra Cosworth four-door in official Ford terms.

From January 1990, revised badges were adopted for the

Sapphire Cosworth 4x4 was subtly different from the front, retaining the original bumper, splitter and fog lamps but including new clear front indicators and bonnet vents.

Flush-fitting fuel flap was remotely released from inside the cabin on 4x4 models, rather than the earlier car's finger handle.

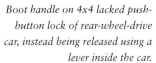

Boot handle on 4x4 lacked push-button lock of rear-wheel-drive car, instead being released using a lever inside the car.

4x4 model. Now, there were separate pieces for SIERRA, RS and COSWORTH, which made it easier to simply delete the RS section for other countries. Still, there were now new 4x4 badges on each front wing, placed just above the indicator side repeaters.

A Sierra Ghia windscreen was fitted to all Cosworths, boasting not just laminated glass but also a heated de-icing facility, dubbed Quickclear from 1989 onwards. A pair of black semi-concealed windscreen wipers were fitted with XR4x4 blade assemblies, featuring small aerofoils. They sat within a slatted black plastic scuttle panel cover, which attached with screws under plastic caps. Within the panel was a pair of black washer jets, which were electrically heated (whenever the engine was running) from January 1990.

The door glass was, again, the same as a standard Sapphire Ghia's, being bronze-tinted and electrically operated. Well, that was the case in the UK: European-spec Cosworths were fitted with manual windows in the rear doors until the final facelift of August 1991. The glass remained the same throughout production, although the inner door window runners were improved in August 1988.

At the back, there was the usual tinted rear windscreen,

complete with heating elements and integral radio aerial.

The Sapphire's roof panel was a standard part, and in factory-original Cosworth guise usually included a sliding/titling glass sunroof as standard. There were exceptions to this rule, though: orders for marked police cars were white non-sunroof bodyshells, as were Ford Motorsport '909' shells (so-called because of their 909-prefix part numbers), which were supplied untrimmed. It's also probable that some left-hand-drive Sapphire Cosworths lacked a sunroof.

The Sapphire's roof panel was revised in August 1991 (it looked the same but was different internally), and the Sapphire RS Cosworth now received an electrically-operated sunroof as standard equipment.

At each side of the roof was a flush satin black-painted rain channel, complete with plastic sliders that opened to reveal mounting points for a roof rack, sold as an official accessory.

During the early build process, Sierra bodyshells were treated with zinc phosphate ion, dipped in electronically-impregnated cataphoretic primer, and sprayed with a top coat of high-bake enamel paint – solid colours were thermoplastic acrylic, while metallics comprised a polyester basecoat and clear coat system. From 1989 the bonnet was given additional

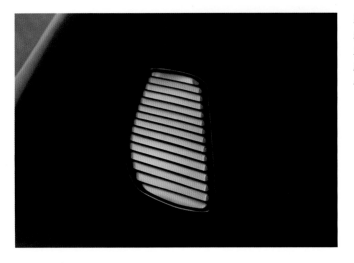

Bonnet vents were introduced for the 4x4 in a new factory pressing. Many rear-wheel-drive machines have since been retrofitted with 4x4 bonnets to aid engine cooling.

Bonnet insulator pad and foil heat shield strip were new for the Cosworth 4x4.

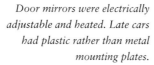

New badges were added to the 4x4's bootlid, complete with RS emblem only on British-bound Sapphires. The Sapphire rear wing lost the satin black paint from its rear part during the final facelift of the last Cosworth 4x4s.

Door mirrors were electrically adjustable and heated. Late cars had plastic rather than metal mounting plates.

zinc-nickel pre-coating to guard against corrosion.

Underneath, the sheet metal was coated with zinc phosphate ion, electrocoat primer and stone-chip protection. High-impact areas and joint overlaps were sprayed or brushed with seam sealer. A strip of floorpan (about 6x2in) between the offside inner sill and chassis rail was painted black after production, to cover bare metal that occurred from stamping in the car's chassis number.

Normally, top coat would be found wafted under the sills, wheelarches (behind the plastic smash guards) and spare wheel well, while the front and rear towing eyes were sprayed satin black – reportedly to cover paintwork missed or marked during the assembly process. Otherwise, the floorpan remained an off-white shade of primer similar to Purbeck Grey or Dove Grey, which was the base colour of every Sapphire bodyshell prior to paintwork.

As already mentioned, a rear-wheel-drive Sapphire Cosworth bodyshell was identical to a regular 2.0 Ghia. But the 4x4 had several differences, reportedly including strengthened C-pillars and extra ribs in the boot floor. Most modifications, though, could be seen on the underside. For example, the transmission tunnel had a bulge at the offside front, the inner wings and

bulkhead were reputedly triple-skinned, and there were half-moon-shaped cutouts in the front chassis rails to give clearance for driveshafts. It's reckoned that some late-model rear-wheel-drive Sapphire Cosworths also received this additional strengthening, although the cutouts were overskinned flush with the rails.

Underbonnet

Mighty powerplant or not, the RS Cosworth was just a standard Sapphire bodyshell even under the bonnet, complete with innumerable drillings in the inner wings for various lesser engines and applications.

That said, the Cosworth's bulkhead was fitted only to cars equipped with ABS (which accounted for many Sierras – it was optional even on the Sapphire 1.6), featuring an inverted-key-shaped cutout for the brake servo unit and four bolt mounting holes, plus a hole for the engine wiring loom to feed into the car.

The entire bulkhead panel was different on cars equipped with air conditioning, complete with large bowl-shaped section that allowed room behind the dashboard for the air con blower mechanism.

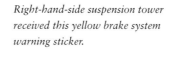

Right-hand-side suspension tower received this yellow brake system warning sticker.

Headlamp adjustment decal was found above the offside front headlight.

Service sticker on top of intercooler has long since vanished from most Sapphire Cosworths.

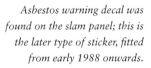

Asbestos warning decal was found on the slam panel; this is the later type of sticker, fitted from early 1988 onwards.

A plastic insulator panel sat between the bulkhead and engine, with a rubber edge protector/seal atop the bulkhead and the car's black-taped wiring loom clipped into place and positioned behind the panel. Behind it, beneath the windscreen scuttle and in front of the driver, was the standard Sierra

fusebox (a big black plastic part with lid) and the windscreen wiper motor and mechanism, all finished in satin black.

At the opposite side, in front of the bulkhead, was the regular Sierra battery tray, painted in body colour and housing a square-post white/clear Motorcraft battery; unlike later Fords there was no cover over the battery. There was an earth strap running from the battery to the nearest bonnet hinge – also painted in the car's body colour, along with the bolts and washers.

A turbo heat shield was attached to the bulkhead on one bolt, with two more through a unique bracket into the offside inner wing. An all-new heat shield was used for the 4x4, and it was again different on cars specified with air conditioning.

Sapphire inner wings were regular Sierra parts, although 4x4 inner wings featured semi-circular cutouts in the chassis rails to allow clearance for the front driveshafts; reports say late rear-wheel-drive Cosworths also featured these chassis rails, although the cutouts were hidden behind flush steel.

The inner wings and slam panel were finished in body colour (unlacquered when metallic), having large round suspension

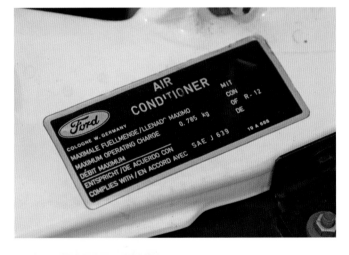

Air conditioning-equipped Sapphires wore this extra decal on the bonnet slam panel.

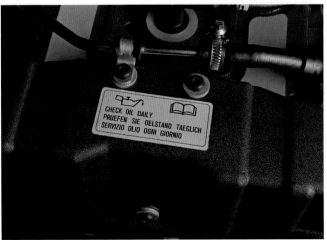

Timing belt cover encouraged owners to check their oil; presumably, problems were anticipated...

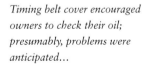

Yellow caps were fitted to fluid reservoirs in May 1989, along with other important items being recoloured in yellow.

towers, bare metal plates and black caps over the damper rods. The offside turret featured a curved brake fluid warning sticker in yellow.

At the offside front of the engine bay was the large plastic airbox, in front of which was the usual Sierra windscreen washer fluid reservoir neck, complete with plastic cap (black until May 1989; yellow thereafter). Meanwhile, the opposite corner was home to the power steering fluid reservoir (clear/white plastic with black cap until May 1989 and yellow cap thereafter), mounted on a black metal bracket.

The coolant header tank was found in front of the nearside suspension turret. Also made from clear/white plastic, on rear-wheel-drive Sapphires the tank was carried over from the original three-door Sierra Cosworth, albeit with its central outlet (previously connected to a coolant level sensor) now blanked off. A black plastic pressure cap was fitted, as was a black-on-white sticker. From May 1989 the cap was swapped for a yellow version, which was otherwise identical.

The Cosworth 4x4's coolant header tank was essentially a similar shape but now featured two outlets at the bottom (about an inch apart) and a larger-bore outlet for the upper hose, which returned coolant from the turbo.

Between the PAS and coolant tanks was the car's ignition coil, mounted in a bare alloy bracket, while the ignition module sat on the nearside inner wing, just behind the suspension tower. On air conditioning-equipped cars, there was also a bare-alloy cylindrical dryer unit positioned alongside the coil.

The Sapphire Cosworth's slam panel was a regular Sierra component, featuring the normal black-coated bonnet prop (and black plastic retaining clip), twin white plastic stoppers (capped with black rubber insulators), VIN tag, build plate and red/white/black asbestos-warning decal, which changed in early 1988 from Mk1 Sierra type (a portrait-shape rectangle with twin-humped top) to a landscape rectangle with rounded corner. Late 4x4s lost the sticker altogether.

In the slam panel's centre was a black-coated bonnet latch mechanism, a unique assembly for the Cosworth. The black-coated bonnet release cable ran from the latch to the cabin via the driver's-side inner wing, retained in black plastic clips.

The slam panel itself was stamped with an undisclosed Ford number above the offside headlamp, while each wing rail was stamped with a Ford oval logo, along with the build year and week number – generally within a month of the car's official build date. The underside of the bonnet was stamped with a similar date code – the week and year – very close to the black plastic bonnet prop retainer. On 4x4 models, black felt insulation was fitted to the underside of the bonnet with black plastic clips, cut around the bonnet vents; special heat-retardant material was added above the turbo.

As usual, twin Ghia-spec horns were bolted to the body crossmember behind the front bumper, at each side of the air intake. Late-model 4x4s (from January 1991) also received a black plastic under-tray beneath the engine.

Front fog lamps were housed in anthracite-coloured surrounds on early cars, or lighter silver on 4x4s. Their glass had a Ford logo and 'England' lettering.

Headlamps were fitted with electric wash/wipe, and front indicators were amber on the rear-wheel-drive car.

Basecoat and no lacquer – the Sapphire's slam panel received regular Ford stampings prior to paint being applied.

Orange indicator repeaters remained throughout Sapphire production; 4x4 badges were found on four-wheel-drive models, naturally.

Clear indicators replaced the amber units on 4x4s, and the Carello headlamps had different lenses.

Lighting

Ghia-type headlamps were specified for the Sapphire Cosworth but, even though they looked the same, they were very slightly different in shape on the mounting lugs due to the unique Cosworth grille.

All Sapphire Cosworths wore Carello H4 60/55W halogen headlamps with integral driving lights, whereas mainstream models were fitted with Lucas or Bosch units. Rear-wheel-drive Cosworths had lenses with large Carello logos, while 4x4s had smaller Carello lettering and a different pattern in the glass.

January 1990 was also the date when left-hand-drive Cosworths gained electric headlamp levelling, complete with motors and adjusting spindles on the lamps, and a switch on the fascia beside the ashtray (beneath the cigarette lighter).

Headlamp wash/wipe was standard on all Sapphire Cosworths, and shared the wiper arms and electric pump (mounted on the front of the common washer fluid reservoir) with the Ghia; the single-speed motors (which functioned only when the windscreen washers were operated with dipped beam switched on) and brackets were unique to the Cosworth.

Alongside the headlamps were the standard Sierra Mk2 indicators, in amber-coloured plastic on the rear-wheel-drive Sapphire and clear/white on the 4x4. Ford logos were moulded into each lamp lens.

Below the headlamps were Scorpio-sourced H3/55W

As usual, the Cosworth's rear lamp clusters were the same as a base-spec Sapphire. All rear-wheel-drive cars had the red/amber/white lights rather than the later smoked clusters.

Smoked rear light clusters were complemented by infill panel behind the number plate on all Cosworth 4x4s. Lesser-model Sapphires received these lamp units at the same time.

halogen front fog lamps, which were also found on other Sierra models. Each had a Ford logo in the centre of the lens, and was recessed into an anthracite/dark silver-painted aperture, retained with a single screw; 4x4s had the apertures painted silver instead.

A standard Sierra-type square indicator side repeater was fitted to each front wing, behind the wheelarch and above the rubbing strip. Within the Ford-logoed amber plastic was a 5W bulb. These units were repeated from the Mk1 Sierra.

At the back of the Sapphire Cosworth were the standard rear lamp clusters in red/white/amber plastic, housing integral reversing and fog lamps at each side. Each was moulded with a series of part numbers plus 'Made in France' lettering and a small Ford logo on the reversing lamp section. The 4x4 received a pair of smoked lamp clusters – again with moulded part numbers but Ford logo and 'Made in France' wording on the fog lamp section – and a matching infill panel behind the rear number plate. All cars had a pair of number plate lamps recessed into the back bumper.

In the Cosworth's cabin were several courtesy lamps with delayed switch-off function, again taken from the Ghia. At the front there was a large rectangular light within the roof-mounted console, complete with a pair of circular rotating map-reading lamps. From 1990 the front footwell kick panels gained small rectangular lights. A headlamps-on warning buzzer was added for four-wheel-drive cars too.

Interior

Designed to be a BMW-beating executive express, the Sapphire Cosworth was equipped with every luxury Ford could throw at it. Well, within the firm's miserly budget anyway.

Starting out as a Sierra Ghia cabin, the Cosworth's primary alteration was its fabulous Recaro front seats. Each had a

reclining mechanism operated by a plastic wheel where the base and backrest joined on the outer side, and the driver's seat was height-adjustable via a wheel and handle at the front. Both seats incorporated sliding base extensions, map pockets on the seat backs and padded, adjustable head rests. Placed prominently on each backrest was a silver-on-black Recaro badge. A pair of foam pads were supplied for owners to bulk out the lumbar region, if desired; they were found in each map pocket complete with instruction sheet. Meanwhile, each seat had a small part number sticker above the fixing bolts.

From the outset the seats were trimmed in Ford's Shadow Halley and Shadow Angora grey velour, which was pale grey cloth on the seat bolsters, with dark/light grey velour centres.

Cloth-trimmed cabin was a bright and inviting environment, especially on early-model rear-wheel-drive Sapphire Cosworth.

Launch-model Sapphire Cosworth featured Recaro front seats in Shadow Halley and Angora grey velour, swapped for a darker Raven velour and Shadow Halley in February 1989.

Cloth-upholstered Recaro front seats boasted Recaro badges from the three-door Sierra Cosworth (along with RS Escorts of the period).

Cloth cabins were complemented by Shadow Halley and Angora grey velour door cards. Early Sapphires had these small, flush-fitting door speakers.

Shadow Halley and Angora grey velour was used for the rear seat of all early Sapphire Cosworths, complete with headrests and folding centre armrest.

Later rear-wheel-drive cars – from 28 February 1989 – were fitted with the exact-same seats but now in Raven Angora and Shadow Halley, which meant the outer sections and bolsters were now a much darker plain grey velour.

Shadow Halley and Raven Angora velour continued into the Sapphire Cosworth 4x4 as standard upholstery until the facelift of August 1991, when it was supplanted by Space and Raven velour. Now the outer sections were the same plain dark grey as earlier 4x4s but the inner panels were grey/red/blue speckled velour, thus the more familiar description of 'rainbow cloth'.

Leather upholstery became optional on the Sapphire

Factory audio equipment in the 1988 Sapphire Cosworth was the Sound 2007 stereo radio/cassette head unit with a separate four-channel power amplifier in the slot below.

Cosworth in February 1989, boasting the same front Recaros as cloth-trimmed cars but with Raven-coloured leather faces and outer bolsters/backs in Raven vinyl. The seats' centre panels were perforated leather, and a large Recaro logo was embossed in the backrests instead of a badge. The headrests were also trimmed in matching smooth leather.

The Sapphire Cosworth's rear bench seat was upholstered to match the fronts, in cloth or optional leather. The cushions were simply retrimmed versions of Ghia/GL seats, complete with integral headrests and split-folding (60/40) facility, with release catches accessible only from inside the boot. In the centre of the backrest was a fold-down armrest, again in matching upholstery.

Sapphire door cards had corresponding covers, being pale grey Shadow Angora velour with padded Shadow Halley inserts until 27 February 1989, after which they were darker grey Raven velour with the same Halley pads at elbow height. Each front door had moulded armrests and lower pockets with hard plastic sections and screw caps; on early cars the plastic was Shadow Grey, which was replaced by (darker grey) Raven in February 1989. Combined door release handles and rocker locking switches were black plastic, while a circular 20-watt premium speaker was fitted flush into the lower corner of each front door panel, complete with black mesh grille.

The Sierra's electric exterior mirror controls had by this point been relocated to the driver's door quarter trim – a black plastic triangle in the front corner. The controller was a round soft-touch/textured knob, which could be switched from left to right. The heated mirror function operated whenever the heated rear windscreen was activated.

Sapphires with optional leather-trimmed seats received door cards covered in Raven vinyl complete with perforated vinyl elbow pads. The hard plastics were the same dark grey

Leather upholstery was launched as an optional extra in February 1989, the cabin meanwhile receiving Raven-coloured dashboard and plastic trim.

Dark grey (Raven) dashboard became standard-fit on all Sapphire Cosworths in early 1989, whether matched to cloth or optional leather upholstery.

(Raven) subsequently fitted to cloth-trimmed cars, while the handle mechanisms and speakers were also identical.

The change came with the 4x4 of January 1990, when the door release handles were swapped for a new design. The apertures looked similar but now the internal locking mechanism was activated by pushing the release lever inwards towards the door, rather than the previous rocker switch. Now a white tab was visible on the handle to show the door was locked, rather than the previous orange of the rocker switch.

The 4x4 also included new front speakers, with bulbous round grilles within a squared-off outer cover.

From August 1991, cloth-trimmed cars had completely new door cards. Now there was a large Space (rainbow) cloth-trimmed section inset into a Ravel vinyl door card. Within the cloth insert was an all-new one-piece armrest in softer-feel Raven plastic. Leather-trimmed models retained the earlier door cards.

In the back the door cards reflected the front, albeit incorporating fold-down plastic ashtrays (alongside the release handles) rather than speakers. That meant grey Angora velour with padded Shadow Halley elbow pads until 27 February 1989, darker grey Raven Angora with the same Halley inserts until August 1991, with Raven vinyl and large Space-fabric

Leather seats featured embossed Recaro logo rather than the separate metal badges found pinned into cloth upholstery.

Raven leather Recaros were a desirable optional extra but only the front faces were leather – the seat backs were Raven-coloured vinyl.

Matching Raven leather was carried through to the back seat, still incorporating a folding centre armrest and integrated headrests.

Leather-trimmed Sapphires had matching door cards front and rear, in Raven vinyl with perforated elbow panels.

inserts thereafter; the armrests were now large Raven plastic one-piece parts too. Raven vinyl rear door cards accompanied all Sapphires with leather seats. Like the fronts, the rear door panels received new internal release levers in January 1990. It's worth noting that left-hand-drive Cosworths' rear doors also housed winding handles to keep the back-seat passengers' arms nicely exercised; electric rear windows weren't found as standard on left-hookers until August 1991.

There was also one other factory trim option for UK Sapphire Cosworths, although it was a non-standard order. Police-specified cars were trimmed with plain black cloth/velour seats, having an embroidered Recaro logo in white or red. Such cars also lacked a sunroof.

The Sapphire Cosworth's dashboard went through four versions: Shadow Grey at launch, Raven from 27 February 1989, Raven with new gloveboxes from January 1990, and

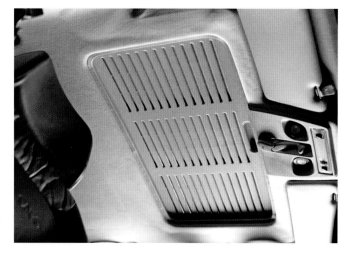

Four speakers were fitted to the Sapphire Cosworth, including a pair in the rear parcel shelf with Raven plastic surrounds.

Road-going Sapphire RS Cosworths were equipped with a manually-operated sunroof with louvred blind. An electric sunroof came in 1991.

a much-revised Raven with curved instrument binnacle and new switches after the facelift of August 1991.

The first dashboard, like the upholstery, was a paler grey colour than later models, being more of a mid-grey than the almost-black Raven used from February 1989 onwards. Indeed, the first Sapphire's dashboard was very similar to the three-door Cosworth's; the shape, colour and texture were almost identical but the Mk1 Sierra's speaker grille had been deleted. The black plastic windscreen demisting vents were slightly wider than before, although the recessed area was roughly the same. Oh yes, and the ECU cover in front of the passenger now lacked the RS logo – presumably due to the deletion of Rallye Sport references in non-UK markets.

Beside the ECU cover was a standard Sierra adjustable heater vent (as seen in the previous model) in plain black plastic with vertical and horizontal slats, plus on/off wheel and

white markings; above it was a narrow horizontal black vent to direct air towards the door glass. The same vents continued until the new dashboard of August 1991, when a smoother-looking vent was used instead, in a very similar style to those of the Mk5 Escort. Now the slats could be angled instead of the whole unit, and the upper narrow vent was also revised, adding vertical slats.

A separate section of Shadow Grey plastic formed the lower dashboard, incorporating an empty speaker grille and large drop-down passenger glovebox. Again identical to the Mk1 Sierra dashboard, the glovebox was Shadow Grey plastic with a black plastic release button; inside was a grey-carpeted base and small round lamp.

With Raven leather trim now an optional extra, all Sapphire Cosworths from 27 February 1989 were equipped with a much darker (almost black but known as Raven) dashboard,

Rear-wheel-drive Sapphire instruments lacked the turbo boost gauge of previous Cosworth models; the fuel gauge's 15, 30, 45 and 60-litre markings were dropped on the subsequent 4x4.

Early cars' three-spoke steering wheel remained the same, regardless of whether cloth or leather upholstery was fitted.

Centre console swapped to dark Raven plastic in early 1989; electric window switches and rear override button were in the panel behind the gearstick.

New five-speed gearknob was fitted to the 4x4, now with provision for lift-up reverse mechanism.

with matching upper and lower sections. The shape of the dashboard was altered where it met the A-pillar trims, too, having a deeper recess on each side.

Another new dashboard came in January 1990, again in Raven but complete with anti-theft alarm sensor in the centre. At this point the engine ECU was moved, and the ECU cover was deleted in favour of a storage slot, seemingly intended to jettison its contents into the lap of front-seat passengers whenever the accelerator pedal was pressed.

Below was an all-new section that lacked the speaker grille but incorporated a wider glovebox with black release handle offset to the right-hand side.

At the centre of the dashboard was a pair of black adjustable heater vents with on/off wheels and white markings. The August 1991 facelift swapped these removable vents for fixed vents like the Mk5 Escort's, now integral with the dashboard binnacle moulding. The new slats could be angled

instead of the entire units.

Immediately below was a much-depleted strip of warning lights for low fuel level on the left, and low windscreen washer fluid level, which would illuminate in yellow. Unlike the Mk1 Sierra, there was no engine management lamp.

Beneath the warning lamps was the usual 'high series' (in Ford language) three-button solid-state multi-function digital clock with green LEDs. From August 1991 there was a new setup with multi-function two-button digital and separate analogue clocks.

Alongside was the familiar graphic information module, showing an illuminated overhead view of the Sierra to advise on low ambient temperatures (with yellow or red warning lights), bulb failures, and doors or boot lid being open.

As before, there was a black plastic lower fascia, which changed shape in January 1990. All types featured twin single-DIN slots; in the upper position was a Sound 2007 electronic

British-bound Sapphire Cosworths were equipped with electric rear windows, operated by buttons at the rear of the centre console storage box.

Facelifted 4x4s retained the rear electric window switches, but the centre console was a slightly different profile.

August 1991 saw a clock layout with two-button digital and separate analogue versions.

Late-model 4x4 instruments lacked numbers on the fuel gauge but gained a white line beneath the red section.

Air conditioning-equipped Sapphire had a new heater blower control with illuminated knob.

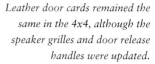

All Cosworths had standard Sierra pedal box, levers and rubbers; the carpet was plush Raven cut-pile with driver's heel mat.

Leather door cards remained the same in the 4x4, although the speaker grilles and door release handles were updated.

Facelifted 4x4 dashboard was radically revised with smoother shape but the cabin retained its moody ambience. This car's original steering wheel has been replaced by a more-attractive earlier version with RS horn push.

Dolby stereo radio/cassette head unit, with a separate four-channel power amplifier in the space below.

From 1989 the Model 2007 was equipped with anti-theft coding, while the 4x4 was offered with premium sound system options: the Model 2008 with RDS, anti-theft coding and separate seven-band graphic equaliser or the Model 2028 compact disc player in place of the graphic equaliser.

All types powered four premium 20-watt speakers (two in the front doors, two in the rear parcel shelf) and were coupled up to an aerial incorporated into the heated rear windscreen.

The Cosworth's standard head unit from March 1991 was the Model 2007 RDS with separate power amplifier, with the Model 2008 options remaining available at extra cost, although the 2028 CD player was swapped for the 2040. By then, there was also a choice of three Ford phones available as factory-fitted options.

A regular Sierra illuminated ashtray sat at the bottom of the fascia; the rear-wheel-drive car's ashtray featured a recessed handle, while the 4x4's had bulges at each side instead. An illuminated heater blower control dial – a rotating knob for a three-speed fan – was positioned alongside the upper DIN slot. Later cars with air conditioning (from around August 1991) also had a different dial (with three settings clockwise and three anti-clockwise) and warning lamp above.

An illuminated protruding cigarette lighter was below the blower control – either separated by a blanking plug (on rear-wheel-drive cars) or immediately underneath (4x4s). Left-hand-drive 4x4s had a headlamp levelling control switch beneath the cigarette lighter, with a basic setting of 0 and position 5 for the maximum angle.

In front of the driver was the main instrument binnacle, which was based on the Sierra Ghia setup. Originally square and boxy black plastic like the Mk1 Sierra's, the fascia was modernised in August 1991 with a curved black binnacle

Front footwell lights were added to the kick panels in 1990.

Sapphire Cosworth 4x4 gained this revised three-spoke steering wheel until it was replaced by a decidedly unpleasant four-spoke design in 1992.

attached to the Raven upper dashboard; there was now also a curved section above the steering column, surrounding the instrument cluster.

On the left-hand section were the regular Sierra heater sliders, which continued into the facelift of August 1991 but with a smoother red/blue graphic featuring more graduations. The dials incorporated large rev counter and speedometer, with smaller fuel and coolant temperature gauges in between; all featured orange needles and white digits.

The rev counter was Sapphire Cosworth-specific, lacking the turbo boost gauge of its predecessor (this wasn't a racing car, after all...) but retaining digits from 0 to 7; for the 4x4 it gained a red section between 6500rpm and the 7000rpm maximum, although some late-model rear-wheel-drive machines had the red line too. All had a small C printed in the lower right-hand corner.

The dials for fuel and temperature were at each side of one central gauge with a seat belt warning lamp in between; only the 4x4 seemed to have a functioning bulb. The rear-wheel-drive car's fuel gauge featured 15, 30, 45 and 60-litre markings for its tank, but they were deleted on the 4x4. From autumn 1991 the fuel gauge had a white line beneath the red segment. The temperature dial stayed the same throughout.

As before, the Cosworth-powered Sapphire boasted a 170mph speedometer, complete with smaller red KMH indicators underneath (reversed, of course, for metric markets). Within the speedo were a mileometer and trip recorder, the latter being reset by a button in the dial.

A strip of warning lamps was positioned across the bottom of the instrument cluster, showing (from left to right) headlamp main beam, oil pressure, direction indicators, handbrake/brake failure and ignition/alternator. Above them was a central ABS failure warning light.

Underneath the instrument cluster was a fascia illumination dimmer control on the left of the steering wheel, and a speed controller for the intermittent windscreen wipers on the right.

A bank of control buttons was positioned to the right of the instruments, controlling (from left to right) the heated rear windscreen, heated front windscreen, front fog lamps and rear fog lamps; each button had an integral warning lamp. Facelift models received the same buttons, now in a square of four: top left was the heated front windscreen, top right was the front fog lamp, bottom left was the heated rear windscreen and bottom right was the rear fog lamp.

Before August 1991 there was a movable heater vent below the row of switches and a thin horizontal demister above. The facelift swapped positions of the window demister to run vertically alongside the control buttons.

Space and Raven Angora velour was standard upholstery on the facelifted Sapphire Cosworth of August 1991, often referred to by owners as 'rainbow cloth' thanks to the colourful trim pattern.

Cloth-trimmed Cosworths had revised door cards from August 1991, including Space upholstery and new armrests.

The driver's-side lower dashboard section was the same colour as the upper dash – Shadow Grey on early cars, then Raven on later models. Rear-wheel-drive Sapphires had a speaker grille (empty) on the outer side, an open-fronted tray under the steering column and a tipping coin tray alongside the centre console. The 4x4 dropped the grille in favour of a tipping driver's glovebox, and an open tray on the left.

The full-width tray was deleted on the 4x4 thanks to its inclusion of a new steering column, which was now adjustable for reach and rake; on rear-wheel-drive machines it was fixed in one (perfect) position. The steering column shroud stayed black plastic throughout, although it was of course updated for the new column.

On top of the shroud was the standard Ford hazard warning switch – a circular push-button in red plastic. As always, a collection of black stalks protruded from the column; on the left-hand side were controls for indicators, main beam and headlamp flashers, while the right had two stalks: one for headlamps/sidelights and another for windscreen wipers and washers.

The usual ignition lock was on the right-hand side, operated from the same Chubb key as the doors, boot lid and petrol cap. An orange plastic lever beneath the column operated the bonnet release mechanism, while 4x4s gained a black lever on the left to adjust the steering column.

Pride of place, of course, was the steering wheel; well, for a limited time anyway. The rear-wheel-drive RS Cosworth carried over the three-door's XR3i-type semi-dished three-spoke wheel, complete with black leather rim, padded spokes, and centre horn push wearing a blue Ford oval badge. The 4x4's steering wheel was also a black three-spoke with leather rim, now having chunkier spokes mounted below the centre line of the wheel. March 1992 brought a soft-feel (instead of leather) four-spoke steering wheel from the Sapphire 2000E, again with centre horn push; sadly, it looked more like the wheel of a Transit tipper truck than that of a 150mph sports machine. But never mind: it was easily swapped for an aftermarket steering wheel from the Ford RS parts catalogue.

Still, at least the Cosworth's gearknob was always covered in black leather. The early Sapphire used the three-door Cosworth's knob, incorporating polished black emblem with the five-speed shift pattern printed in white. The 4x4's version included space for a collar that lifted before you could shift into reverse, but lacked the shift diagram up top, now printed with only the white numbers.

At the same time, the rear-wheel-drive's rubber concertina-type gear lever gaiter was swapped for a black leatherette item. The gear lever gaiter's black plastic surround was a different shape from before, encased in a new centre console – although it looked very similar it was a new profile for the enlarged 4x4 transmission tunnel.

Early Cosworths had a Shadow Grey centre console, switched for Raven from 27 February 1989. All types housed a raised section behind the gearstick where the electric window rocker switches were found; UK-spec cars featured four switches, while European examples had just the fronts. Between them was a locking button to stop the rear windows being operated from the back of the car.

Behind the switches was an oddments tray, along with a standard Sierra Mk2 handbrake lever, incorporating black plastic handle and black push-button. It was fitted within a lidded storage box at the back of the centre console, complete with armrest trimmed to match the car's upholstery – either cloth or leather. Inside were slots for cassette tape storage. Meanwhile, on UK-spec cars a further pair of electric window rocker switches were fitted to the back of the console, accessible for rear-seat passengers. Some overseas markets were treated to the option of heated front seats from August 1991; their switches were either side of the handbrake on the centre console.

Up front, the Sapphire Cosworth was fitted with a standard Sierra 2.0 pedal box, with the usual pedals and brackets in black with black rubbers. A new clip on the clutch cable was the only modification.

In each front footwell was a hard plastic kick panel, in Shadow Grey on early cars, and Raven from February 1989. The 4x4 gained small rectangular lights in the kick panels.

Each panel overlapped black door rubbers, along with plastic door scuff plates, attached with black screws. Shadow Grey was used until 27 February 1989, when Raven was introduced instead. Thin black plastic outer sill protectors were also fitted to later models, from around June 1991.

The 4x4 added a lever between the driver's seat and inner sill, which pulled upwards at the front to release the petrol cap and up at the back to pop open the boot lid.

True to its Ghia specification, the Cosworth was equipped with a plush deep-pile carpet; Shadow Grey was the shade until Raven took over in February 1989. A new carpet was used for the 4x4 to cover its bulging transmission tunnel. As always, there was a plastic flap in the carpet beside the driver's seat, under which was the car's VIN, stamped into the floorpan.

Standard seat belts were fitted to the Sapphire Cosworth all-round, including two inertia-reels with height-adjustable mounts in the front, two lap/diagonal inertia-reels in the back and a static lap belt in the centre rear. In line with regular Sierra updates, the front seat belt assembly was revised in February 1991, while the back belts remained the same.

Early Sapphire Cosworth A-pillar trims were identical to those found in the three-door Sierra Cosworth, in Shadow Grey 86 plastic. Raven plastic took over in February 1989, with a further revision for shape in August 1991. In contrast, B-pillar and C-pillar trims were Dawn Grey, much the same as base-spec Sapphires.

The headlining was also Dawn Grey, complete with Dawn Grey grab handles above the passengers; the driver's side was

European-spec Sapphire Cosworth's cabin was similar at first glance but was slightly downmarket, having manually-operated rear windows. This is a 1988 model with Shadow Halley and Angora trim.

fitted with a pair of Dawn Grey plastic bungs.

The headlining was universal among Sapphires fitted with a sunroof, complete with Dawn Grey plastic inner surround/ overhead console (Ghia spec, with swivelling map reading lamps), sliding roof blind and winder handle assembly – all in Dawn Grey.

A new overhead console was used from August 1991 onwards to accompany the Cosworth's now-standard electric sunroof; a revised Dawn Grey headlining was fitted too.

Meanwhile, a regular Sierra's dipping rear-view mirror was bonded to the top of the windscreen, in standard black

plastic. Alongside was a pair of Dawn Grey sun visors, with mirror and illumination on the passenger side.

Finally, behind the rear head rests was a carpeted parcel shelf, incorporating a pair of premium-level 20-watt speakers with black grilles; the parcel shelf and speaker surrounds were dark grey/Raven.

Inside Boot

The Sapphire Cosworth's luggage compartment was much like that of any lesser model, complete with split/folding rear seat backs, which allowed long loads into the passenger space. Perhaps the body would have been stiffer with a steel bulkhead, but the Sapphire was already more rigid than the three-door Sierra anyway.

Under the boot floor was a full-sized spare alloy wheel and 205/50x15 tyre, held down by a black metal hook through one of the wheel nut holes, screwed into the wheel well. Due to its extra depth compared with a standard Sierra wheel, the Cosworth's spare was surrounded by a grey foam pad to artificially raise the floor level.

Above the pad was a unique fleece carpet in dark grey (Anthracite 86), with matching Anthracite 86 trim over the wheel housings and Anthracite 86 fasteners. The rear seat backs were finished in satin black paintwork. Above them, under the rear parcel shelf, was a pair of levers, which pulled out to fold down the seats.

The boot hinges – which were body-coloured – were trimmed with black plastic shields for the wiring loom.

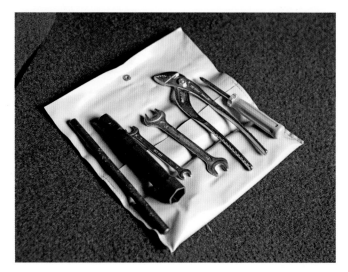

Heavy-duty springs helped to lift the lid, with the right-hand-side spring being made tougher in February 1989.

Across the back panel were plastic shields for the rear lights and, bolted into place with wing nuts, a black jack and wheelbrace. A tool kit wasn't standard but was available from dealers as a Ford accessory.

Along the top of the panel was a gold-passivated boot lock striker, exactly the same as the part used in other Sapphires. There was also a small rectangular 5W luggage compartment lamp towards the left-hand side, in clear textured plastic.

Colour schemes and interior trim

Colour	Code	Introduced	Discontinued	Interior colour
Black 69	A	August 1988	February 1993	Raven
Diamond White 73	B	Launch	February 1993	Raven
Smokestone 90	M	August 1988	February 1993	Raven
Radiant Red 89	P	August 1988	February 1993	Raven
Mercury Grey 87	Q	Launch	August 1988	Raven
Flint Grey 89	T	August 1988	August 1990	Raven
Crystal Blue 87	U	Launch	August 1988	Raven
Nouveau Red 92	X	August 1991	February 1993	Raven
Magenta 88	1	August 1988	August 1991	Raven
Moonstone Blue 86	5	August 1988	August 1990	Raven
Moondust Silver 91	6	August 1990	February 1993	Raven
Ebony Black 91	7	August 1990	April 1992	Raven

Black

Diamond White

Smokestone

Radiant Red

Mercury Grey

Flint Grey

Crystal Blue

Nouveau Red

Magenta

Moonstone Blue

Moondust Silver

Ebony Black

ROUSE SPORT RS COSWORTH

One of only six rear-wheel-drive Rouse Sport RS Cosworths (with around half that number still in existence), this Diamond White 302-R is build number three, constructed by Ford in October 1989 and completed by Andy Rouse Engineering on 1 August 1990. Currently owned by RS enthusiast Damon Sargent, the 302-R is an ex-concours-winning car, having been comprehensively restored over many years by a Ford mechanic using all new original parts. The Raven leather upholstery is original but the vented bonnet is from a Sapphire 4x4, and the CD player came from a 1993 version.

Barely distinguishable from the front, the Rouse Sport's only alteration was its colour-coded RS500-style splitter. A standard Sapphire Cosworth driver may notice the Rouse Sport's wider tyres in his mirrors, but it wouldn't have remained there very long.

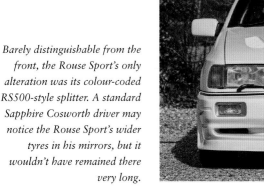

Factory originally, in RS Cosworth terms, is pretty straightforward. If the car is as it was when it left the production line in Genk – or that extra-special Tickford assembly area set aside for RS500s – it's safe to say it qualifies.

But what about specially-built competition machines based on Ford Motorsport shells, with part codes starting in 909? While we wouldn't deny them the Rallye Sport badge, it's stretching credibility to suggest they could ever be factory-original. Likewise, contemporary tuning packages such as the 175mph BBR Mogul 400 or the Turbo Technics Micro-Technics Cosworth, which boasted 250bhp. Period modifications, maybe, but definitely aftermarket.

Which leaves us with a rather special car that was not just inextricably linked to the British Touring Car Championship (BTCC) but was also available brand new from selected Ford dealers: the Rouse Sport RS Cosworth.

No lower on the suspension than a standard Sapphire Cosworth, the Rouse Sport RS sat visually closer to the ground thanks to a colour-coded front splitter, rear bumper extension and chunkier side skirts.

With 260bhp and a very limited production run, the Rouse Sport was faster than any standard Sierra and substantially rarer too. And, as its name revealed, it was created by a team that was perhaps more responsible than any other for raising the public's perception of the Ford Sierra from jellymould repmobile into world-conquering competition car.

Andy Rouse Engineering was led by a British tintop racing legend Andy Rouse, who, until surpassed by Jason Plato in 2011, was the most successful BTCC driver of all time, with 60 overall wins to his credit.

Yet, perhaps even more importantly, Andy also happened to be a brilliant at the technical stuff. Andy started his career as an apprentice with an agricultural engineering firm before bagging a job in 1971 as a race mechanic with Broadspeed, run by saloon car racer and tuner Ralph Broad.

At the time, Andy had been competing in autocross, driving self-built specials, and had recently begun to try his hand in Formula Ford. But thanks to Broadspeed's experience with Ford Escorts, Andy was encouraged to enter saloon car racing in 1972, when he scooped the Escort Mexico crown.

Impressed by Andy's success and knack with track setups, Ralph promoted Andy to the British Saloon Car Championship. Class honours behind the wheel of an Escort RS1600 in 1973 were repeated in a Triumph Dolomite Sprint in 1974, along with the championship title in 1975.

The following year found Andy doubling up as driver and race development engineer for the ill-fated Jaguar XJ12C, after which Broadspeed went into liquidation. Andy then

seized the team's talent, bagging key Broadspeed staff to establish Andy Rouse Engineering in 1981.

In the meantime, he'd switched back to racing Blue Oval-badged cars, spending five seasons with three-litre Capris. Andy won consecutive championship titles in 1983 (driving an Alfa Romeo GTV6) and 1984 (Rover Vitesse) before his team won favour with Ford to build its impending track star: the turbocharged Sierra.

But it wasn't an RS Cosworth. Well, not yet anyway. When Ford approached Andy, it was with the American Merkur XR4Ti, which, in road-going trim, was a mixture of Sierra

Extended rear wing looked little different from this angle; only from the side was its full outline apparent.

101

Bolder bodykit than the regular RS Cosworth was completely colour-coded, including the C-pillar trims and extra-large rear wing.

XR4i bodywork and Pinto-type 2.3-litre engine boosted by a Garrett T3 turbo, and all bolted together by Karmann in Germany.

Despite being a mere stand-in until the Cosworth arrived, Andy's team ensured the XR4Ti was outrageously successful. The car achieved homologation on 1 April 1985, after which Andy drove it to victory nine times in its first year, along with overall championship success. He scooped five more wins and

class honours the following year, by when it was time for the Cosworth to take over.

Unofficially backed by Ford, Andy Rouse Engineering built some of the BTCC's most memorable machines, its ICS- and Kaliber-sponsored Sierras spitting flames across our TV screens on Sunday afternoons from 1987 until 1990.

Alongside Robb Gravett and Tim Harvey, Andy was responsible for throwing the Sierra into a nation's hearts during the height of Cosworth competition. Andy alone grabbed class honours in 1988 (including another nine overall victories) and '89, third in class during 1987 and second spot in the RS500's final year, 1990.

Great times indeed – especially for Andy. He said, "It was the end of the Sierra racing period, but the best for our business. We employed around 30 people, had two engine dynos, ten guys building race engines, and were sending crates of stuff all over the world."

By that point, the Rouse Sport road car had become a reality. Andy had realised his reputation as a driver and engineer could add some kick to the four-door Cosworth, and devised a plan to create an exclusive edition of the super saloon. The relationship between BMW and Alpina (known as a manufacturer, rather than tuner) was serious inspiration.

Unofficially sanctioned by Ford, the idea was to develop a series of modifications for the Sapphire Cosworth that could be sold as a complete package. Andy and his team of race engineers spent six-to-nine months speccing parts to make the car faster and more refined.

Special reminder under the fuel flap to fill up with suitable petrol for a Rouse Sport remapped engine.

The 302-R's engine bay looked largely like a stock Sapphire Cosworth's, complete with the original YBB powerplant and Weber yellow injectors.

A rear-wheel-drive Sapphire prototype was built and tested extensively on UK roads; despite Andy's background, circuit analysis wasn't considered because the car was never intended to be a track machine. "It was an executive express," said Andy, "it was tuned for the road."

Many hours were spent on dynos to perfect the optimum engine and management tweaks for everyday driveability. Rather than outright power, the goal was versatility throughout the rev range.

According to Andy, "We tried all sorts of things and came to the conclusion that a big turbo and high boost weren't the answer.

"We used a hybrid T25 (a new turbo on the market from Garrett), made a casting to adapt the turbo to the manifold and remapped the ECU with a new chip. We only made 260bhp but built up pressure much quicker. The RS500 needed 100mph in fifth to come on boost, but ours started to build at 2000rpm."

The performance figures were remarkable, averaging out at a 28 per cent improvement. Tested with Andy at the wheel, 30-to-50mph took 2.2 seconds, 50-to-70mph a mere 2.9 seconds, and 80-to-100mph was 39 per cent better than standard, at 3.7 seconds.

Torque was increased to 300lb ft at 4000rpm (the standard Cosworth peaked at 214lb ft), which led to Rouse Sport naming its Sapphires the 302-R and 304-R, for rear-wheel-drive and four-wheel-drive machines respectively. Conversions were developed for both cars because Andy was privy to more

than a little insight into the incoming Cosworth 4x4 before it was launched.

In practice it meant the 302-R and 304-R were available concurrently because, despite Ford replacing one with the other, plenty of older Sapphires were kicking around dealership showrooms when the 4x4 appeared.

Everything was assembled at the firm's 12,000sq.ft Coventry

Even from this angle, the engine bay looked like a regular RS Cosworth's, with YBB powerplant in the case of this 302-R. A closer look reveals the tiny T25 turbo from Garrett.

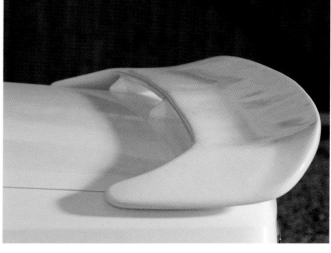

Functional rear wing was substantially larger than standard, and moulded by Andy Rouse Engineering/Rouse Sport. It was reckoned (by Andy himself) to aid stability at high motorway speeds.

The key to the Rouse Sport's driveability was this smaller-than-standard T25 turbo, which built boost more quickly, resulting in a more responsive drive. The turbo damper on this 302-R is an aftermarket add-on.

factory, alongside those all-conquering BTCC RS500s.

"The road cars were built by the same guys who did the race cars, in the same workshop together," remembered Andy. "It was a bit special at the time."

The job of promoting the Rouse Sport RS Cosworth was entrusted with Alan Gow, who later went on to become chairman of the Motor Sports Association, in charge of the BTCC. Andy recalled, "Alan came to work for us from Australia after buying our Kaliber race cars with Peter Brock, which then became the Mobil Cosworths. Alan looked after our sales through the dealers – they loved these cars because they made more money out of the conversions than the retail price."

A total of 18 Ford dealers around the UK were involved in the scheme, which allowed customers to buy a Rouse Sport 302-R or 304-R brand new, complete with Ford's 12-month,

unlimited-mileage factory warranty. The cost was £4450 plus VAT on top of Ford's list price, which at the time was £25,960 – although bartering with salesmen could easily see thousands slashed off.

Quite a sum, admittedly, but its rivals were sedate machines from Jaguar and Mercedes, or sportier BMWs. Not that any driving enthusiast should have chosen a German saloon, when ultra-popular BTCC TV coverage showed them being trounced every weekend by simple Sierras. And besides, none would be as fast as a Rouse-tuned Sapphire.

Ordering a 302-R or 304-R was as simple as any other new Ford, which included choosing colour and trim from the dealer's all-model Ford catalogue, then selecting Rouse Sport options on top of the standard package.

Along with the 260bhp/300lb ft powerplant, each car came with a reworked RS bodykit, which comprised Rouse-

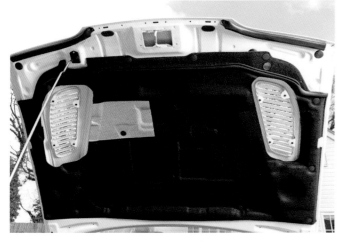

Underbonnet insulation was found on 304-Rs, complete with reflective turbo heat shield.

Unique plaque was found on the timing belt cover of every Rouse Sport RS Cosworth, whether 302-R or 304-R.

Rouse Sport front splitter was based on RS500 design but produced in fibreglass, which proved fruitful for the after-sales spares department. High-output headlamp bulbs were focused on fast road use. The orange indicators were found only on the 302-R; clear versions were fitted to the 304-R instead.

Deeper back bumper valance was a Rallye Sport part from Ford's accessories brochure, colour-coded to match each car apart from the dual black inserts.

designed-and-moulded side skirts (complete with small flared sections on the back doors), RS500-style front splitter (in fibreglass rather than rubber), bigger rear spoiler (chiefly for the looks but also useful at motorway speeds, reckoned Andy) and deeper rear valance (which was a Rallye Sport part from Ford's accessories brochure). Each bit was painted body-colour by the Rouse team, along with the stock Sapphire C-pillar trims.

The front splitter, in particular, was a sound investment for the firm because it was breakable rather than bendable like the RS500's; there were no other suppliers, so it became an often-requested replacement part.

Identification was with a silver Rouse Sport sticker under the nearside rear lamp unit, a silver 302-R or 304-R decal beneath the offside rear lamp, silver Rouse Sport stickers on the rubbing strips beneath the side repeaters and silver 302-R or 304-R tags on the rubbing strips on the back doors.

Andy also added a few detail touches from a driver's perspective, including high-output headlamp bulbs and double-edged wiper blades.

Side skirts were moulded by Andy Rouse Engineering/Rouse Sport, complete with additional mouldings on the rear doors, designed to clear the wider rear tyres. Decals were applied to the rubbing strips on each rear door, declaring 302-R or 304-R depending on whether the car was two- or four-wheel drive.

Side skirts kicked up at the front edges onto the wings, intended to work with the wider tyres; Yokohama 225/50ZR15s helped the handling and bulked out the car's stance too.

Unusual dual-insert design was due to the lower rear valance being additional to the standard rear bumper, with the original upper section remaining visible. It was found by Rouse Sport in Ford's Rallye Sport accessories brochure.

Rouse Sport decal was applied to the nearside rear panel, regardless of model. Decals were always this silver-coloured vinyl.

Rouse Sport model name stickers were found beneath the offside rear light, in 303-R or 304-R guise. The blue oval badge was standard Ford stuff. Model names were self-explanatory – 302-R was 300lb ft and two-wheel drive, while 304-R meant 300lb ft with four-wheel drive. A mere half-dozen 302-Rs were produced.

The cockpit was also heavily focused on comfort behind the wheel, built around unique, big-wing Recaro front seats. "The seats were radical at the time," said Andy. "They were made for us from the originals by a specialist automotive retrimmer in Leicester, who stripped them down and added new foam shapes. We got the leather from Ford's source in Argentina – we had to buy lots of hides!"

Of course, leather upholstery wasn't standard on a Sapphire Cosworth, and the regular Rouse Sport was likewise offered with cloth trim on those big-wing Recaros; a mere handful of the cars were so equipped, probably due to nine in ten contemporary Cosworth customers opting for leather upholstery (a £280 option on a 302-R or 304-R). Again, Ford materials were used according to the customer's wishes.

Rouse Sport dashboard, steering wheel and controls were unchanged from the standard Sapphire RS Cosworth on which it was based unless wood trimmed was specified (not shown).

Custom-made Rouse Sport seats were a massive selling point, including deep shoulder supports. Cloth trim was standard, but the Raven leather option seen here was usually specified at an additional £280.

Rear seat remained standard Sapphire Cosworth, whether trimmed in cloth or leather from the Ford factory.

As a hidden luxury, the cabin contained additional noise insulation. Andy recalled, "We doubled the soundproofing under the carpets – we bought the standard panels from Ford, cut them to fit and overlaid them. It made quite a difference to the comfort inside."

Andy Rouse Engineering also offered mahogany-trimmed dashboard and door cappings (plus an Italian wood gearknob on the 302-R), which were a popular addition to modified sports saloons of the period. Not so with the Rouse Sport, though, because it was an expensive option and only a couple of Sapphires got wood.

All cars were fitted with luggage retaining straps in the boot, presumably to keep businessmen's briefcases in place while hitting 150mph en route to important meetings.

Each car received a silver-on-black Rouse Sport badge on the passenger side of the dashboard and similar badges on each front seat where a Recaro emblem normally sat.

At the bottom of the driver's B-pillar there was a blue-on-silver plaque, listing the car's model, build number, chassis number and build date. Meanwhile, another blue-on-silver plaque was attached to the top of the timing belt cover, declaring, 'Rouse Sport use and recommend Shell Gemini 15W/50 oil.' And inside the fuel filler flap was a message to use, 'super unleaded or 4 star petrol only.'

Fantastic factory Recaro seats were made even more magnificent with Rouse Sport wing backs, modified by a trimmer in Leicester using genuine Ford hides or cloth, depending on the buyer's preference. The badges were in place of the usual Recaro emblems.

Rouse Sport badge was fitted to the passenger-side dashboard of all cars; this 302-R's ECU cover is a non-standard part, sourced from a three-door Sierra RS Cosworth.

Each car came with a letter to the owner and a note of authenticity signed by Andy Rouse.

There was one other alteration made by Andy, for which the results were reckoned to be excellent: the swap from Ford's standard-fitment Dunlop or Bridgestone 205/50x15 tyres to 225/50ZR15s from Yokohama – the supplier to the Rouse race team. Although there were no other chassis changes, adding wider rubber to the Sapphire was a wise choice. "They had much better grip and straight-line stability," said Andy. "And they looked better."

The Rouse Sport press demonstrator, a Moonstone Blue 304-R registered G808 DKV (run by Alan Gow in 1990, later rolled on a racetrack, reshelled and eventually broken up in 2012), had its polyurethane front wheelarch liners reshaped with a heat gun to accommodate the bigger rubber, but most (if not all) customer cars remained standard. G808 DKV also boasted uprated suspension bushes, which weren't offered to buyers. In contrast, the firm's glossy brochure mentioned optional alloy wheels but, according to Andy, none were specified.

A contemporary *Autocar* road test praised the choice of Yokohamas as, "An astoundingly successful modification…

The car is so well balanced that those tyres earn a very good living… Turn-in is sharper, grip is in abundance, and one can forgive the Yokohama tyres' slight tendency to tramline – particularly under braking – just for the massive reserves of safety they provide."

Autocar was also extremely favourable about the tested 304-R's performance, apparently expecting a barely-disguised road racer but finding a civilised saloon with 'new-found docility.' Yet it was clearly a package so quick and so driveable that virtually nothing on 1990's roads could keep up.

Autocar reported, "Where the standard car is flat until about 3500rpm, the Rouse Sport is already up and running… The Rouse is deceptively quick and constant vigilance of the speedometer is required. One moment's inattention and it'll have you up to 100mph between corners. Such margins are the mark of a truly great car."

Understandably, many orders were taken for Rouse Sport RS Cosworths before assembly began. Andy recalled, "They sold all over the country. Every Monday morning we'd turn up at work to find cars outside waiting to be converted."

Even so, the planned production run of 100 cars sadly stopped at 78, namely six 302-Rs and 72 304-Rs, but not including the rear-wheel-drive prototype.

The first 304-R was delivered to its owner on 1 June 1990, with seven more cars the same month – three of which were 302-Rs. Unfortunately, numbering was not consecutive, because Alan Gow fiddled with the figures to allow customers to choose their preference.

According to Andy, "We used all the numbers up to 62, then random numbers thereafter according to customers' requests. These were 70, 84, 87, 88, 91, 95, 98, 99 twice, and 100.

"Number 90 was a 302-R, number 99 was built in July 1992, and number 100 was delivered on 14 June 1991. The very last car was built on 26 July 1992." All were conversions of new, Genk-built Sapphire Cosworths, and no three- or five-door Sierras carried the Rouse Sport badge.

Special Rouse-Sport plaques were fitted to the lower B-pillar of each car, detailing model type, build number, chassis number and build date.

ROUSE SPORT
MODEL: 302-R
BUILD N° 003/100
CHASSIS N° KK 00754
BUILD DATE: 1/8/90

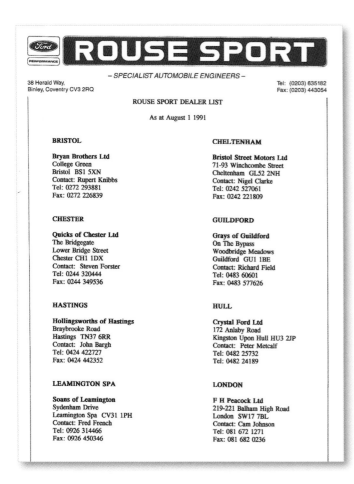

Official nationwide list of Ford dealers responsible for retailing the Rouse Sport RS Cosworth in August 1991.

Not a Cosworth – thus not necessarily relevant for this book – there was also one other Rouse Sport Sapphire, the 250-R. Designed around the rear-wheel-drive, twin-cam Pinto-engined GLSi, it featured a full bodykit, wing-backed seats and a T25 turbo, meaning 215bhp and 250lb ft torque. The sole 250-R was regrettably broken up in 2014.

The entire Rouse Sport RS Cosworth project was cut short during 1992, in part due to Andy Rouse Engineering's tie in with Toyota, competing with Carinas for the BTCC in 1991 and '92, before returning with Ford's Mondeo BTCC team during the next two seasons.

There was also the small matter of Ford replacing the Sapphire RS Cosworth with the Escort, which – with its in-your-face attitude – Andy felt was unsuitable for the same treatment as the subtle Sapphire.

Of course, the Escort would later sport a small turbo similar to Andy's spec, with comparable driving characteristics. Funny how things turn out...

Boot compartment looked standard at first glance, but included fatter spare tyre (a Yokohama 225/50ZR15) and luggage retaining straps, which can just about been seen here beneath the carpet.

ESCORT RS COSWORTH

Concours champion, continual cup winner and arguably the best Escort RS Cosworth in the country, Mark Barber's June 1993 Big Turbo is a pure museum piece that the owner has never driven. Although it's covered just 28,444 miles, Mark's Radiant Red Escort has been restored twice – most recently in Mark's hands, when he stripped it to a bare shell, replaced innumerable parts, and even sourced a fresh set of wheels with the correct build dates. The brake callipers are refurbished every year and the discs renewed, but otherwise this Escort will remain as close to factory condition as possible, including every inch of original paintwork.

The Escort RS Cosworth. The final incarnation. The third in a thrilling trilogy. For many Blue Oval enthusiasts, the Escort RS Cosworth was the ultimate fast Ford. It had the power, the handling and the motorsport pedigree. And most of all, it had the iconic, genre-defining, wild styling that inspired the Max Power generation.

The Escort RS Cosworth was for rallying what the Sierra was for the circuit and the Sapphire was for the street – an uncompromising combination of race-bred mechanicals and humble Ford accessibility, tailored perfectly to take on the world and win.

The Escort RS Cosworth grew from Ford's need to regain some lost ground in the performance car sector. A PR reason to improve the image of an underwhelming range of current-model Escorts. An answer to the incoming Japanese international rallying onslaught.

Because, although the Sierra RS Cosworth, XR4x4 and Sapphire Cosworth 4x4 achieved limited success on the rough stuff, the mid-sized machine was considered too bulky for rallying's tight turns, and not stiff enough for serious durability. The smaller Escort was traditionally the ideal size for the sport, and – thanks to the revered Mk1 and Mk2 – there was significant evidence to back it up.

The problem was that since 1980 the Escort had been front-wheel drive, which was fine for low-powered rallying but couldn't compete with the big boys, who were by then getting grip at all four corners.

The concept of introducing a concoction of Escort bodywork and Sierra running gear arose long before the Sapphire Cosworth 4x4 saw the light of day; they were simply

Auralis Blue was a very late-spec Cosworth colour, available only for the final year of production – which, naturally, meant Small Turbo setup. Chris Barlow's 50,000-mile, October 1995 Escort is a winning combination of original and restored, having been a lightly-modified everyday driver before being renovated and returned to standard by serial RS owner Mark Barber, whose Radiant Red Escort is also featured on these pages.

the right size of car and the best mechanicals.

Despite resistance from Ford bosses, reluctant to make radical alterations to mainstream models, the plan to squeeze the as-yet-unannounced Sapphire Cosworth 4x4 engine, transmission and axles into an Escort body was authorised in summer 1988. The switch from a front-wheel-drive, transverse-engined layout to four-wheel-drive and north-south engine setup was a big step in production car terms, from both engineering and marketing standpoints.

A semi-official Mk4 Escort RS Turbo mule (registered E386 YVX) was built by TC Prototypes in Northamptonshire under the instructions of Ford bigwigs Stuart Turner and Mike Morton. Codenamed ACE14 (A for Group A, CE14 from the new Escort platform's internal code), the car was developed between July and October 1988, including appraisal at Boreham by rally ace Stig Blomqvist. It was already very quick and very effective.

Ford Special Vehicle Engineering (SVE) was given the task of designing the road-going Escort RS Cosworth, which required more than 400 unique components. Half the body panels were new, and the rest were modified from existing Mk5 Escort and Sierra parts; only the Escort's roof, doors and pillars remained.

The Sierra three-door's winning approach of deep spoilers and wild wings was applied to the Escort, developed during 200 hours in a Cologne wind tunnel. At the front were a three-position adjustable front splitter and wheelarch spats, while a monstrous rear aerofoil was as dramatic as it was purposeful.

Yes, the drag coefficient had risen from the standard Mk5's 0.33Cd to 0.38Cd but the Escort RS Cosworth was to become the first mass-production car to generate front and rear aerodynamic downforce (45 Newtons at the nose and 190 Newtons at the rear at 112mph). Such was the effect of the rear wing that it limited the car's top speed to a mere 140mph – a hefty 4mph slower than without.

Remarkably lofty ride height was a pointer to the Escort RS Cosworth's rally heritage. Luxury model is identifiable by its rear head rests and hinged back windows, while the large door mirrors mean this is an early car.

The bodywork encompassed wide wheelarches to house 18in rims, albeit reduced to 8x16in alloys in road trim, and SVE sprinkled magic on much of the Sapphire 4x4's running gear – from revised suspension settings to a new intercooler.

Because the car was to be an unusual concoction of shortened Sierra floorpan and radically-altered Escort body, assembly on the regular Ford factory lines was ruled out in favour of outsourcing to a specialist. Karmann in Osnabruck, North Germany had already proved itself capable of the task, having been responsible for production of the Escort convertible and Merkur XR4Ti.

The first complete Escort RS Cosworth prototypes were constructed in 1990, including a dozen Karmann-built machines and a rally version. By August 1991 another ten road cars had been produced for publicity and service departments, and by January the following year a further 76 pre-production cars had been created, including 25 for press evaluation. It's rumoured that these cars wore tags under the bonnet declaring a Karmann build number.

Full-scale assembly finally began at Karmann on 27 April 1992, using the defunct XR4Ti facilities; left-hand-drive Escorts came first, with British-bound cars having to wait. The official launch took place on 5 May 1992, and UK sales began a couple of weeks later, on 22 May 1992.

Unlike previous RS Cosworths, the Escort was offered to buyers in a choice of three models: Roadsport (generally referred to as Motorsport), Standard and Luxury. It was also possible to purchase enough top-spec components to build an entire competition car, from seven-speed gearboxes to Ford decals. Most notably, a seam-welded group N Escort Cosworth bodyshell was available off-the-shelf as a Ford Motorsport part; such machines are generally referred to as 909s due to their shells being listed with a part number beginning in 909. Officially, though, they were called Motorsport Escort RS Cosworth bodyshells; for those who say they aren't proper Rallye Sport models, it's probably worth noting the RS part of Ford's nomenclature.

As for those fully-built production cars, the Roadsport was a basic, stripped-out machine with less kit than any previous RS Cosworth. Sadly now almost wiped out of existence thanks to a mixture of owner upgrades and competition use (imagine that in the Porsche market; a Roadsport/Motorsport would command huge premiums), the Roadsport was lighter (1300kg compared to 1375kg for the Luxury version) and lacked a radio, sunroof or central locking. Officially offered only in Diamond White (although other colours were produced in very limited numbers, primarily for overseas markets), there were no fog lamps and even the door mirrors were unpainted.

A Standard Escort RS Cosworth came in a choice of colours (Diamond White, Radiant Red, Polaris Grey, Pacifica Blue and Mallard Green were offered from launch) but was otherwise similar to the Roadsport. Karmann-made (non-Recaro) seats and manual windows were included, but the Standard added headlamp washers, front fog lamps, remote boot release, radio/cassette player, alarm and central locking. Generally, Recaro seats were fitted to Standard models, at a small extra cost. Indeed, it's confusing to determine a car's specification today because a host of optional extras meant substantial crossover with the Luxury.

Of course, we're not talking limousine levels of opulence. The Luxury added Recaro seats, electric front windows, opening rear quarter windows, heated windscreen, sunroof and heated mirrors. An option on the Luxury (which proved enormously popular) was leather upholstery. Otherwise the seats were trimmed in the same Hexagon-patterned cloth (grey on grey, red on grey or green on grey) as lesser models

Like the original Sierra RS Cosworth the Escort was built for competition, which meant motorsport homologation was a must. A yearly production of at least 5000 cars was initially required to enter Group A but the figure was reduced by FISA (the sport's governing body) to 2500 for 1993, when Escorts were scheduled to begin rallying.

To qualify, each production car had to be fitted with essentially the same specification as its competition counterpart. For the Escort this meant a big Garrett T03/T04B turbo (quite oversized for a road car running low boost pressure) strapped to a Cosworth YBT powerplant, which was a revised version of the Sapphire's YBG boasting 227bhp.

The first 2500-or-so cars were also supposed to be supplied with a water injection kit to comply with homologation.

Aggressive as ever, even this car's subtle Auralis Blue bodywork doesn't disguise its intentions. The smaller door mirrors mean this is a late-model machine built in 1995.

Little more than a dummy system, it was neither plumbed in nor complemented by the correct engine ECU. There's also evidence to suggest not all cars were thus equipped.

Ford's intention was to ditch the so-called Big Turbo model after Group A and N homologation had been achieved in January 1993 (by that point, 3448 Escort RS Cosworths had been built) but it carried on until June 1994. In the meantime, Ford dropped the Motorsport (or Roadsport) model (in early '93), offered an Aero Pack deletion no-cost option (which removed the upper rear wing and lower front spoiler) and added a Monte Carlo (known as Martini in some markets) limited edition; see the following chapter for a detailed description.

There were also new paint colours, including Ash Black and Moondust Silver in place of Polaris Grey, with Imperial Blue superseding Pacifica Blue.

In June 1994 the Small Turbo appeared, looking almost identical on top but featuring significant changes beneath the skin. Most notably, there was a dinky Garrett T25 turbo, and the Weber-Marelli fuelling and ignition system fitted to all previous Cosworths had been swapped for Ford's run-of-the-mill EEC-IV engine management, complete with individual coil packs and a revised throttle body. Significantly less tuneable, the Small Turbo was nevertheless an impressive road car, using its 217bhp YBP powerplant to deliver far better response at low revs in a notably more user-friendly package.

Other changes came too – including driver's airbag and new fuel filler flap – but the formula remained much as before: incredible handling, supercar performance and jaw-dropping looks, all with a humble Blue Oval badge.

The final Escort facelift of January 1995 brought enough alterations to the mainstream range to warrant a Mk6 tag. But rather than updating the Cosworth's body panels, Ford stuck with the original styling, tweaking details such as the door mirrors and badges in an attempt to conform.

Sadly, though, it wasn't to last. Ford announced the impending demise of the RS Cosworth in September 1995. Was it due, as suggested, to upcoming emissions laws and drive-by noise tests turning the YB engine into a dinosaur? Was it down to the crippling insurance premiums of the joyriders' all-time favourite transport? Or was it simply because sales had slowed, and there was no more need for a motorsport-based machine in a recession-hit market?

By the end of its life, 7145 Escort RS Cosworths had been produced, and it's reckoned that more than 5000 were Big Turbo cars (5186 YBT engines were built). Ford considered other options to boost sales and keep the line running, including a couple of normally-aspirated, rear-wheel-drive prototypes based on aero-deleted Escort RS Cosworth bodyshells, one fitted with a 150bhp RS2000 powerplant and another using the Scorpio's 2.9-litre V6, an MT-75 gearbox and five-stud hubs. Frustratingly, neither car could be produced at substantially less cost than the Cosworth, and the plans were quickly shelved.

RS Cosworth production officially ended in January 1996: according to Ford historians, the last ever Escort RS Cosworth left the Karmann factory on 12 January 1996, with the chassis number WF0BXXGKABSP93313 (a December 1995 build date). Apparently a Diamond White, right-hand-drive machine, it had 'last car' stamped on its build plate and was registered in the UK as N912 FVX; it was subsequently stolen and never seen again.

Much the same can be said of the RS Cosworth. Although other fast Fords came and went, the Escort remained the poster car of Blue Oval enthusiasts. It was simply unbeatable.

We'd already witnessed wild wings on the original Sierra RS Cosworth, but the Escort's whale tail took things to a whole new level. This was a mass production car from a mainstream manufacturer, remember, and it was based on a remarkably forgettable machine.

A more familiar sight by the time the Small Turbo model appeared, the Escort RS Cosworth was nevertheless still staggeringly bold from the back. Note this 1995 car's revised badges and central Ford oval.

Engine – Block, Sump and Oil System
Big Turbo (YBT)

Cosworth's completely re-engineered block for the Sapphire 4x4 was such a step up from production Ford castings that it was still more than man enough for the rally-bound Escort.

Indeed, the YBT's entire bottom end was unchanged from its predecessor, being built around a 1992-spec 200 block. That meant a 90HM6015AB casting, which lacked the earlier blocks' rear core plug, and also had no drillings for a mechanical fuel pump drive, which was a throwback to the engine's Pinto origins.

Externally, it looked similar to other 4x4 Cosworth units. The iron casting was painted satin black, and featured the usual 200-block strengthening points around the base. There were the same raised digits – reading 200 – on each side of the crankcase adjacent to number two cylinder, not far below the cylinder head; as before, the 20 represented 2.0 litres and the extra zero was for 1990, which was the model year of the casting's introduction.

A smaller 200 was found in raised numbers in front of the offside engine mount, accompanied by a Ford oval and the casting's part number. A machined flat surface was above them, where the Ford engine number was stamped by hand. It comprised two letters to represent the build year and month,

followed by a five-digit serial number that corresponded with the car's chassis number.

Cosworth also stamped its own unique engine number into the front of the cylinder block, just above the water pump. In this case it was YBT followed by a series of numbers; this serial never matched Ford's numbers on the block or VIN plate.

There was also a production date cast on the side of the block, found in a raised oval. Its format was a pair of digits relating to the day and week of manufacture, a letter relating to the month (A for January, B for February etc) and another two digits being the year (92 meaning 1992 and such like).

Being cast especially for Cosworth engines, the Escort's 200 block featured fewer variations than earlier Sierra powerplants. But by this point in production all were good, strong blocks.

Inside the YBT, the bottom end wasn't as thoroughly balanced as 205-block Cosworth engines. It included the Sapphire 4x4's five-bearing forged-steel crankshaft with nine flywheel bolts, and long nose, interference-fit front pulley. Two different crank pulleys were found on the Escort – the single poly-vee version for cars without air conditioning, and the twin poly-vee where air con was specified.

The Sapphire's forged heat-treated connecting rods

Early Escort Cosworth engine bay, with 227bhp YBT powerplant and Weber-Marelli engine management.

remained in the Escort engine, along with the regular 4x4 pistons, which had 1mm offset gudgeon pins and 4cc larger bowls than the first rear-wheel-drive YB pistons. The original 8:1 compression ratio was unaltered.

Underneath was the usual oil spray bar, directing fluid in jets to each piston for cooling as it reached the bottom of its stroke. The bar was brazed onto the oil pickup pipe, which was fed from the side of the usual 4x4 oil pump, with upper supporting spigot, externally-visible circular raised noggin and five bolt fittings.

The 4x4 Sapphire's Modine oil cooler/heat exchanger was fitted between the oil filter housing and cylinder block face, along with the same high-capacity oil filter. Similarly, the Sapphire's revised breather system was retained, complete with twin outlets and pipework, which ran from beneath the inlet manifold to the intake airbox. A new gold-passivated oil pressure switch and T-piece was fitted at the nearside rear of the cylinder block.

The Sapphire Cosworth 4x4's oil sump was kept for the Escort, cast in bare alloy with tunnels for front driveshafts to pass through, plus a revised baffle plate. The sump gasket was carried over too, made from aluminium between two sheets of cork. Despite the Escort's apparently smaller engine bay, it retained the Sapphire's awkward-to-reach dipstick position

at the nearside rear; it was the same metal rod with yellow plastic handle, which reached into a wider tube than the YBB engine's version.

Because the Escort's floorpan was taken from the Sapphire 4x4, its YBT was located on the same alloy crossmember, which was also the part used on the Sierra 2.0 twin-cam 4x4. The engine mounts were identical too, featuring the twin-cam 4x4's circular rubbers within oval alloy plates, which then bolted into the crossmember with long studs.

Engine – Block, Sump and Oil system
Small Turbo (YBP)

When Ford refined the Escort RS Cosworth as a responsive road car, it wasn't just a swap to a smaller turbo that took place. There were innumerable other alterations to the engine, not least of which were found in the bottom end.

The 217bhp Cosworth YBP became standard fitment in June 1994, complete with new cylinder block, now listed with the part number 93HF6010AA. Its appearance was pretty similar to earlier blocks, with satin black-painted iron casting, the familiar 200-block strengthening, no rear core plug and no drillings for a mechanical fuel pump drive.

As before, the YBP block featured a cast '200' in raised digits on each side of the crankcase at cylinder number two,

Late-model Small Turbo underbonnet view, compete with tiny Garrett T25 for improved throttle response.

slightly below the cylinder head. Just in front of the offside engine mount was a smaller 200, along with a Ford oval and the casting's part number. Ford's engine serial number was hand-stamped on a machined flat surface above them; as was traditional, it consisted of a pair of letters representing the build year and month, followed by a five-digit number that matched the car's VIN/chassis number.

A production date was cast on the side of the crankcase in a raised oval. It featured two digits for the day and week of manufacture, a letter relating to the month (A for January, B for February) and another two digits representing the year (95 meaning 1995, for example).

Not to be left out, Cosworth also hand-stamped a unique serial number onto each YBP engine, above the water pump on the front of the block. Its format was YBP followed by a series of numbers, which did not match Ford's VIN.

The YBP cylinder block casting also boasted revised core plug locations and a minor increase in boss size at the engine mount positions. The engine mounts themselves, though, were unchanged from the Sapphire 4x4, composed of Sierra 2.0 twin-cam 4x4 circular rubbers inside oval alloy plates that were bolted into the crossmember with long studs. The alloy crossmember, too, was the same, being identical to that of the four-wheel-drive Sierra 2.0 twin-cam.

Inside the block was where most changes were found. The original 4x4 long-nose crankshaft was still in place (with new front pulleys, which differed between air conditioning-equipped and non-air con cars), turning the same forged steel connecting rods. Yet the pistons were new, being dimensionally identical to preceding 4x4 components but with half-moon cutouts in their skirts (all previous YB pistons were flat across the bottoms). The cutouts were introduced to make clearance for the YBP's new under-piston cooling jets, which would otherwise have made contact with the skirts. Now, rather than a spray bar from the oil pump, this block boasted individual pressure-driven jets drilled and screwed into the main oil gallery, which resulted in a better and more focused spray pattern.

Because the spray bar had been deleted, a unique Cosworth oil pump was no longer required, and the YBP engine reverted to a standard Ford Pinto oil pump. Still, the oil system incorporated other improvements, including a windage tray inside a new alloy sump, and new   oil filter hoses.

The triple-layered sump gasket was retained from the earlier Escort, as were the Modine oil cooler/heat exchanger, oil filter housing, high-capacity oil filter, updated breather system and oil pressure sender setup. Likewise, the Sapphire 4x4's metal dipstick and tube with yellow plastic handle remained.

Cylinder Head – Big Turbo (YBT)

The early Escort RS Cosworth's entire YBT engine was essentially a transplant from the Sapphire Cosworth 4x4, and the cylinder head formed part of that package. Well, almost.

Its 92HF6090AA head was an aluminium alloy casting, produced by Cosworth at its Worcester foundry in the regular 16-valve, twin-overhead camshaft design. Following the familiar Ford part numbering pattern, the 92 represented the component's design year (1992), 6090 was simply the reference for a cylinder head, and AA meant the first version of the part.

Even so, the YBT head was a mere manufacturing revision of the YBG/YBJ's, seen primarily at the head bolt pillars, where the casting tapered inwards without leaving a burr. Otherwise, there was little to distinguish the head from earlier versions.

It featured a 46cc combustion chamber volume, 23mm ports, and the same four valves per cylinder (35-to-35.2mm inlet head diameters, and 31-to-31.2mm sodium-cooled exhaust valves), which were arranged in a vee formation, with inlet and exhaust valves at opposing sides. As before, valve sizes were stamped in 5mm digits on the rear of the cylinder head, referring to oversized valve guides, seats and tappets, where fitted; a letter A represented oversized tappets.

The Escort's camshafts were also the same standard Cosworth type, each with 8.544mm lift. They were fitted with the usual pulleys from the older eight-valve CVH engine, still in bare metal and attached to the cams using gold-passivated bolts. There was a grey alloy belt tensioner, also fitted with gold-passivated bolts, and a Uniroyal glassfibre-reinforced toothed rubber timing belt with printed white lettering.

They were encased in an Escort-specific timing belt cover made from textured black plastic. It differed from the Sapphire 4x4 cover in having a more rounded upper section, and also lacked the previous Ford and Cosworth logos. The cover attached to the engine with three black Torx-headed bolts and washers.

The YBT-engined Escort was fitted with the familiar Cosworth alloy cam cover. Although there was a new part number (V92HF6582AA was cast inside the cover) it was essentially the same, albeit now finished in textured satin blue paintwork rather than the Sapphire 4x4's red or green. As before, the DOHC 16-V TURBO and Ford COSWORTH sections were skimmed back to bare alloy, while the oil filler cap aperture had a screw-thread fitting. The cap itself was the same as the Sapphire 4x4's part, in black plastic with yellow ENGINE OIL lettering and an oil can diagram in inside a yellow circle, flush with the surface rather than early caps' raised characters.

There was no turbo damper fitted to the YBT, so the cylinder head had no provision. There was, however, a pair of lifting eye brackets at the nearside front and offside rear manifold studs, shorter in length than Sierra/Sapphire items and now finished in satin black rather than the previous Cosworths' passivated coating.

YBT engine was topped with blue cam cover but was otherwise very similar to the Sapphire Cosworth 4x4's YBG.

Cylinder Head – Small Turbo (YBP)

Another heavily-revised component, the YBP's cylinder head was noticeably different inside and out. The casting was virtually all new, now with a 93HF6090AA part number due to its 1993 design, although it wasn't released until June 1994. It was also compatible with all previous YB cylinder blocks, but many of its ancillaries were not.

The 93HF6090AA head had slightly smaller ports (by roughly 0.5mm each) than its predecessors, and lacked the previous bolted-on water outlet on the intake side; instead, the heater stub had moved to the front of the head underneath the inlet manifold, directly above its Modine oil cooler, which simplified the system by removing unnecessary pipework.

The other major external alteration was provision in the casting for an EGR (exhaust gas recirculation) setup, including new drillings for EGR pipework and a flange at the back of the cylinder head; it was not tapped because the proposed EGR system was never implemented.

Of course, the YBP's cam cover had a radically different appearance from earlier engines, ousting the traditional Cosworth cover in favour of a modernised design with smoother, rounded profile that swept upwards at the front to meet a textured black plastic timing belt cover (itself almost identical to the YBT's timing belt cover but without the two uppermost mounting holes).

Unlike previous cam covers, the YBP's had a new bolt pattern, meaning the parts weren't interchangeable. It featured a smooth painted silver finish and large central removable plastic panel wearing a blue Ford oval and a Cosworth logo; beneath the plastic panel were the ignition coils and HT leads. Its oil filler was now fitted with a knurled black plastic cap

YBP powerplant was modernised with smooth cam cover and plastic inserts above coil-pack ignition system.

featuring a printed yellow circle and oil can symbol.

Within the head was a pair of regular YB 8.544mm-lift camshafts and the original valves, featuring 35-to-35.2mm inlet head diameters, and 31-to-31.2mm exhaust sizes. The layout remained identical, with four valves per cylinder arranged in a vee, inlet and exhaust valves opposite each other. Again, the combustion chamber volume was 46cc, and the stock Cosworth hydraulic lifters remained in place.

At the front of the head, each cam was equipped with a CVH cam pulley, left bare and affixed with a gold-passivated bolt. There was also an alloy belt tensioner (attached with gold-passivated bolts) and a Uniroyal glassfibre-reinforced toothed rubber timing belt with printed white lettering.

The usual lifting eye brackets were left in their previous positions, one on the offside rear manifold stud and another at the nearside front. Both were finished in satin black.

Cooling System

Mostly inherited from the Sapphire Cosworth 4x4, the Escort's cooling system nevertheless featured a few crucial alterations.

At the front of the car was its radiator, of the usual Sapphire Cosworth type but slotted into the Escort-shaped nose; it comprised a black-coloured aluminium core and black plastic end tanks, marked with a Ford logo and part number. There was a new black plastic fan shroud, positioned around twin electrically-driven cooling fans (in, yes, black plastic), triggered by a thermal switch from the Sapphire Cosworth. Later cars (from October 1992) received a revised radiator complete with extra brackets to accommodate an air conditioning condenser, regardless of whether or not the system was fitted.

Air con itself was an optional extra on Luxury models, not offered on Standard or Roadsport versions. It necessitated a host of changes to the cooling system, including Sapphire 4x4-sourced pump, compressor and clutch, all-new pipework, unique condenser, dehydrator, heater/blower assembly, wiring loom, and even the upper bulkhead panel.

The 4x4 Sapphire Cosworth donated its water pump (with deeper body and bigger impeller than the YBB engine) and three-bolt thermostat housing with outlets for a bleed hose and coolant feed pipe to the turbo, and containing the same 88-degree wax thermostat.

The pump was turned by a pair of matched belts from the crank pulley, which, like the Sapphire 4x4, differed between air conditioning-equipped Escorts (a twin poly-vee) and those without (a single poly-vee).

Coolant flowed from the pump through a series of hard metal pipes and black rubber hoses with white-printed part numbers, many of which were new for the Escort Cosworth. All were attached using Ford-stamped hose clips.

Until June 1994 there was a removable two-bolt coolant sensor housing and blue sensor on a stub at the rear of the cylinder head, under the inlet manifold. For Small Turbo Escorts the stub was repositioned at the front of the head, logically positioned just above the Modine oil cooler, accompanied by shorter coolant pipes.

The Escort's coolant reservoir was taken directly from the Sapphire Cosworth 4x4; it was a clear/white plastic tank mounted on the nearside inner wing, featuring twin lower outlets and a large-bore upper hose, which returned water from the turbo via a new plastic pipe that was clipped to the bonnet slam panel; the turbo coolant inlet and outlet hoses were renewed when the Small Turbo appeared in June 1994. The header tank's screw cap was the same as before, too, in yellow plastic.

The Escort Cosworth also boasted a new Behr intercooler with air-to-air and water-to-air cooling, the latter using water from the engine cooling system; its mounting position left it at a different angle from the Sapphire, too, but the route – fed by hose from the turbo, through the intercooler, then back out, much colder, via a hose to the inlet manifold – remained as before.

A replacement air-to-air intercooler was fitted to Small Turbo cars, from June 1994, complete with new hoses and the addition of an air charge temperature sensor in its outlet.

The other major difference was found between launch and autumn/winter 1992. The Escort RS Cosworth was homologated with water injection, so the initial 2500 cars were supposed to be supplied with suitable equipment to comply with the rules. But that's not exactly the way it turned out: in June 1993 Ford reported that 427 Escorts had left Karmann without the water injection plumbing in place, while 2634 had the components on board.

Still, in reality it was merely a dummy system, which was

neither plumbed in nor capable of being used – the kit wasn't up to the task, and even the engine ECU had the wrong chip to run water injection.

Such homologation-spec Escorts featured a blanking plug screwed into the intercooler instead of a water jet, and some cars also came with pipework routed to the space beneath the back seat, where a water injection pump and pipework were cable-tied but unfitted. Rather than supplying expensive water injection components, Ford gave owners a simple headlamp washer motor; well, at least it looked the part.

There was also a grey water-injection bag in the car's boot, contained within a Ford-marked plastic bag, left loose instead of being coupled up.

To make matters even more complicated, quite a few non-homologation Cosworths were fitted with the early intercooler and blanking plug but lacking any of the other water injection accessories.

Fuel System

Run-of-the-mill Ford components here, a few all-new parts there, and a handful of bits from its Sierra predecessor: that was the Escort Cosworth's fuel system.

Its 65-litre petrol tank, mounted beneath the boot floor using a pair of steel straps and two 13mm bolts, was a unique part blow-moulded in black plastic by Kautex to fill the available space, meaning ten litres more capacity than a regular Mk5 Escort tank. In the top was a circular plate with pipes for feed and return, marked white and red respectively, held in place by a castellated steel ring that covered a large access hole to reach the in-tank fuel pump and integral sender unit – essentially a regular Escort 1.6 EFi component that was barely up to the task.

The filler neck (from offside rear wing to tank) was revised for the Cosworth version of the Mk5 Escort, and suitably refreshed in June 1994 when the bodywork swapped from flush-fitting filler to a recessed cap behind an opening flap.

Petrol was delivered through a standard fuel-injected Escort (Bosch) fuel filter assembly just in front of the tank via typical Ford fuel lines in green-coated steel, attached to the underside using black plastic clips. The pipes swapped to hard black plastic in the engine bay, along with quick-release couplings and a braided rubber fuel return. There was also a model-specific fuel vapour carbon canister behind the front wing's wheelarch liner.

Most of the Sapphire Cosworth 4x4's Weber-Marelli multi-point fuel injection and electronic management was used at the engine of the Big Turbo Escort Cosworth. That included the Sapphire's alloy inlet manifold and plenum chamber, along with its 60mm throttle body (with recessed adjuster) and an integral elbow, which was supported by a nearside engine mounting bracket.

The throttle body was home to an idle speed control valve and a black Weber PF09 throttle position sensor, while an inlet

air temperature sensor was fitted to the plenum chamber, plus vacuum connectors for the fuel pressure regulator, air charge bypass valve, 2.5 bar MAP sensor and crankcase ventilation filter from the Sapphire 4x4. The throttle cable came from the original three-door Sierra Cosworth, while left-hand-drive Escorts used the cable from a Pinto 1.3-engined Sierra. The cable ran from the accelerator pedal, through the bulkhead, under the offside inner wing rail and bonnet slam panel, then through a passivated bracket at the throttle body.

There was a bright nickel-finished fuel rail similar to the Sapphire's, although it now featured an integral non-adjustable fuel pressure regulator with short black hose. It fed a set of four dark blue Weber fuel injectors (identical to those used in the Sapphire 4x4)

At the offside front of the engine bay was a black plastic airbox, designed specifically for the Escort Cosworth and containing a new paper filter element. Its lid featured a Ford oval logo and five horizontal ribs, and was attached to the base with five wire clips. It had several outlets, connected to black hoses for the inlet manifold and air bypass valve; the largest joined an induction hose to the turbo, which attached with a Ford-branded Jubilee-type clip and featured a T-piece to a dump valve between the turbo and intercooler. Meanwhile,

Big Turbo models featured Weber-Marelli engine management, fuel injectors and control sensors.

YBP engine's airbox was unchanged but the inlet pipework was revised for the T25 turbo.

beneath the airbox was a feed scoop, taking cold air from beneath the offside headlamp.

The Small Turbo Escort RS Cosworth had numerous noteworthy alterations resulting in its swap from Weber-Marelli to Ford fuelling and management. A new, less restrictive plenum and inlet manifold was used, complete with relocated vacuum ports on each side and a new idle speed control valve and connector, mounted to the manifold rather than the throttle body. Talking of which, the Small Turbo featured a larger throttle body (now around 65mm), a Ford-made (rather than Weber) throttle position sensor and MAP sensor, plus a revised fuel rail and all-new injectors – now high-impedance type (Weber injectors were low-impedance).

The air cleaner assembly and hoses looked similar to the earlier Escort's and remained in place at the offside front of the engine bay, but were now new made to accompany the smaller turbo, although the paper element stayed from before.

Most noticeably, there was a mass air flow (MAF) meter fitted into the intake pipework just after the airbox, affixed to a black tube that connected to the airbox on four gold-passivated nuts and bolts.

Exhaust System

Unlike the rest of the Escort RS Cosworth, the exhaust system was almost entirely exclusive to the car.

Almost? Well, the Big Turbo's exhaust manifold was essentially the one-piece part from the Sapphire Cosworth 4x4, albeit with a different part number. It was bolted to a new Garrett AiResearch T3/T04B turbocharger (sometimes referred to by Ford as a T35), complete with 0.63 exhaust housing. Basically, it combined the turbine of the T3 with the compressor of the larger T04B.

A black-painted Garrett actuator was mounted directly to the compressor housing in a nine o'clock position. A silver sticker with black Ford logo was on the turbo, and a silver 'caution' decal was stuck to the rim of the actuator, plus a rubber hose and hard black plastic pipe linking it to the boost control solenoid.

An oil feed reached the turbo through steel-braided hose from the engine's oil pressure switch adaptor, and it returned to the engine's sump via a black rubber hose and a pair of clips. The turbo was also water-cooled, through a pipe from the thermostat housing, which returned to the header tank via a black rubber hose clipped to the bonnet slam panel. There was no turbo damper.

Above and over the turbo was a large black plastic heat shield wearing the word TURBO in raised letters, attached on two bolts and one nut. Its peak shrouded a large-bore rubber

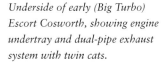

Underside of early (Big Turbo) Escort Cosworth, showing engine undertray and dual-pipe exhaust system with twin cats.

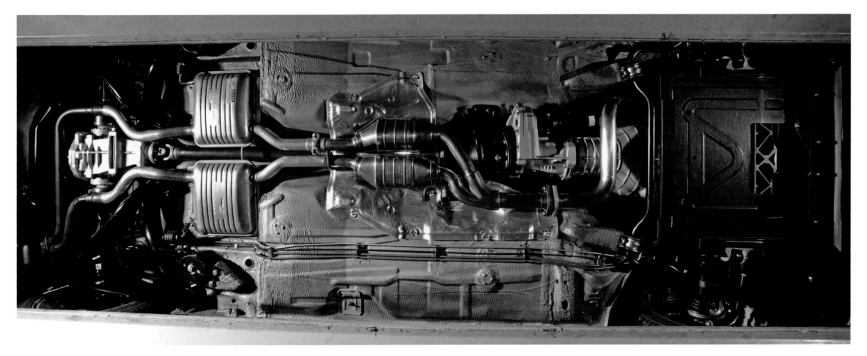

Bosch dump valve was fitted to the Big Turbo model but omitted from later cars, which used an internal system.

Big Turbo meant exactly that – a hefty Garret T3/T04B, which was essentially too laggy for low-boost road use.

hose that fed the turbocharger with intake air from the airbox; air was then pushed through the turbo to the intercooler from a lower hose that was equipped with a black plastic Bosch bypass valve, which was also connected to the intake hose via a T-piece.

Behind the turbo, a large-bore front pipe swept underneath the gearbox and connected to a single exhaust pipe that split into two, each including a catalytic converter pressed with a Ford logo and part numbers. The cat section then bolted to another pair of pipes and dual square centre boxes (again, featuring Ford markings), which wrapped around the rear differential and returned to a single pipe. From there, the two pipes fed into a squarish rear silencer complete with polished oval tailpipe. Each section wore a pale blue paper sticker with a Ford logo and the part number.

The exhaust was hung from the body on one regular Ford Sierra/Transit rubber and four from the standard Mk5 Escort, along with special C-shaped exhaust mounting bracket and supports on the rear floor crossmember. A large heat shield was fitted between the entire catalytic converter section and the car's floorpan.

Of course, much of the setup changed for the last-generation RS Cosworth, fitted with a YBP powerplant and colloquially referred to as the Small Turbo.

Being sized between the Sapphire's T3 and the RS500's T4 turbos, the original Escort's T3/T04 turbocharger was essential for Group A homologation but too big for a road car, leading to excessive lag under acceleration. The Small Turbo Escort RS Cosworth of June 1994 was Ford's answer, long after the requisite homologation numbers had been achieved.

Here, the T3/T04 was binned in favour of a tiny Garrett T25, complete with T03 compressor wheel and internal dump valve in the compressor housing. Again, a black Garrett actuator was fitted in a nine o'clock position, but now bolted to a bracket rather than directly to the compressor housing.

New inlet trunking from a revised airbox sat ahead of the turbo, now shorter to make room for an airflow meter, and lacking the T-piece for a separate dump valve. The original Escort Cosworth's heat shield sat above the turbo, while revised inlet and outlet coolant hoses were used.

Behind the turbo there was a visually similar manifold but with a smaller bore and flange to suit the little T25 turbo. The rest of the exhaust system was the same as the previous Escort RS Cosworth.

Ignition System – Big Turbo (YBT)

Owing much to the Sapphire 4x4, the original Escort Cosworth's ignition system featured several crucial differences.

Most notable of all was the ECU (electronic control unit), which was swapped from a Weber-Marelli level eight (L8) to a P8, now featuring adaptive spark and fuel control, and closed-loop boost control (meaning constant adjustment of the turbocharger boost level, allowing for overboost beyond the pre-set 0.8 bar for short periods). Externally, the P8 looked similar to its predecessor, with smooth sides to the metal case and no mounting flange. But unlike the L8, the P8 lacked a drilling at the mixture screw hole; it wore a white sticker with the part number IAW048/P8 or IAW48/P8. The Escort's ECU was fixed to the passenger-side A-pillar behind the glovebox and kick panel area.

121

The YBG-engined Sapphire 4x4's Marelli breakerless distributor found its way onto the Escort, positioned beneath the inlet manifold, with the same phase sensor underneath its rotor arm and topped with a conventional distributor cap rather than the angled type of earlier Sierras.

The black silicone HT leads were also taken from the Sapphire 4x4, all four held in a bundle above the fuel rail with a black plastic clip. Each lead fed through the rocker cover and connected to a platinum-tipped AGPR12PP8 spark plug, unique to the Escort RS Cosworth. The king lead ran from the distributor cap to the Escort's high-output breakerless ignition coil, a Motorcraft-branded component with black body and red label; it was attached to the nearside inner wing in a bare metal bracket, just in front of the car's coolant reservoir. An accompanying Marelli ignition module was attached to the inner wing on a bare metal plate alongside the coil.

The engine ECU was also supplied with signals from a variety of sensors, many of which were carried over from the Sapphire Cosworth 4x4. The same air charge temperature (ACT) sensor was fitted to the plenum chamber, along with the familiar idle speed control valve above the throttle body and a black PF09 throttle position sensor on the side.

The Sapphire 4x4's engine coolant temperature (ECT) sensor was screwed into the Escort's cylinder head beneath its inlet manifold, the YBG's lambda sensor screwed into the exhaust downpipe, and the previous engine speed/TDC sensor bolted to the engine beneath the crankshaft pulley. Again, the original wastegate control solenoid (Amal valve) was fitted to the slam panel above the intercooler, and connected by a hose to the high-pressure side of the turbo. It included a white top with a two-pin electrical connector and silver Behr decal on the side, while the sides had hoses coupled up to the airbox, inlet manifold and wastegate actuator.

The main difference was a new Escort-specific 2.5-bar MAP sensor, mounted to a passivated bracket on the front chassis rail below the coolant header tank. But that was nothing compared with what came next…

Ignition System – Small Turbo (YBP)

For the Small Turbo model of June 1994, Ford ditched the traditional Weber-Marelli engine management system in favour of its own EEC-IV setup. It was a radical revision, being more economical to produce and offering advanced wasted spark and closed-loop fuelling features, meaning arguably superior levels of usability, reliability and control. Unfortunately, it was considerably more difficult to remap by aftermarket tuners, which may even – in some small part – take some blame for the Cosworth's eventual demise.

At the heart of the EEC-IV system was Ford's own ECU, fitted into the A-pillar like the original Escort RS Cosworth, now with a new wiring loom held in place with one central bolt. Its metal case looked very different from a Weber-Marelli ECU, and had 'EEC-IV' printed on a white label, along with

four-digit code reading COSY.

Now, for the first time, the conventional distributor and coil arrangement was cast aside and replaced by wasted-spark ignition system, with a pair of coil packs each firing two spark plugs, fitted directly onto plugs numbers two and four. The spark plugs were the AGPR12PP as before, although with a wider gap to suit the wasted spark setup. A Ford Motorcraft ignition amplifier was affixed to the nearside inner wing instead of the Marelli version.

In place of the distributor was a phase sensor with integral viewing window to check the ignition timing; like the distributor it was gear-driven from an auxiliary shaft, and slotted into the same hole beneath the inlet manifold.

All the other sensors were changed too. The crankshaft/TDC sensor was unique to the Small Turbo, with a 36-1 trigger wheel; a new air charge temperature sensor was found in the intercooler outlet; there was a new idle speed control valve, now mounted to the inlet manifold and coupled up with a standard Ford two-pin plug; a new EEC-IV throttle position sensor was connected using a standard Ford multiplug; a unique coolant temperature sensor was found at the front of the cylinder head under the inlet manifold, along with new, shorter hoses; a different oxygen sensor was used, screwed into the turbo exhaust housing beneath the turbo heat shield; a Ford 2.5-bar MAP sensor was fitted instead of the Weber part.

Crucially, the Small Turbo also boasted a mass air flow (MAF) sensor, which was positioned in the inlet pipework between airbox and turbocharger, complete with gasket, whereas all earlier Cosworths had none.

Electrical System

Like pretty much everything else about the Escort RS Cosworth, its electrical system was a mixture of Mk5 Escort, Sierra/Sapphire Cosworth and all-new parts.

Unfortunately, the fuse box came from a run-of-the-mill Escort, complete with a multitude of inherent weaknesses to cause problems for future owners. Like other Mk5 Escorts, the Cosworth's fuse box was positioned under the dashboard, equipped with standard ATO fuses and relays.

The Cosworth's wiring loom, though, was completely different. Unlike the Sapphire's loom, it was fully integrated into the car and unable to be removed; instead, it featured two large multi-plugs (in front of the coolant header tank) to allow the engine to be released from the car.

As you'd expect, the wiring loom changed during production; initially it was a different loom for cars with or without air conditioning, but from August 1993 there was one new section, along with accompanying immobiliser circuitry; the Motorsport/Roadsport model had no immobiliser. Naturally, left-hand-drive Escorts required alternative looms, while the whole lot was replaced in June 1994 when new connectors were requited for the EEC-IV engine components.

Visually, most Escort Cosworth wiring was similar, being

wrapped in traditional black Ford loom tape and clipped to the car in a series of black plastic brackets and clips.

The Escort's battery lived in the same position as its Sierra predecessor and Escort Mk5 body, beneath the windscreen scuttle panel and clamped to a steel tray on the nearside upper bulkhead. As standard it was a square-terminal 500A/70RC or 590A/90RC, depending on territory, and was capped with a black plastic cover complete with Ford logo. The cables were unique lengths for the Cosworth.

The Escort RS Cosworth retained the Sapphire 4x4's Magnetti Marelli M78R 1.4Kw starter motor, along with the Bosch NI-90A 90 amp alternator (with blue label), albeit equipped with a revised alternator heat shield. The regulator assembly remained the same throughout Cosworth production.

As before, the alternator was fitted on a heavy black bracket at the offside front of the engine, along with a black adjusting plate. It was driven by twin belts from the crankshaft pulley.

The Escort Cosworth was fitted with dual-tone horns on a single bracket behind the front bumper, along with a single alarm horn on the bulkhead; the standard alarm system was upgraded in August 1993, along with immobiliser circuity and a new red master key to accompany the regular Chubb ignition key.

Transmission

Following on from the Sapphire 4x4, the Escort RS Cosworth was fitted with an almost identical Ferguson-patented four-wheel drive system, boasting 66/34 torque split between rear and front axles.

As before, there was an MT75 five-speed gearbox, with MT meaning manual transmission and 75 relating to the distance (in millimetres) between the main and layshaft centres. An all-synchromesh unit (including reverse), the Escort's MT75 gearbox contained its predecessor's gear ratios, which originated in the Sierra 2.9 XR4x4: first was 3.61:1; second was 2.08:1; third was 1.36:1; fourth was 1:1; fifth was 0.83:1.

Like the late-model Sapphire Cosworth 4x4, the Escort's MT75 'box featured a slightly longer output shaft to mate up to a new rubber propshaft coupling.

The MT75 featured a ribbed aluminium alloy casing and bellhousing, inside which was the usual Cosworth 242mm clutch assembly. The first batch of 2500-or-so Escort RS Cosworths were fitted with a unique homologation flywheel, designed to allow for a 7.25in twin-plate clutch (which wasn't fitted); the rear face of the flywheel was identical to that of the rear-wheel-drive Sierra Cosworth, machined and hollowed-out. Later Escorts then swapped to the heavier flywheel found in the Sapphire Cosworth 4x4, with flat rear face.

The Sapphire Cosworth 4x4's clutch cable was carried over, while a Granada gearchange rod and Mk5 Escort RS2000 gearshift and stick assembly got everything moving smoothly.

A black-painted steel rear mount was used to attach the

gearbox to the Escort's floorpan, complete with rubber insulator. Behind the gearbox was a chain-driven aluminium alloy transfer box, distributing torque to the front and rear wheels through an epicyclic centre differential with viscous coupling to reduce slip.

A Hi-Vo transfer chain (with 31-tooth chain wheels) and a short propshaft (which ran along the right-hand-side of the engine, and wore a white paper sticker with bar code) fed power to the front, where an aluminium differential case was

MT75 gearbox and four-wheel-drive transmission was carried over from the Sapphire Cosworth 4x4.

Front hubs and driveshafts were Sapphire Cosworth 4x4, with 29mm anti-roll bar.

Rear differential was from the Sapphire Cosworth 4x4 but the boot floor and plastic petrol tank were all-new for the Escort.

Cosworth 4x4 propshaft (with circular centre insulator); the front section of the shaft was identical but the rear piece was shorter to account for the Escort's reduced wheelbase. The prop's front bearing originated in the Ford Transit, while the centre bearing was standard Sierra.

As before, the Sierra XR4x4 V6/Sapphire Cosworth 4x4 7in viscous coupling limited-slip diff was fitted inside the usual bare alloy differential casing. The internals were the same too, with 3.62:1 final drive ratio and 47 crownwheel teeth to 13 on the pinion, although the Escort's viscous couplings were said to be set stiffer than before.

The usual Cosworth differential mount (a large, gold-passivated part containing a rubber bush) supported the rear axle from the Escort's floorpan, while the Sapphire's unequal-length driveshafts (longer on the left-hand side) took power to the rear wheels. Unlike the Sierra, the Escort's driveshafts were painted black, equipped with black rubber gaiters, stainless steel clips, and blue Torx-headed bolts through to the hubs. Each shaft wore an orange sticker declaring L.H or R.H. for left-hand or right-hand fitting respectively.

Suspension and Steering

Despite its radically different styling and notably improved roadholding, the Escort RS Cosworth's underpinnings were sourced almost entirely from the Sapphire Cosworth 4x4. Indeed, benefits of the Escort's stiffer bodyshell, shorter wheelbase and aerodynamic package couldn't be ignored – although it could also be argued that a few minor tweaks made just as much impact.

At the front, almost all of the suspension was the same. There were black-painted, Sapphire-sized MacPherson struts with Fichtel and Sachs gas-filled twin-tube dampers, albeit running revised rates for the Escort. Each damper body wore an oval yellow sticker with the part number (different for

bolted to the right of the engine sump. It contained a 6.5in diameter spiral-bevel final drive open differential. Meanwhile, an extension shaft in a support bearing ran through the sump (underneath the crankshaft) and mated to Sapphire Cosworth 4x4/Sierra XR4x4 equal-length driveshafts, equipped with constant velocity joints at each end. The driveshafts were painted black, with a red sticker with black part number around the circumference; each end was fitted with a black rubber gaiter and stainless steel clip.

From the back of the transfer box, torque was taken to the rear wheels through a modified late-model Sapphire

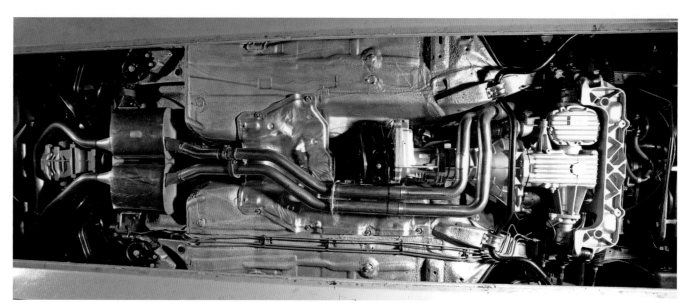

Underside of late-model Escort RS Cosworth. This car's Auralis Blue paintwork would originally have ended at the chassis rails.

left and right) printed on in black. The 21kg/Nm front coil springs (black with grey? paint splashes), upper retaining plates and bearings were identical to the Sapphire's but the Escort's mounting rubbers were stiffer than before.

At the lower end of the Escort's struts were unpainted Sapphire 4x4 hub carriers, with pinch bolts to attach the track control arms rather than the original three-door Cosworth's tapered ball joints and castellated nuts. The (unpainted) track control arms' inner ends fitted into the Sapphire 4x4's alloy engine crossmember, while the black-painted anti-roll bar was 29mm diameter. The usual Ford Scorpio bushes and fittings remained in place.

The Escort RS Cosworth's power-assisted steering system was a mixture of Sapphire 4x4 and Mk5 Escort components. The rack was produced by ZF TRW rather than Cam Gears; it was finished in satin black, and wore black rubber gaiters clipped onto each end, with bare-metal track rod ends. The rack mounting bushes to the crossmember were standard Sierra components.

A Sapphire Cosworth 4x4 steering shaft coupling mated to an Escort Cosworth-specific adjustable steering column, produced in two versions depending on whether or not an airbag was fitted into the steering wheel. The PAS pump was new for the Escort – said to be modified for increased sensitivity and response – and mounted onto a black-painted, late-model Sapphire Cosworth bracket at the turbo side of the engine, complete with Mk5 RS2000/Granada pulley, model-specific hydraulic hoses and Sapphire fluid reservoir and cap.

The Escort Cosworth's rear suspension was similarly

Sapphire 4x4-based, again with revised shock absorber settings (still black-painted Fichtel and Sachs gas-filled single-tube telescopic dampers wearing white identification labels around their lower shafts) and harder coil springs, rated at 62kg/Nm and finished in satin black with grey? paint splashes.

Like the Sapphire, the Escort was equipped with a modified Ford Scorpio rear beam (again painted black) with black rubber bushes and Sierra strengthening plates attached to the floorpan. The Escort added stronger semi-trailing arms than before (stencilled with a white S inside a square), along with uniball joints, as was traditional for Ford Cosworths.

The rear hubs and bearings came from the previous model, left unpainted, but there was a beefy new anti-roll bar, now measuring 22mm diameter. Its mounting points to the Escort's body were the same as its predecessor, inboard of the trailing arms.

Brakes

Disappointing – that's one word for an Escort RS Cosworth's braking setup. Lousy – well, that's another. Even when trying to be diplomatic, the best description is probably 'economical'.

To be fair, the Escort's stopping system wasn't all bad, but Ford's continued use of Sapphire Cosworth 4x4 cut-price callipers was unacceptable for a car of this calibre. Unlike the first Sierra Cosworths, which were fitted with four-pot front brake callipers, the Escort came with single-piston floating callipers from the Granada, along with new carrier brackets and uprated pads. As before, the callipers and carriers were supplied in a gold-passivated finish, and clamped around 278mm x 24mm ventilated discs.

Like most Ford products, the majority of suspension components were finished in satin black paint.

Escort Cosworth rear suspension was lifted from its Sapphire 4x4 predecessor, albeit it with new mounting points. Note Karmann's 'hand-crafted' work on the side skirts.

ABS braking system was similar to the Sapphire 4x4 setup; Escort suspension turrets had extra bracing to the inner wings.

Escort Cosworth front brakes were identical to the Sapphire 4x4's; plastic liners were fitted over black-painted inner wheelarches.

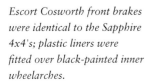

Fortunately, the Escort retained the Sapphire Cosworth 4x4's 273 x 20mm vented rear discs matched to the same single-piston callipers and carriers (gold-zinc plated), black-painted splash guards and uprated brake pads.

The handbrake mechanism consisted of Sierra or Sapphire lever (depending on model) and Sapphire 4x4 cable, the brake pedal was from the Mk1 Sierra, and the brake light switch was commonly seen in any pre-1992 Escort Mk5.

Little else was affected by the change from Sapphire to Escort bodyshell, with an almost-identical front/rear split dual-circuit braking system featuring ATE (Teves) Mk2 electronic ABS, as originally fitted to Granada models.

In the engine bay, on the bulkhead in front of the driver,

Rear brakes were also taken from the Sapphire Cosworth 4x4. The inner wheelarches were coated in black paint over the original body colour.

was a Granada's gold-passivated brake booster assembly and alloy single-piston master cylinder featuring blue ATE decal, along with black-painted electronic ABS pump and accumulator, the latter wearing a yellow warning sticker and series of yellow stamps. Above the cylinder was a clear/white plastic brake fluid reservoir with white plastic screw cap and yellow electrical connector; on the side of the tank was a yellow sticker with warning triangle and handbook icons.

An alloy and gold-passivated ABS actuation assembly was mounted on the nearside inner wing, where the car's green-coated steel brake lines connected. At each wheel the steel pipes switched to rubber flexible hoses, all of which were the same as the parts found on the previous Sapphire Cosworth.

The Escort's ABS control module, relays and fuses were positioned in the nearside rear quarter panel, and a set of Scorpio sensors and toothed rotors were fitted at all four wheels. The rear sensors were mounted in the end castings of the suspension arms, with integral wiring.

Wheels and tyres

One wheel design was used throughout Escort RS Cosworth production (excluding limited-editions, but we'll come to those in another chapter), and what an inspirational wheel design it was. Like the Cosworth's whale-tail rear wing, the Escort's wide soft-spoke alloys became iconic the moment they were released, prompting a host of aftermarket lookalikes, perhaps even leading to the rise of large-diameter rims on mainstream production cars.

Unremarkable today, maybe, but by 1992 standards the Escort's 8x16in wheels were positively massive. Ford designed and Ronal-made, with an offset of ET25mm they gave a wider track than previous Cosworth models, protruding further out

A design classic – the Escort RS Cosworth's soft-spoke 8x16in alloy wheels were built by Ronal in ET25mm offset, widening the car's track and filling out the boxy wheelarches. Remaining unchanged throughout production, dating is done by checking the stamps beneath the centre caps. Pirelli P Zero tyres in 225/45 ZR16 were standard fitment.

to fill the Escort's boxy wheelarches. The wheels' five spokes sat within a narrow outer rim, which was absent from similar (and often assumed to be the same) five-spoke Mondeo alloys.

Each wheel was finished in Moondust Silver and fitted with a removable centre cap featuring Ford oval logo; the caps also differed from Mondeo versions, having a more concave surface. Beneath the cap, and between the bolt holes, were the casting identifiers, including Ford oval logo, part number and size (8Jx16x25).

The nuts were of the usual Ford alloy wheel variety, incorporating rotating conical washers.

Ford's choice of tyres for the Escort Cosworth was the Pirelli P Zero in 225/45 ZR16 size, with Dunlop Performa 8000 directionals (with green markings on the inside of right-hand-side tyres and red markings on the left) also approved.

The Escort's spare wheel was found in the luggage compartment, attached to the raised boot floor with a special mounting plate and wing nut. The spare was a black-painted steel 3.5x16in, ET25mm space-saver, wrapped in a Pirelli 125/80R16 tyre. A yellow 50mph warning decal was stuck to the wheel's outer face, with a matching 80km/h decal at the opposite side.

Bodywork

Was it a bird? Was it a plane? Was it a load of plastic stuck to a chopped-up Mk5 Escort bodyshell and slung over a shortened Sierra floorpan?

Well, not exactly. But it wasn't far off.

Ford said there were 400 unique components produced for the Escort RS Cosworth, and more than 50 per cent of the body panels were brand new. The remainder were made up of existing Escort and Sapphire parts, many of which – even pressed steel pieces – were modified by Karmann from standard stuff.

The basic ingredients were an early Mk5 Escort three-

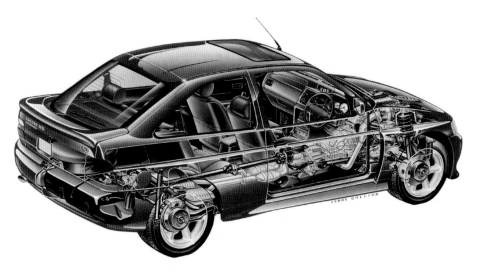

Cutaways of early Big Turbo version in Luxury spec with leather trim (above) and late-spec Small Turbo with Aero Pack delete option (below). Karmann stitched a three-door Escort shell to a cut-down Sierra underside.

127

Chassis number was hand-stamped into the floorpan from below, then coated in black brush paint to protect the surface.

door upper section and Sapphire Cosworth 4x4 lower half, including chassis rails, suspension mounts, inner wings and longitudinally-mounted engine bay and transmission tunnel. Clearly, the Escort was a smaller car than its Sapphire stablemate, so 100mm had to be removed from the floorpan's length, and serious alterations made to the external panels for full clearance. The result was only marginally longer than a regular Mk5 Escort, and that figure came from the Cosworth's bumpers and spoilers rather than fundamental changes. Most importantly, it was substantially stiffer than its Sapphire predecessor, with Ford quoting more than double the torsional rigidity for the Escort Cosworth shell.

Despite sounding like a cut-and-shut from a dodgy dealer beneath some backstreet railway arches, it was a completely bespoke bodyshell, constructed by Karmann by stitching a bare Escort body to two-thirds of a Sierra underside, which was chopped down by 18in beneath the back seat, just in front of the rear axle. An entirely new rear floor section was then hand-welded into place, including fresh chassis rails, mounting points and boot floor. Its was now triple-layered rather than the original twin skins. And although all the suspension bolted into the same locations, only the rear turrets were the Sierra steelwork.

A variety of shells were produced for road and competition use. Standard Escort Cosworth road cars were available in

Roadsport model wore plain black door mirrors and handles, along with RS500-type grilles instead of front fog lamps.

any colour (well, any colour from Ford's catalogue) and had a non-sunroof body. Unless, of course, a sunroof was specified (officially, it was not an optional extra) – in which case the shell was identical to that of a Luxury model. Standard models also lacked the Luxury's opening rear windows, but they were easily retrofitted.

The Motorsport (or Roadsport, as it was initially called) road car was a different matter. It was generally sold only in Diamond White (although other Ford shades were reportedly produced in small numbers at special request) and had no sunroof option. Built from launch until 1993, the Roadsport was available as a fully kitted-out (albeit poverty-spec) car from Ford showrooms, road-ready but also suitable for clubman motorsport. But it wasn't simply a stripped-out Standard model: the Roadsport also featured a riveted panel in the boot floor to enable easy access to the in-tank fuel pump; it was coated in seam-sealer at the factory but easily removable at a later date.

All of these cars – Standard, Luxury and Roadsport – were stamped with Ford chassis numbers on the floorpan, generally viewed through a flap in the carpet between the driver's seat and inner sill. They also had underseal.

In contrast, Ford offered a selection of Escort Cosworth bodyshells off-the-shelf, officially recognised as Ford Motorsport replacement parts. As with most such competition-orientated components, Motorsport bodyshells carried a part number beginning in 909, leading to later enthusiasts referring to them as '909s'. The official name was a Motorsport Escort RS Cosworth bodyshell.

The general idea was to use these shells to update tired Sapphire 4x4 Group A or N rally machines or rebuild damaged Escorts, but it's worth bearing in mind that most world-class championship rally cars – including Ford's own contenders – were scratch-built from 909 Motorsport bodies.

The 909 was offered as a bare or trimmed (with doors, glass, lights, instrument panel and so on) shell in primer or Diamond White. Each shell featured the aforementioned removable fuel pump inspection panel, but was seam-welded and lacked the underseal of road-going Roadsport Cosworths, along with seam sealer on the important panel overlaps. Some shells were supplied with FIA-approved roll cages, and were available in right-hand-drive or left-hand-drive guise. Naturally, a chassis number wasn't present, although a build plate riveted to the slam panel declared MOTORSPORT GROUP N.

Regardless of its ultimate destination, every Escort RS Cosworth bodyshell followed a set theme. The front inner wings and chassis rails were based on the Sapphire 4x4's, mated to Mk5 Escort-type outer panels and unique parts. The front panel, lower crossmember and towing eye mount, radiator support section and brackets were new, although the bonnet slam panel was from the regular Escort (albeit different for cars with or without air conditioning). The slam panel was hand-stamped with the date of production.

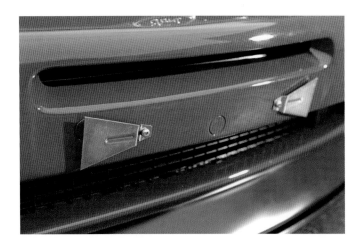

Unique number plate fixing plates were found on Escort Cosworths but often thrown away when the plates were renewed.

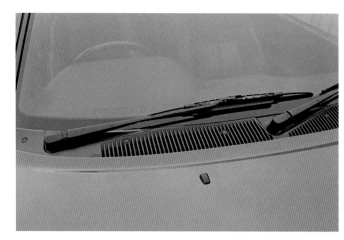

Run-of-the-mill Mk5 windscreen wipers were one of the RS Cosworth's few regular Escort components, although the linkage was revised. Heated washer jets were standard on the Luxury model.

A bulky front bumper was tailored for the Cosworth, complete with wide cooling slots (the larger lower vent having a black plastic mesh grille) and apertures for Sierra Cosworth-sourced indicators and fog lamps. The Roadsport/Motorsport model ditched the fog lamps in favour of RS500-type grilles, although Ford admitted there was no cooling advantage for Group N use.

All Cosworth front bumpers were finished in body colour except for the black plastic air splitter, with wheelarch deflectors (which reduced drag by ten per cent) and three-position lower extension, designed to be retracted for use on gravel surfaces and extended for tarmac rallies and racetracks, where maximum downforce was required. The deleted Aero Pack option (offered from early 1993 after the first 2500 cars had been homologated) ditched the adjustable lower section and wheelarch spats but retained the main black plastic splitter across the width of the car.

On the right-hand side of the bumper was a removable circular towing eye cover, also painted in body colour. On

Standard and Luxury models a pair of headlamp washer jets were mounted in mouldings across the bumper top. Each was a duel black jet in black oval surround, which was unique to the RS Cosworth. The jets were fed from a common motor on the windscreen wiper reservoir – again, a special component – and (mainly) regular Escort pipework and fittings.

The Escort Cosworth's body-coloured radiator grille was unique to the model, incorporating a Ford oval badge (at first the early version in mid-blue, followed by the darker blue oval in 1995) and a black plastic mesh inner section. It remained the same throughout production, avoiding the ignominy of being hampered with the awkward smiley-faced grille of mainstream Escorts in autumn 1992 (Ford tried the styling on a prototype; it wasn't good).

Likewise, the Escort Cosworth's bonnet continued unchanged, being similar to that of the standard car but featuring pressed cut-outs for a pair of oval bonnet vents, clipped into place from underneath. The bonnet catch was unique, too, but the two bonnet-mounted windscreen washer

Three-position adjustable splitter was essential for motorsport homologation, intended to be extended for tarmac rallies and retracted for the rough stuff.

Adjustable splitter continued unchanged until the end of production, complete with spats around the corners of the front bumper. Late-model Escort RS Cosworth kept the earlier car's headlamps and Sierra-sourced indicators and fog lamps.

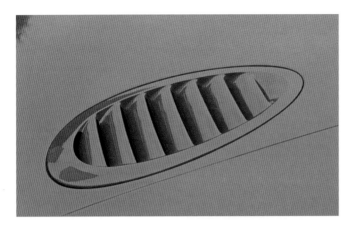

Oval bonnet vents quickly became fashionable on modified cars of the 1990s, but on the RS Cosworth were crucial for encouraging extremely hot air to exit the engine bay.

Functional front wing vents were attached with three black screws. The indicator side repeater was standard Mk5 Escort kit.

Cosworth doors were the same as any other three-door Escort Mk5, and the handles and locks were also regular parts. Handles were colour-coded on the Standard and Luxury but bare plastic on the Roadsport model.

jets were the usual black plastic items found on normal Fords. The Luxury model gained heated washer jets.

Behind the bonnet was a standard Mk5 Escort scuttle panel, complete with black plastic windscreen wiper shroud with circular plastic screw cap covers. The wipers, too, were stock Escort stuff, in satin black with aerofoil on each side. The wiper motor was also taken from the regular Mk5 but a new linkage assembly was used for the RS Cosworth.

A standard Escort Mk5 laminated and tinted windscreen was found in the Cosworth, with a Quickclear heated windscreen included on the Luxury model.

Of course, the outer wings were radically altered,

incorporating boxy extensions to cover the Cosworth's meaty 8in alloy wheels – or wider still for circuit work. At the rear edge of each front wing was a black plastic air outlet grille (to aid underbonnet cooling), attached with three black screws. A special wheelarch liner, again in black plastic, sat within the inner arch.

Regular three-door Mk5 Escort doors were retained, gaining internal side-impact protection beams from early 1995. The normal black plastic handles were used for the Motorsport/ Roadsport, while Standard and Luxury versions had colour-coded handles instead.

The usual Ford Chubb door locks were fitted, with black plastic outer caps; a pair of matching keys were supplied – one torch key and one spare, plus T-handle master/pattern. From August 1993 the keys included a transponder for a factory-fitted immobiliser, and there was a red master key instead of the previous T-handle. All keys operated the doors, tailgate, ignition switch and fuel cap. Roadsport/Motorsport models lacked the torch key, along with the electric central locking of the Standard and Luxury variants.

The Cosworth was also supplied with standard Escort Mk5 door mirrors. Most were colour-coded to the car's bodywork, but Roadsport models' mirrors were the unfinished grained black plastic of base-model Escorts. Each mirror was manually adjusted using a lever inside the car.

Colour-coded door mirrors were fitted to the Standard and Luxury, the latter benefiting from electric adjustment and heating elements. These early mirrors were replaced by slimmer versions for 1995.

January 1995 brought slimline door mirrors, intended to keep vague elements of the Cosworth's styling in common with the newly-introduced Escort Mk6.

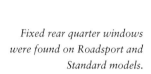

Sekurit glass was fitted to all Karmann-built Escort Cosworths, complete with simple dating code – here the four dots mean April and the 5 represents 1995; clearly, windows were stockpiled some time before cars were produced.

Fixed rear quarter windows were found on Roadsport and Standard models.

Standard-model RS Cosworths were also fitted with manual mirrors, now boasting body-coloured mirror housings. The Luxury kept the colour-keyed capping but added electric adjustment and heating elements to the mirror glass.

The January 1995 facelift – when the regular Mk5 Escort became the Mk6 – brought a smaller, sleeker door mirror design. By this point the Roadsport was long gone, but the Luxury was still the only Cosworth to feature electric mirrors as standard.

It's often thought that such facelifted features coincided with the switch from big turbo to small turbo, but there was a substantial overlap between the Cosworth's mechanical upgrades and the aesthetic alterations that accompanied the incoming Mk6 Escort of January 1995. In fact, a large number of Escorts left the Karmann factory with small turbocharger and large mirrors, along with other pre-facelift features.

The door window glass was from the standard Mk5 Escort three-door, tinted and wearing white Sekurit markings complete with date code of a month or two within the car's build date. Standard and Motorsport/Roadsport models featured wind-up windows but on Luxury versions the glass was electrically operated.

For the Small Turbo model of June 1994, some European markets gained a small black-on-silver HTT badge stuck to each door, referring to a high torque turbo.

New sills were added to the Escort shell for the Cosworth, attached underneath to the Sapphire floors and strengthened at the rear where the chassis shortening had taken place.

Atop each sill was a curved side skirt, made from polyurethane by Phoenix and colour-coded to the car's bodywork. Each skirt was formed in two pieces, with a joint beneath the driver's door; the rear section featured two small arrows to point to jacking point locations. The skirts were screwed, clipped and riveted into position, with black plastic caps at the trailing edges, while the undersides were hacked away to clear the rear suspension mounts. On later cars – probably from January 1995 – a length of rubber trim sealed the joint between skirt and steel sill; each sill was pressed with holes for the seal's clips.

RS Cosworth rear quarters were significantly wider than standard, although they retained the original Mk5 Escort's swage lines. The offside rear wing incorporated a regular Escort fuel filler cap, functioning from the car's ignition/door lock key. On Standard and Luxury models it was colour-coded to the car's bodywork, but with a grained black finish on the Motorsport/Roadsport machine. From May/June 1994 the flush-fitting cap was replaced by a Mk6 Escort-style fuel filler flap complete with lug for opening.

Standard and Roadsport models were fitted with fixed tinted rear side window glass, printed with white Sekurit markings and date code. The Luxury gained pop-out opening

Standard Escort door rubbers and outer sills, mated to broad Cosworth side skirts.

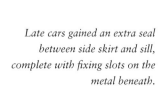

Late cars gained an extra seal between side skirt and sill, complete with fixing slots on the metal beneath.

Flush-fitting fuel filler cap was colour-coded on the Standard and Luxury, but left black on the Roadsport. It was replaced by an opening flap in summer 1994.

Opening fuel filler flap became part of mainstream Escort bodywork before finding its way to the Cosworth in summer 1994, around the same time as swapping to the Small Turbo engine.

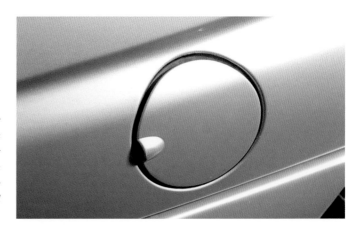

rear quarter windows, complete with Sekurit markings and black plastic caps over the hinges.

An almost-standard Mk5 Escort back panel wrapped across the rear of the RS Cosworth, the alteration being the addition of fuel tank strap mounting brackets. Similarly, the rear floor crossmember (with exhaust supports) was new, and the boot floor was radically different from either a stock Escort or Sierra. There were reinforcements to the wheelarches and new rear lamp brackets too.

A stock bumper reinforcement (with threaded hole for a towing hook) was mounted to the rear panel, wrapped in a colour-coded rear bumper, which was again unique to the RS Cosworth. It featured a circular colour-coded towing eye cover on the right-hand side, a number plate lamp and a wide slot incorporating an oval aperture for the exhaust tailpipe.

The ultimate whale tail – the Escort RS Cosworth's rear wing generated aerodynamic downforce, reducing the car's top speed by 4mph in the process.

In case it's escaped your attention, it's worth noting that the Escort Cosworth wore a slightly enormous rear wing, which was well-known for providing huge amounts of aerodynamic downforce, not to mention an immense ability to make onlookers stop and stare.

The two-piece arrangement was resin transfer moulded by Italian firm Sotira, a process that made it 50 per cent lighter than polyurethane by injecting foam and resin into a 1.5mm thick fibreglass-reinforced plastic skin. It comprised an upper whale-tail combined into one part with a central pillar, along with a lower boot-lid spoiler at a crucial distance apart, and all colour-coded to the car. Each piece was moulded with a Ford logo, part number and date stamp on the underside, where it attached to the bodywork. The wing was affixed with two bolts at each side, its upper pillar fastened down through the centre of the lower spoiler, which was attached using a pair of bolts at each side plus doubled-sided tape across the leading edges.

Of course, the oversized appendage was needed only for motorsport homologation. So after the requisite number of cars (2500) had been built Ford offered the Escort RS Cosworth with an Aero Pack delete option, which was ideal for owners more concerned with driving the car than being noticed; and not just noticed by envious neighbours – the Cosworth's whale tail was a magnet for attention from police and their counterparts on the other side of the law.

Whale tail remained standard – and very popular – even after the introduction of the Small Turbo model and Aero Pack deletion option. It's key to the Escort Cosworth's identity, after all.

Aero Pack deletion was more popular in mainland Europe than the UK. This wingless beast is a German car in Imperial Blue with Luxury trim. Note the early mirrors and badging alongside late-type fuel filler flap.

Aero Pack deletion was less obvious from the front, lacking only the extendible section of the adjustable lower splitter.

Officially a no-cost option, Ford dealers were told to knock £300 off the price for anyone choosing to go wingless. When they did so, the adjustable front splitter, spats and upper rear wing weren't fitted, leaving the lower spoiler in place on the tailgate, complete with grommet-filled hole for the wing's central pillar, and retaining a wiper cutout.

Aero Pack deletion made its debut at the Geneva motor show in March 1993, with wingless cars available in the UK from May 1993. Despite a more pleasing appearance to many people's eyes, Aero Pack deletion was rarely specified; such was the nature of choosing to buy an aggressive, hardcore rally reprobate rather than a discreet hot hatchback.

It's widely reported that the RS Cosworth's tailgate was a regular Mk5 Escort component but that's not quite the case. Although it was very similar, and opened on regular hinges, the Cosworth's hatchback lid was adapted for the whale tail's fixing bolts, with an indented section on the internal structure at each side of the upper tailgate. A pair of holes were made in the steelwork by Karmann, along with one locating dimple. Obviously, cars with deleted Aero Pack didn't have the drillings.

All Cosworths had the standard Escort heated rear window with tinted glass and wiper with electronic washer. The wiper sat within a recess in the lower spoiler, while the washer jet was above the window. Standard and Luxury models benefited from remote tailgate release.

Early Escort Cosworths were fitted with a blue oval Ford badge on the right-hand side of the tailgate, along with separate chrome ESCORT, RS and COSWORTH badges on the nearside; the Escort badge was the same as any regular Mk5, while the RS matched the logo seen on the RS2000. From January 1995 they were superseded by a smaller new Ford oval (in darker blue) in the centre of the tailgate (above the lock), with individual chrome letters declaring ESCORT RS on the left-hand side and the previous COSWORTH plaque on the right. The Escort characters were standard Escort stuff, with the RS simply taken from the appropriate letters in Escort.

As for the RS Cosworth's roof, it was just a standard Mk5 Escort panel, although a pair of side rail reinforcements were added above the rear quarter windows. Standard and

Escort badge was the same as any other Mk5, while the RS emblem was shared with the RS2000. Iconic Cosworth logo had been seen before on the Sapphire.

New-look badging, maybe, but the 1995 Cosworth's individual lettering was even cheaper to produce, being the same as any other Escort model – conveniently, the R and S are also found in the model name.

The RS Cosworth's Ford oval badge and rear lights were shared with even the most basic Mk5 Escort.

Late-model RS Cosworth brought with it a new, smaller Ford badge mounted above the boot lock in the centre of the tailgate.

Oval exhaust tailpipe exited through a cut-out in the rear bumper. This meant contemporary tuners couldn't fit a traditional drainpipe-sized tube into the slot.

Motorsport/Roadsport models wore a plain roof, while the Luxury was equipped with a tinted, tilting/sliding glass sunroof – manually operated on early cars but optionally electric, a feature that became standard in January 1993.

Similarly, Standard and Luxury cars received a roof-mounted radio aerial above the windscreen, but the Roadsport had a blanking plug in the roof instead.

RS Cosworth paintwork was in a solid finish as standard, with metallic colours or black available as extra-cost options. The top coats were high-bake enamel – thermoplastic acrylic for solid colours and polyester basecoat plus clear coat for metallics.

Before painting, the Escort's body was treated with zinc phosphate ion and dipped in electronically-impregnated cataphoretic primer, with the underside also coated in stone-chip protection and seam sealer on joint overlaps and high-impact areas; all Cosworth road cars (including the Roadsport) received the stone-chip paint and seam sealer, but 909 Motorsport shells did not. The final finish on the floorpan was off-white primer (like Ford Purbeck Grey or Dove Grey) over the stone-chip protection, with overspray from the top coat wafted under the sills.

The Escort's chassis number was stamped into the floorpan from underneath, and Karmann applied a thick layer of black paint to the area. The inner wheelarches, meanwhile, were coated with textured black paint and the fronts were fitted with plastic liners.

Air conditioning was an optional extra on Luxury models, adding this warning sticker to the bonnet slam panel.

Underbonnet

For anyone familiar with the front-wheel-drive Mk5 Escort, opening the RS Cosworth's bonnet came as a bit of a shock. Rather than the usual transverse engine and gearbox layout, the RS's longitudinally-mounted motor filled the engine bay. Surprisingly, it looked completely at home – especially considering the fact that almost everything in sight was taken straight from the Escort's bigger brother.

Sapphire 4x4 inner wings were blended into Escort bodywork, along with reinforcement plates connecting them to the suspension towers. Each Macpherson strut was topped with a circular, bare metal plate and black plastic cap over the damper rod.

The inner wings and entire engine bay were finished in body-coloured paintwork, albeit basecoat without lacquer for metallic shades. The bonnet slam panel was a standard Mk5 Escort part, and home to the RS Cosworth's bonnet release mechanism, which was unique to the car, finished in black and screwed in from the front. The release cable also came from the regular Mk5, running under the slam panel and inner wing rail, through the bulkhead towards an orange lever on the steering column.

The Cosworth's bonnet prop and grommet were also standard Mk5 stuff, swinging from the underside of the slam panel and held into a black plastic clip on the nearside of the slam panel; the prop was zinc plated on early cars, and black-painted from around January 1995. At each side of the slam panel was a black plastic bump stop with rubber insulator (the same parts found on normal Escorts), and an alarm microswitch sat nearby on the offside of the panel.

The slam panel also housed the VIN plate and body-coloured build plate, on centre left and right respectively. In the middle, just visible, was a factory-made date stamp. A couple of stickers were also present, depending on model. A circular warning decal depicting a lit match was commonly found on the right-hand side (from summer 1992), and a black-on-yellow air conditioning information label was used (where fitted) closer to the VIN plate. Headlamp adjuster stickers (black text on a small, white label) were also often found on the slam panel, above the nearside headlamp, just in front of the bonnet prop retaining clip.

Behind the slam panel, the right-hand side was filled with airbox, while the nearside housed reservoirs for the power steering fluid (from the Sapphire), washer fluid (unique to the Escort Cosworth, feeding its windscreen and headlamp washers) and engine coolant (from the Sapphire Cosworth 4x4), all wearing yellow plastic caps. The coil (on Big Turbos; it was of course deleted on the Small Turbo) and ignition amplifier were screwed to the inner wing between the three tanks.

A new bulkhead – finished in body colour and wearing a black plastic insulator over felt sound deadening material – was at the back of the engine bay, topped by a new upper

bulkhead compete with large rubber seal to separate it from the engine compartment; the upper bulkhead section was a different panel for cars with and without air conditioning.

Within this section was – on the left-hand side – the Escort's battery, sitting on a body-coloured metal tray and topped with a ribbed black plastic cover. On the right-hand side was the horn for the Escort's anti-theft alarm and, towards the centre, the windscreen wiper motor – a regular Escort part but having a special linkage for the RS Cosworth.

The body-coloured bonnet hinges retracted beneath the scuttle panel, which was topped with a black plastic grille. The underside of the bonnet was fitted with a fabric insulating pad, shaped around the bonnet vents and bump stops, and attached with black plastic clips.

Beneath the engine was a black polyurethane underbody shield, which protected the sump and steering rack from stones, and supposedly helped to rid the engine of excess heat.

Underbonnet insulation was applied to the Standard and Luxury, specially shaped around the factory-pressed vent cut-outs. Early cars had a galvanised bonnet prop, which was switched for black paint on later models.

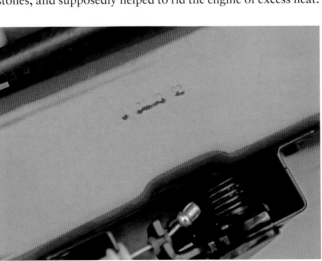

Date stamp on bonnet slam panel, found behind the release mechanism.

RS Cosworth headlamps were sourced from the Mk5 Escort RS2000, while the fog lamps and indicators came straight from the three-door Sierra RS.

Tried-and-tested Cosworth emblem and Mk5 rear lamps were unchanged for the facelifted Escort RS of 1995, although the badge had now been moved to the right-hand side.

Lighting

For once, the Escort RS Cosworth was run-of-the-mill; nothing about its lighting was unusual.

The 60/55W H4 headlamps were the same as the parts found in the Escort RS2000 or XR3i Mk5 – and, indeed, every other Mk5 with integral long-range driving lamps as standard. Produced by Carello, right-hand-drive cars had clear glass, while left-hand-drive cars wore clear or amber lenses. A headlamps-on warning buzzer was included on the Standard and Luxury from May 1994.

Below the headlamps were 55W H3 halogen fog lamps, as found in the original three-door Sierra Cosworth and XR4i. Each lamp had clear glass and a Ford logo, although some markets had amber lenses available. The Escort Cosworth Roadsport lacked fog lamps, which were supplanted by RS500-type grilles instead; that said, fog lamps were optional.

A pair of orange indicators were recessed into the front bumper beside the fog lamps, again sourced from the Sierra Cosworth Mk1.

Escort Cosworth front wings were fitted with square 5W orange plastic side repeaters behind the front wheels, again the same as other Fords of the period. Likewise, the rear lamps were identical to those found on every other Mk5 Escort, complete with integral fog lamps. There was a single number plate light mounted in the middle of the back bumper.

The Roadsport's interior lamp assembly was typical of 1980s' Ford cars – such as the Fiesta, Sierra and Escort Mk3 – while the Standard and Luxury boasted a central light with individually-switched map reading lamps and delayed switch-off function. The boot lamp was the same part found in other Mk5s; as expected, it was omitted from the Roadsport.

Headlamp washers were supplied on Standard and Luxury but omitted from the Roadsport.

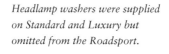

Single Mk5 Escort number plate lamp was recessed into special RS Cosworth back bumper.

Luxury trim meant exactly that – fancy seats, plush velour carpet and plenty of standard kit. Leather upholstery was optional, and this car's audio equipment was extra too. Everything else came standard in 1993.

Luxury spec, late-model style, here with grey Hexagon upholstery. Little was changed but the steering wheel was an obvious exception.

Interior

At a glance, the RS Cosworth's cabin looked much like that of any other Mk5 Escort, with plenty of hard plastics and a familiar dashboard layout.

But it was actually a very different environment. Not just because of the sporty seats and improved driving position but also due to the majority of the components being built specifically for the RS Cosworth.

Most important of all were the front seats, which came in two basic varieties: basic sports seats or Recaro. The basic seats were produced by Karmann as a cheaper alternative to the Recaros traditionally found in Ford RS models. Fully-reclining and equipped with adjustable head restraints

from the Mk1 Sierra, these Karmann seats were fitted with common-or-garden levers and plastic parts used in other Mk5 Escorts. They were upholstered in Raven velour with Hexagon (hexagonal-print) cloth centre sections in red, grey, green or blue depending on exterior bodywork colour. The seat backs lacked map pockets, although it's possible they were added to later examples. The seat bases were updated in October 1993, although not to any noticeable extent.

Officially, Karmann front seats were factory-fitted to Standard and Roadsport models; the Standard gained lumbar support and adjustable driver's seat height, again using regular Ford components. However, Recaro seats were offered at extra cost, and most Escort Cosworths around today have had

Perforated Raven leather Recaro seats were pretty much the perfect place when the Luxury was launched in 1992.

Cloth upholstery was offered in Raven with grey (seen here), red, green or blue hexagons; blue was extremely rare, fitted only to Karmann seats rather than these Luxury-spec Recaros. Note the passenger airbag, an optional extra from late 1993.

Luxury back seat in Raven leather, complete with rear head restraints and folding armrest.

Cloth-trimmed Luxury-model rear seat, offered with grey (seen here), red or green hexagons; Standard back seat lacked headrests and armrest, but was additionally available with exceptionally rare blue hexagons.

Recaro logo was embossed into Ford's traditional Raven-coloured Cosworth leather.

them fitted – either by the supplying dealer or later owners.

Some early left-hand-drive RS Cosworths were fitted with Karmann seats covered in Raven perforated leather, with matching door cards; they had heating elements too, which generally weren't available on Standard or Roadsport models.

The right-hand-drive Luxury model boasted Recaro front seats, but other markets sometimes featured the basic Karmann versions. Recaros were fully reclining with adjustable head rests, lumbar support and driver's seat height. All wore map pockets on the seat backs, along with bold Recaro logos on the front of the backrests.

Recaros were supplied with Hexagon fabric upholstery – in Raven velour with grey, red or green hexagonal print, depending on body colour – or perforated Raven leather at extra cost (Luxury models only).

Expanding map pockets were found in the seat backs of Luxury-model Recaro seats. Alternatively, they could act as sick bags for nervous passengers.

Map pockets were included in seat backs of Recaros regardless of cloth or leather upholstery. Centre armrest was cloth-trimmed to match.

Door cards matched seat upholstery, in this case Raven leather. Deep, carpeted door pockets were found only on the Luxury.

Raven cloth door cards accompanied Hexagon trim.

The Cosworth's rear seat also differed depending on model. On all cars the seat base came from the Mk5 Escort Cabriolet but on the Roadsport and Standard there was a basic 60/40 split/folding backrest, while the Luxury added adjustable rear headrests and a folding soft-feel centre armrest. The upholstery was, as expected, matched to the front seats – in Hexagon fabric on all models, with the option of Raven leather for the Luxury.

Escort Cosworth rear seat belts were the three standard black items found in regular Mk5 Escorts (a pair of inertia reels plus one centre static lap belt), while early cars also shared stock Escort belts up front. From October 1992, though, unique front seat belts were listed instead. The RS Cosworth also featured a non-standard seat belt height adjustment assembly on each B-pillar, plus black metal rails along the inner sills.

As you'd expect, the Cosworth's door cards and rear quarter panels matched the seat material, finished in grey velour or Raven vinyl, the latter including perforated inserts. Each front door card had an upper plastic section in Raven vinyl/plastic, incorporating a black oval speaker grille (including 20W speaker) alongside a black plastic internal door release. Below was a Raven plastic handle, which was separate from the moulded armrest. Standard and Roadsport machines also added manual window winder handles, again in Raven plastic; these parts were common to the regular Escort Mk5.

The Luxury added deep door pockets, covered in cut-pile Raven carpet to match the cabin's floor. The Standard and Roadsport made do with basic Escort Mk5 door bins, which were much shallower and left bare in Raven-coloured plastic.

Meanwhile, each front door had a black plastic quarterlight trim where it met the window corner. Standard and Roadsport models featured a black plastic lever within each piece, which controlled manually-operated exterior mirrors. In contrast, the Luxury was equipped with electrically-adjusted mirrors, which were operated by a round soft-touch/textured knob (as found in other high-spec Escorts) protruding from

the quarterlight trim; the passenger-side piece was blank. Electrically-operated mirrors were also heated, functioning when the car's heated rear windscreen was switched on.

In the back of the Escort, the inner quarter panels featured an upper plastic section in Raven vinyl/plastic, complete with rotating ashtray in black plastic. The lower section was either grey velour or Raven vinyl, depending on whether cloth or leather upholstery was specified. Rear-seat passengers in the Luxury were able to open the back windows using a latch on the C-pillar and hinges on the B-pillar; this facility was absent from lesser models, which made do with fixed glass.

A Raven-coloured carpet covered the Cosworth's floor, in cut-pile velour for Standard and Luxury variants or a basic non-woven velour for the Roadsport. All featured a heavy-duty heel pad for the driver's feet. Beneath the cut-pile carpet

A familiar fascia for any Mk5 Escort owner, but the RS Cosworth somehow rose above the sum of its cheap plastics and extra gauges to become a thoroughly enticing environment.

Unique RS Cosworth instruments were produced by Aston Martin supplier John McGavignan. Early Escorts had this type, with sidelight warning lamp in the lower strip instead of above the fuel gauge.

Airbag-equipped cars gained a warning lamp on the dashboard, which moved the sidelight indicator to a new oval area above the fuel gauge.

was a set of unique under-carpet sound-deadening pads and floorpan insulation, which was lacking from the Roadsport. Raven velour overmats were often found in Luxury models as a dealer-fitted extra.

All cars had a Raven plastic flap in the carpet between the right-hand-side inner sill and driver's seat (or passenger seat, in left-hand-drive cars), beneath which was the car's chassis number, stamped into the steel floorpan from below

The carpet was retained at each side by Raven plastic scuff plates (revised in August 1993), attached with black screws and overlapping black door rubbers. A pair of Raven plastic kick panels sat in the front footwells, attached on Raven clips.

All Escort Cosworths had essentially the same dashboard, made up of regular Mk5 components, unique parts, and

Air conditioning was an optional extra on the Luxury, necessitating an entirely new fascia panel for its new central blower switch.

fittings from a variety of other Ford cars. The main fascia panel was the usual Mk5 Escort dash in Raven grained plastic, with a visible VIN number (when viewed through the windscreen) affixed to the passenger side on a plastic mounting, printed with an airbag symbol and Ford logo.

Most importantly, the RS had a new instrument cluster within the Escort's familiar black plastic surround: the Cosworth boasted an impressive selection of electroluminescent white dials (which shone metallic silver in some conditions) from Aston Martin supplier John McGavignan. Each dial wore black digits and symbols along with red needles, and needed no backlight bulbs, instead glowing green on the faces.

A large semi-circular speedometer was positioned in the middle, reading up to 170mph in black around the outer edge, with 270km/h inner figures. A black-on-white mileage readout was sited within the display, with an offshoot trip recorder – again black-on-white figures, with red tenths digit – and reset button at the bottom.

To the left of the speedometer was a rev counter, reading up to 7000rpm, with 6500rpm red segment. A fuel gauge sat on the right of the speedo, complete with red empty marker, and a water temperature dial was on the far side, including a red upper warning section.

A collection of warning lamps was found within the binnacle: between the rev counter and speedometer was a green-flashing circular direction indicator warning lamp, while a matching circle sat to the right of the speedometer, illuminating blue to warn of main beam. A strip of warning lamps ran across the bottom of the instrument cluster, showing (from left to right) handbrake/brake failure (red), ABS failure (yellow), ignition/alternator (red), sidelights (green), oil pressure (red), washer fluid level (yellow) and low fuel (yellow). The Roadsport made do without warning lamps for low fuel or washer fluid.

From around October 1993 the dials were revised, with an oval shape instead of a circle to the right of the speedometer, now featuring an extra warning lamp for the sidelights, which was moved from the strip below to make room for an airbag warning lamp (in yellow) between the ignition/alternator and oil pressure lights.

Eventually, another new set of instruments accompanied the Small Turbo, having a revised rev counter for the new EEC-IV system, along with an engine management warning light on the far left of the strip in the bottom of the cluster.

The Cosworth's instrument binnacle sat within a special fascia panel, again made from hard, black plastic. To the right of the driver (on right-hand-driver cars; flip it for left-hookers) was a regular Escort adjustable air vent, below which were regular Mk5 push-buttons (including yellow 'on' lights) for heated front windscreen (where fitted; it was standard kit on the Luxury) and front fog lamps (again, where fitted – only the Roadsport went without). If the car wasn't equipped with a heated windscreen and/or fog lamps, it wore basic Escort blanking plates instead.

To the immediate left of the main instruments was a multi-function LCD clock, with green-illuminated display of time or ambient temperature, plus red and green frost warning lights.

A pair of standard Escort Mk5 push-buttons for rear fog lamps and heated rear window were mounted beneath the clock, while a pair of adjustable heating/air vents took centre stage. Below the vents was a trio of standard-looking Escort heater blower control knobs, albeit backed up by unique-to-the-Cosworth heater hoses, pipes and distribution valves.

Air conditioning was offered as an optional extra on the Luxury, which meant a whole new fascia assembly, including central blower knob with more positions and warning light.

The RS Cosworth was also fitted with a new upper dashboard cover, which incorporated a curved section complete with embossed Cosworth badge and centrally-mounted instrument binnacle. Colloquially called a 'banana pod', Karmann fitted the set of dials somewhat roughly into the Escort dashboard, chopping a hole using a hacksaw or similar. Still, it remained unseen once the pod was fitted.

A 1.3 bar turbo boost gauge sat in pride of place within a black plastic cowling, flanked by battery voltage gauge on the left and oil pressure dial on the right; each instrument had a white electroluminescent display, along with red needles.

The fascia in front of the passenger came in two types – normal Raven grained plastic, or with an optional SRS airbag from autumn 1993. On the far side was the usual Mk5 Escort adjustable heater vent.

The passenger also gained a fold-down glovebox, again in grained Raven plastic, with black plastic handle. A small glovebox lamp was found in Standard and Luxury models, but absent from the Roadsport version.

The driver's lower fascia panel was completely different from the regular Escort part. Made from Raven grained plastic, it housed the fusebox, which was accessed via a regular Escort fusebox door to the right of the steering column. Meanwhile, above the driver's other knee was a small rotating dimmer switch for the dashboard lights.

The Cosworth's steering column protruded from the

Raven plastic lower fascia featured Granada-sourced ashtray and differing audio equipment, depending on model; here's the 2007 RDS radio/cassette and optional 2040 CD player.

Standard and Luxury models boasted long centre console with lid; the front section contained a switch panel behind the gearstick, on Luxury models having a remote boot release between a pair of electric window buttons.

Just in case passengers were wondering why the Escort they were riding in was travelling at warp speed.

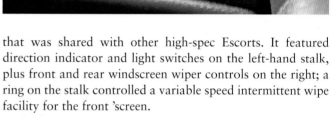

Passenger airbag was an extra-cost option from autumn 1993, when this steering wheel airbag became standard-fit.

lower fascia panel. Adjustable for reach and rake, it came in different versions for Escorts with and without a driver's airbag (from around October 1993), which received a revised upper alloy casting. All columns used a Sierra-type steering shaft coupling but unique wiring loom, which added an immobiliser transponder in August 1993.

The column was wrapped in a black plastic shroud, which was also home to an orange bonnet release lever, as found in other contemporary Fords. On the right was the ignition lock, which operated from the same key as the doors, tailgate and fuel filler cap.

Similarly, the conventional red hazard warning button was found in the top of the shroud, and a pair of column stalks were built into one multiple-function column switch assembly that was shared with other high-spec Escorts. It featured direction indicator and light switches on the left-hand stalk, plus front and rear windscreen wiper controls on the right; a ring on the stalk controlled a variable speed intermittent wipe facility for the front 'screen.

The first Escort RS Cosworths were equipped with a three-spoke Raven leather-rimmed steering wheel complete with perforated hand grips at each side of the rim. The spokes were black grained plastic, and in the middle was a horn push with Ford badge and white horn symbol. A pair of buttons on the spokes also operated the horn.

Later cars (from early 1993) swapped to a plainer wheel, as seen in other Escorts of the period but with a Raven leather rim. Again, it had three spokes (two thin and one fat), and again they were in a black grained finish. The central horn push remained, now wearing only a Ford oval emblem.

The wheel was replaced by a new three-spoke version in autumn 1993, again with Raven leather rim but now housing a standard Escort airbag, complete with embossed Ford logo, 'SRS airbag' lettering across the bottom spoke, and horn pushes for each thumb, complete with embossed symbols.

Below the steering column was a Mk1 Sierra 2.0 pedal box, as fitted to the original Sierra Cosworth, featuring black pedal levers and black rubbers. There was a three-door Cosworth accelerator cable, Sapphire 4x4 clutch cable and a black brake light switch from the pre-1992 Escort Mk5.

An unusual gearchange assembly was found in the Escort Cosworth, using RS2000 4x4 stick and linkage mixed with a Granada gearchange rod, special soft-feel gaiter and black leather gearknob, topped with a silver-coloured emblem with the five-speed shift pattern printed in black. Like the Sapphire 4x4, the Escort's knob had space on the underside for a collar that lifted before reverse could be selected.

Around the gearstick was a grained Raven plastic centre

Electric mirror control came from regular Mk5 Escort.

Roadsport model had no need for audio equipment or any luxuries – note the switch blanking plates for electric windows, boot release, heated windscreen and front fog lamps.

Interior light with map reading lamps was found in a variety of other high-spec Fords.

console in two sections. The front piece extended to the dashboard, housing a pair of standard DIN radio slots. A selection of head units was offered for the RS Cosworth, some of which were optional at extra cost.

From launch, the standard equipment included a Ford 2007 RDS stereo radio/cassette player in the upper slot, complete with Keycode anti-theft coding and eight 20W speakers. The lower slot was left empty but for a flocked-type insert, as found in base-spec Granadas.

The Luxury also had the option of a Model 2040 CD player in the lower slot or premium sound system, which included a Model 2008 RDS head unit with Keycode, eight speakers (60/40W front; 40/25W rear) and Model 2040 CD player. From summer 1992 the choice of equipment was the standard 2007, or options of a Model 2028 CD player or premium pack including Model 2008 head unit plus 2028 CD player.

Later Luxury models could be specified with the faithful 2007 radio-cassette as standard, an optional 2040 CD player, or with an additional 2050 unit, complete with boot-mounted six-disc CD autochanger.

The Roadsport RS Cosworth had no stereo equipment, and no official factory option of head unit or speakers. Instead was a pair of empty slots.

Beneath the head unit apertures was a special ashtray assembly, conjured up from Escort, Sierra and Granada components. The Raven ashtray and housing were from the Granada, while the cigar lighter and element assembly were Sierra stuff.

Early Escort Cosworths were equipped with a Vecta immobiliser, added at the Karmann factory by Vecta staff (and not particularly well). All such cars had a slot for the immobiliser key in the console beside the gearstick, along with warning light. The immobiliser was swapped for a Wipac device in 1993, which had a bigger slot but no light.

From August 1993 the Cosworth was factory-fitted with an immobiliser and transponder key, which worked alongside the Wipac unit.

Behind the gearstick was a small removable panel with switches or blanking plugs, depending on model. The Luxury had a pair of regular Escort Mk5/Granada electric window switches flanking a button for the remote tailgate release, sourced from the Granada. Standard models kept the boot release but lacked the electric window controls, while the Roadsport had blanks for them all.

Behind the front console was the rear section, again in grained Raven-coloured plastic. The Roadsport's console

Tilting/sliding glass sunroof was fitted only to the Luxury model, gaining electric operation in January 1993. The headlining was Dawn Grey, and non-specific to the RS Cosworth.

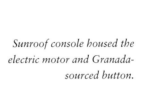

Dawn Grey sunroof console and sun visors; the passenger's sun visor gained a mirror on Standard and Luxury models.

Sunroof console housed the electric motor and Granada-sourced button.

Rear parcel shelf was simply sourced from the regular Escort Mk5, trimmed in Raven fabric.

was a short, fuss-free affair without a centre armrest. It wrapped around a Mk1 Sierra handbrake lever with ribbed handle and black release button.

In contrast, the Standard and Luxury boasted a long console, complete with storage box that surrounded a Mk2 Sierra handbrake lever with smooth handle and black release button. The storage box featured two blanks or heated seat buttons (optional at extra cost on the Luxury). The lid formed a centre armrest, which differed depending on the car's trim – cloth or leather. Inside was a storage box for cassette tapes.

The rest of the RS Cosworth's cabin was regular Mk5 Escort kit, sourced from one version or another. The A-pillar, B-pillar and C-pillar trims were Raven plastic with black screws, and at the top touched a stock Escort Cheviot fabric headlining in Dawn Grey.

The sun visors were also Dawn Grey, in two types depending on model. The Roadsport had basic visors, while the Standard and Luxury added a mirror on the passenger side. Cars from autumn 1993 had an airbag warning sticker on the driver's-side visor, visible when closed.

A standard, black, Mk5 Escort rear-view mirror was stuck to the windscreen, and all cars had three Dawn Grey grab handles – one for each passenger; the driver's side had a pair of Dawn Grey blanking plugs.

Of course, two different headlinings were used: one was a plain piece, for the Roadsport and Standard, while the Luxury gained a large aperture for its tilting/sliding glass sunroof.

A Dawn Grey cowling was fitted around the sunroof, which changed in January 1993 when the operation went from manual (with Dawn Grey winding handle) to electric (previously an optional extra), with console-mounted button. Different mechanisms were used for each type of sunroof, but both used the same Dawn Grey blind and sealing rubber.

Boot

Harking back to the days of the original RS Escorts of the early 1970s, the Cosworth's luggage compartment was a dead giveaway of the car's motorsport heritage.

Rather than loads of luggage space, a spare wheel was laid on the boot floor, and there was little respect for convenience.

For the modern RS, though, there was a 3.5x16in ET25mm space-saver, in painted black steel and wearing a pair of yellow warning stickers: a 'max 50mph' label sat opposite an 80km/h version. The tyre for all cars was a Pirelli 125/80R16.

The spare wheel was screwed into place with a large black washer and grey wing nut, which threaded into a specially-

Spare wheel and toolkit covers were found in the Standard and Luxury but omitted from the Roadsport model.

Spare wheel was a space saver, which fitted around a body-coloured bulge in the floor for the fuel tank.

pressed boot floor, complete with hump for the fuel tank. The floor – uncarpeted and finished in body colour – was a unique part for Roadsport and Motorsport models, having a riveted panel for access to the in-tank fuel pump, which was coated around the edges in seam sealer at the Karmann factory.

A curved chunk of grey polystyrene was wedged between the spare wheel and the car's back seat, and included a basic toolkit of black jack, handle and wheelbrace, along with a gold-passivated towing hook, which could be screwed into the front or rear bumper bar. Surprisingly, even the towing hook was unique to the RS Cosworth, being longer than some others in the Ford range and a different diameter thread from the rest.

On Standard and Luxury models the toolkit had a removable lid, in thin grey plastic, which was carpeted to match the boot floor; it was omitted from the Roadsport.

The entire load compartment was carpeted in Shark Grey material, including the wheelhouses and rear seat back.

Raven-coloured plastics were used on the load sill and inside panel of the tailgate, along with rear parcel shelf supports (which housed 20W speakers as standard, or premium 40/25W replacements). There was also a Raven-carpeted parcel shelf, dangling from the tailgate on rubber straps, along with a pair of uprated gas lifting struts to take the weight the whale-tail rear wing.

Standard and Luxury models added a courtesy lamp in the luggage compartment, while a Luxury could also be bought with a six-disc CD changer installed in the boot. On some cars, lifting the inner side trims has revealed production date stamps inside the body panels; it's likely they're present on all Escort RS Cosworths.

Late-model Luxury showing position of CD autochanger.

Boot-mounted CD autochanger was optional or dealer-fitted accessory.

	Roadsport	Standard	Luxury
Body-coloured door mirrors	No	Yes	Yes
Electric door mirrors	No	No	Yes
Body-coloured door handles	No	Yes	Yes
Central locking	No	Yes	Yes
Body-coloured fuel cap	No	Yes	Yes
Electric front windows	No	No	Yes
Opening rear quarter windows	No	No	Yes
Headlamp washers	No	Yes	Yes
Heated windscreen	No	No	Yes
Front fog lamps	No	Yes	Yes
Aero Pack deletion	No	Optional	Optional
Sunroof	No	No	Yes
Recaro front seats	No	Optional	Yes
Karmann front seats	Yes	No	No
Karmann front seats with height and lumbar adjustment	No	Yes	No
Leather upholstery	No	No	Optional
Heated front seats	No	No	Optional
Rear seat head rests	No	No	Yes
Rear seat armrest	No	No	Yes
Air conditioning	No	No	Optional
Cut-pile carpet	No	Yes	Yes
Carpeted deep door bins	No	No	Yes
Centre console with armrest	No	Yes	Yes
Glovebox illumination	No	Yes	Yes
Courtesy light with delay	No	Yes	Yes
Map reading lights	No	Yes	Yes
Load compartment light	No	Yes	Yes
Passenger vanity mirror	No	Yes	Yes
Low fuel and washer fluid warning lights	No	Yes	Yes
Lights-on warning	No	Yes	Yes
Spare wheel cover	No	Yes	Yes
Remote tailgate release	No	Yes	Yes
Passenger airbag	No	Optional	Optional
RDS radio/cassette	No	Yes	Yes
CD player	No	No	Optional
RDS radio/cassette with CD changer	No	No	Optional
Radio aerial	No	Yes	Yes
Ford phone	No	Optional	Optional
Removable fuel pump access panel	Yes	No	No

Colour schemes and interior trim

Colour	Code	Introduced	Discontinued	Cloth	Leather
Diamond White	B	Launch	December 1995	Grey Hex or red Hex	Raven
Ash Black	V	January 1993	December 1995	Grey Hex or red Hex	Raven
Radiant Red	P	Launch	December 1995	Grey Hex or red Hex	Raven
Imperial Blue	H	January 1993	December 1995	Grey Hex or blue Hex	Raven
Mallard Green	4	Launch	November 1994	Grey Hex or green Hex	Raven
Pacifica Blue	J	January 1993	November 1994	Grey Hex	Raven
Polaris Grey	N	Launch	June 1994	Grey Hex	Raven
Black	A	Launch	January 1993	Grey Hex	Raven
Moondust Silver	6	January 1993	December 1995	Grey Hex or red Hex	Raven
Zinc Yellow	U or Z	January 1993	December 1995	Grey Hex	Raven
Petrol Blue	C	November 1994	December 1995	Grey Hex	Raven
Dark Aubergine	E	November 1994	December 1995	Grey Hex or red Hex	Raven
Auralis Blue	5	November 1994	December 1995	Grey Hex or red Hex	Raven

Diamond White

Ash Black

Radiant Red

Imperial Blue

Mallard Green

Pacifica Blue

Polaris Grey

Black

Moondust Silver

Zinc Yellow

Petrol Blue

Dark Aubergine

Auralis Blue

ESCORT RS COSWORTH MONTE CARLO

Jewel in the crown: Escort RS Cosworth Monte Carlo build 164, a May 1994 machine in Jewel Violet, in the capable custodianship of Neil Arnold. Other than mildly lowered ride height and a handy power increase, this ultra-low-mileage (around 8000 recorded miles) Monte is almost exactly as it left the factory.

Hardcore full Monte frontal appearance was as aggressive as any other RS Cosworth, especially when equipped with standard Aero Pack.

Limited editions and run-out models are nothing new in the Ford world. The big Blue Oval has a real knack of drawing attention – and resulting sales – from sticking glitter, sparkle and sometimes extraordinary parts onto otherwise run-of-the-mill machines.

That's not to say you can level such an accusation at any homologation special, of course. The Sierra RS500, for example, deserves its rank at the top of the Cosworth tree if only because it allowed the existence of a simply outstanding motorsport legend.

As for Ford's seemingly monthly habit of launching imaginatively-named limited-editions, the merits of Fiesta Flights and Mondeo Veronas generally have more in common with using up old stock or testing the market than any real development of the marque.

Classic Escort RS Cosworth styling plus a few neat touches gave the Monte Carlo additional allure, not least when finished in rare Jewel Violet metallic paint – a shade that was almost exclusive to the Monte. Ash Black and Mallard Green were the two other colours offered on the UK-bound Escort Monte Carlo.

But then there are the celebratory specials. The Fords that appear as promotional exercises yet can't help but burst through their money-making intentions with pure petrol-headed passion. The Fords that become not just desirable but essential to the brand.

Take the 1970 Escort Mexico as a case in point. Borne of an attention-grabbing victory on the 1970 World Cup Rally (which ran from London to Mexico, thus the name), the sporty Escort became an overnight sensation that exists to this day. It's impossible to estimate how many humdrum Fords were sold on the back of the Mexico's reputation, but you can bet it was more than a few.

Such success could never escape Ford's heritage-clinging talents – witness the woeful Mk6 Escort Mexico decal special of 1995, a rare backfire from the Blue Oval's marketing team – and it led to a rather special spiritual successor: the Escort RS Cosworth Monte Carlo.

Now, the Monte Carlo wasn't the first limited-edition RS

Regular Escort RS Cosworth rear view but wearing some subtle alterations – notably new decals and repositioned Ford emblem.

Something special – the Monte's appearance on 16in OZ Racing alloy wheels was simply breathtaking, and all the more unusual when drenched in Jewel Violet paintwork.

Stunning side profile. Sexy Jewel Violet paint complemented the regular RS Cosworth's curves.

Cosworth. Around the time of the model's launch in 1992, Italy was treated to a very low run of 120 Escort Cosworth Miki Biasion editions, named after the Italian two-time world rally champion and Ford works hero Massimo 'Miki' Biasion.

The Biasion was a mixture of the basic Roadsport and Standard models of Escort Cosworth, in a non-sunroof Diamond White body with colour-coded door mirrors and fuel cap. Inside was a pair of Hexagon cloth-trimmed Recaro seats, along with manual windows, an absent stereo and no internal tailgate release button. The only special extra was a silver-coloured plaque on the dashboard instead of the usual Cosworth badge, complete with Miki Biasion's signature and the car's build number. It's reckoned that all were produced between June and September 1992, and none were supplied to any other country.

Ford in the UK also tried its hand at a couple of celebratory RS Cosworths, with varying degrees of success. The limited-appeal Acropolis of autumn 1993 was an unfortunately colourful Escort, named after Biasion's victory on the '93 Acropolis rally but visually inspired by the contemporary modified car market.

Its garish paintwork – probably Zinc Yellow – had contrasting black details, including black bonnet vents, Acropolis graphics on the sides and rear wing, along with

Nose down and wing held high – the Monte was Ford's final incarnation of the iconic RS Cosworth stance. Aero Pack was standard kit; very few Monte buyers went for the no-cost option of Aero Pack deletion.

black vinyl on the B-pillars and outlines around the non-opening back windows.

The colour scheme continued to the standard 16in alloy wheels, which were also yellow but with black Ford logos on the centre caps. Interestingly, there was no RS Cosworth badge – just an Acropolis sticker – and the rear lights were tinted dark red. The square indicator side repeaters were swapped for orange ovals from the contemporary Mondeo, which were presumably planned to follow throughout the Ford range. Meanwhile, the interior was fitted with Recaro A8 bucket seats and – it's believed – an alloy gearknob.

Not exactly a production car (the planned 200 units stalled at one), the left-hand-drive, one-off Acropolis was nevertheless a factory-built Escort RS Cosworth, and it survived the decade as a French rally machine, still wearing its Acropolis stickers for at least some of that period.

Meanwhile, Ford pursued its plans with a few more prototypes. At least one Karmann-built Escort was converted to rear-wheel drive and equipped with a normally-aspirated Escort RS2000 DOHC two-litre engine and Granada MT75 gearbox, suspension, hubs and brakes. It was an Aero Pack-deleted Luxury model, and on its nose was a facelifted Escort bonnet with oval grille. A very similar machine, also made by Karmann, was fitted with a Granada 2.9-litre, 24-valve V6

engine and rear-wheel drive.

Another yellow car (which remains in Ford's Heritage collection) was mildly tuned, and fitted with an alloy gearknob and bucket seats with a rather funky trim featuring embroidered Motorsport logos; it's assumed the exact-

Escort Acropolis of 1993 was the Monte's direct descendant. This one-off marketing exercise went on to become a rally car in its own right.

led to Ford's first official limited-run Escort RS Cosworth available in the UK – the Monte Carlo.

Built by Karmann alongside the regular Escort Cosworth, the Monte was named in tribute to Francois Delecour's victory on the 1994 Monte Carlo rally. Available from February 1994 in a numbered run of 200 examples, the Monte was mechanically standard but fitted with OZ Racing alloy wheels, much like the then-current Ford rally car. On the road-going Monte, though, they were 8x16in, stamped with an OZ logo, ET25mm offset, size and Ford part number between the spokes, and wore Ford centre caps.

Muscular front and rear wheelarches were carried over from the regular RS Cosworth, bulging out over 8in-wide alloys, now made by OZ Racing.

same Recaros were taken from the Acropolis car and seen in another prototype, bearing in mind the seats' shells were finished in metallic burgundy paint…

This prototype, yet another Aero Pack-deleted car, was also hampered with an oval grille and equipped with the Acropolis's tinted rear lights and oval repeaters. It was topped off with a rather fetching shade of metallic red called Jewel Violet.

It was the cumulative result of these styling exercises that

There were no other major external alterations; the Monte Carlo was offered with or without the Aero Pack, and in a choice of three colours: Mallard Green, Ash Black or the Jewel Violet that premièred on the aforementioned prototype. New silver stickers were attached to the doors and tailgate,

The full Monte – silver door decals sat behind functional front wing vents, as found on the standard Escort RS Cosworth.

What better reason to introduce a car called Monte Carlo than an outright win on the 1994 rally. Never accuse Ford of missing a marketing opportunity.

Monte fascia was familiar to any Escort Cosworth owner, and not too dissimilar from a standard Mk5 Escort. The instruments and controls were identical to other Cosworths of the period.

reading Monte in Ford Motorsport font; on the tailgate it replaced the usual Ford badge, which was swapped for a smaller, Australian-sourced version and repositioned in the centre, above the boot lock.

Its cabin included Raven Flow cloth upholstery, as seen in the Escort Si and RS2000, not to mention the earlier Zinc Yellow prototype. The front seats were otherwise regular Luxury-spec Recaros, now with Motorsport logos embroidered on

one thigh support per seat, plus a Recaro emblem stitched into the rear of the backrest beneath the head restraint.

The Monte's steering wheel was different from the regular Cosworth's, having an airbag fitted as standard but boasting diamond-shaped perforated sections at each side of the leather rim. Like the previous prototypes there was a shiny alloy gearknob, now with matching alloy button in a specially-produced handbrake lever.

Luxury with cloth was the Monte's trim level, meaning plush carpets, electric windows and central locking. But now there was new fabric upholstery, a different steering wheel, gearknob and handbrake handle. Leather trim wasn't an option.

Recaro recliners were the same front seats found in other Luxury-level Cosworths, albeit in multicoloured Raven Flow upholstery from the contemporary Escort RS2000.

Ford's 1990s' Motorsport brand donated the italic font on the thigh support of each front seat.

Monte Carlo steering wheel was unique, with stock Escort airbag but diamond-shaped perforated sections on the leather rim.

Luxury-spec rear seat included headrests and folding centre armrest. Raven referred to the grey velour sections, with Flow cloth inserts.

Luxury trim meant long centre console, electric windows and internal boot release. Monte meant chrome handbrake button and alloy gearknob.

Pedal box was unchanged from the regular Escort RS Cosworth – which itself was carried over from the early Sierra.

Electric tilting/sliding glass sunroof with internal blind was standard kit on the Monte Carlo. Dawn Grey headlining was identical to other Luxury-spec Escort Cosworths.

Tricornered seat recliner knob was peculiar to Recaro seats of the period.

Chassis number was stamped into the floorpan from below, visible through this flap beside the right-hand-side front seat.

Door sill trims were Ford sticky-backed plastic, as seen in other Mk5 Escorts.

Legendary Recaro logo was embroidered into the backrest of each front seat for the sake of passengers.

Auxiliary gauge pod came straight from the standard RS Cosworth, complete with dials for battery voltage, boost and oil pressure.

A proper limited edition – 200 Monte Carlos were created, in a choice of three colours. Rarity was guaranteed…

Cosworth YBT powerplant packed 227bhp from T3/T04B turbo and Weber-Marelli engine management. Later Montes were fitted with the June 1994 YBP engine revision, including T25 turbo, Ford EEC-IV management, silver cam cover and 217bhp.

Crucially, there was also a new upper dashboard cover with a unique badge. Instead of the previous Cosworth logo, the Monte's name plate was black with white Motorsport script, and individually numbered from 000 to 200; number 000 was a Jewel Violet pre-production Monte owned by Ford and fitted with Motorsport decals rather than the later Monte versions.

And that's where it all gets confusing. The planned markets for the Monte Carlo were Great Britain, France, Belgium, Germany, Holland and Italy. But Ford in France opted out of naming the car Monte, settling instead for a simple Motorsport tag and disregarding the numbering system; it's reported that 100 examples were produced.

Meanwhile, Ford decided the Italian market would prefer the car to be named Martini in honour of the rally team's sponsor, and stuck Martini badges over the numbered dashboard plaque. It's not known whether Monte Carlo build numbers were duplicated to replace these now-Martini-badged cars.

Production continued until June/July 1994, by which point

Blue cam cover was unchanged for the early Monte, finished in blue like all other YBT engines.

Garrett T3/T04B turbo was found on the majority of Monte Carlos. This heat shield and airbox were identical to other Big Turbo models.

the Small Turbo Escort RS Cosworth had been introduced. Therefore, around 20 Montes received YBP engines with T25 turbocharger and EEC-IV engine management instead of the earlier YBT setup with T3/T04B turbo and Weber-Marelli ignition that formed the bulk of Monte production.

In total, it's reckoned that a mere 73 Montes were right-hand drive for the British market, including a handful of Small Turbo versions. Generally, the Small Turbos had later build numbers than Big Turbo cars, although there were undoubtedly one or two exceptions.

But that wasn't the end of the story because Italy, by this point, had decided it wanted more. So a further 100 Monte-spec Martinis were built by Karmann specifically for the Italian market, now offered in Diamond White or Petrol Blue paintwork, and all with YBP powerplants. But one thing they certainly lacked was a numbered plaque on the dashboard, instead wearing a Martini badge – often in some random place on the fascia – with nothing underneath.

Celebration was the generic Ford moniker for Monte and Martini models of Escort RS Cosworth. Note the Motorsport decals on this left-hand-drive car's doors.

Left-hand drive Monte with Aero Pack deletion option, probably for the German market. This Ford press car was possibly the same Jewel Violet machine used for photos of the Celebration, simply wearing different door decals.

Martini was the tag for the Italian-market Monte Carlo, and lacked decals on the doors; this photo features an Ash Black press car.

Cockpit of left-hand-drive Monte Carlo or Martini, complete with Ford Motorsport seat badges. Note the left-hand-drive centre console with Wipac immobiliser.

Colour schemes and interior trim

Colour	Code	Introduced	Discontinued	Trim
Mallard Green	4	February 1994	July 1994	Raven Flow
Jewel Violet	T	February 1994	July 1994	Raven Flow
Ash Black	V	February 1994	July 1994	Raven Flow

BUILD PLATES

Factory-built RS Cosworths were fitted with a pair of identity tags, which were found riveted to the bonnet slam panel.

To the left of the bonnet release spring (when looking from the front of the car) was a standard VIN plate, as used on many Ford cars from 1979 onwards. The plate remained roughly the same throughout Cosworth production, although one box (in the lower right-hand corner) was altered when emissions compliancy became important.

All Cosworth VIN plates had the words FORD-WERKE AKTIENGESELLSCHAFT across the top, being the product of Ford Germany rather than Ford UK. Each plate was reverse-stamped, and contained crucial information about the car, including the engine, transmission, trim, body colour, unique identification number and so on.

Also on the slam panel but on the opposing side of the bonnet release spring (on the right when looking from the front of the car) was the Cosworth's body-coloured build plate. Reverse-stamped and fitted to the slam panel before any other part of the body was constructed, this plate was intended to aid factory workers during the build process, including references to body colour, trim and specification, along with the car's unique identity number. Because it was added so early on the assembly line, this build plate was riveted and painted in the car's body colour.

The prime exception to this rule is the Escort Cosworth. Although Ford's obligatory VIN plate was in place on the slam panel, a much lesser-detailed body plate was at the other side, declaring only the chassis number and paint code. This was simply because the cars were built by Karmann in Germany, where Ford's production coding process wasn't used.

For today's Cosworth owner, all build plates provide vital information about a car's history, specification and authenticity. Bear in mind, of course, that such plates are easily removed and riveted onto any old slam panel. Only documented evidence and educated guesswork will confirm a car's true identity.

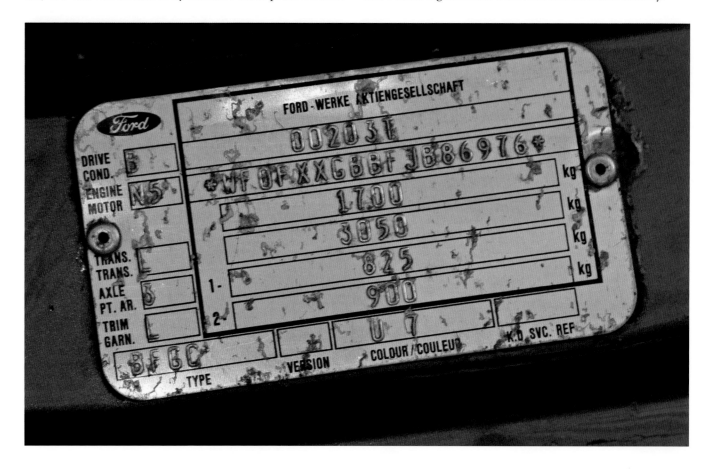

Chassis Plate

DRIVE COND

1 or A = left-hand drive

2 or B = right-hand drive

Untitled box

Type approval number, as required in some territories.

00203T – Sierra/Sapphire

00209T – Escort

ENGINE MOTOR (Sierra and Sapphire)

Inline engines

First digit	Second digit	Third digit
G - 1100cc		
J - 1300cc		
F - 1400cc	A – LC	
L - 1600cc	C or E – HC	T – w/o fuel economy
R - 1800cc	R – injection type	
N - 2000cc	5 – injection with turbo	S – with fuel economy
	S – fuel economy type	
	B or U – OHV	
	U or J or 6 – CVH	
	7 – DOHC	
	D or K or O – Zetec	
	T or F – diesel	

Vee engines

First digit	Second digit
N - 2000cc	Y - HC
Y - 2300cc	R - injection type
P - 2800cc	

Diesel engines

First digit	Second digit
l - 1600cc	T - no code value
Y - 2300cc	

ENGINE MOTOR (Escort)

First digit	Second digit OHV	CVH	DOHC	Diesel	Third digit
G – 1100cc					
J – 1300cc	B/U	U			High compression/increased perf
F – 1400cc		J	7		EFi
L – 1600cc		6			SPi
R – 1800cc				T	N/A
N – 2000cc				F	Turbo

Vehicle identification number

*	WFO	B	XX	G	B	B	F	AE	00001	*
A	B	C	D	E	F	G	C	H	K	L

A – Asterisk was a legal requirement

B – World manufacturer origin
- SFA - Brentwood, Essex, UK
- WFO - Cologne, Germany
- VS6 - Almussafes, Spain
- UNI - Cork, Ireland
- XLC - Amsterdam, Netherlands
- TW2 - Azambuja, Portugal

C – Body type
- A – five-door hatchback
- B – three-door hatchback
- C – two-door coupé
- D – three-door estate
- E – three-door hatchback
- F – four-door saloon
- L – convertible
- N – five-door estate
- T – two-door saloon
- V – van
- W – three-door estate

D – XX was constant

E – Product source
- E – Brentwood, UK
- G – Cologne, Germany
- W – Almussafes, Spain
- C – Cork, Ireland
- C – Amsterdam, Netherlands
- C – Azambuja, Portugal

F – Assembly plant
- A – Cologne, Germany/Dagenham
- B – Genk/Halewood
- C – Saarlouis/Langley
- E – Cork
- K – Rheine
- M – Rheine (Federal Sierra)
- N – Amsterdam
- P – Valencia/Azambuja

159

G – Model

    A – Escort/Orion

    B – Taunus/Cortina/Sierra/Mondeo

    E – Capri

    F – Fiesta

    G – Granada/Scorpio

H – Body type

    A – five–door hatchback

    B – three–door hatchback

    C – two–door coupé

    D – three–door estate

    E – three–door hatchback

    F – four–door saloon

    L – convertible

    N – five–door estate

    T – two–door saloon

    V – van

    W – three-door estate

J – Manufacture date

Year code	Year	Jan	Feb	Mar	Apr	May	June	July	Aug	Sep	Oct	Nov	Dec
F	1985	J	U	M	P	B	R	A	G	C	K	D	E
G	1986	L	Y	S	T	J	U	M	P	B	R	A	G
H	1987	C	K	D	E	L	Y	S	T	J	U	M	P
J	1988	B	R	A	G	C	K	D	E	L	Y	S	T
K	1989	J	U	M	P	B	R	A	G	C	K	D	E
L	1990	L	Y	S	T	J	U	M	P	B	R	A	G
M	1991	C	K	D	E	L	Y	S	T	J	U	M	P
N	1992	B	R	A	G	C	K	D	E	L	Y	S	T
P	1993	J	U	M	P	B	R	A	G	C	K	D	E
R	1994	L	Y	S	T	J	U	M	P	B	R	A	G
S	1995	C	K	D	E	L	Y	S	T	J	U	M	P
T	1996	B	R	A	G	C	K	D	E	L	Y	S	T

K

Vehicle serial number

The remaining figures were the car's own individual serial number, in order of vehicles produced during the month. Numbering started at 00001 for all types of cars built during each month, rising to 99999 depending on the number produced.

L

Asterisk was constant.

Untitled box (gross vehicle mass)

Maximum legal laden mass.

Untitled box (gross train mass)

Maximum combined mass of vehicle and trailer or caravan.

1 – (permitted front axle load)

Maximum permissible load on the front wheels of the vehicle.

2 – (permitted rear axle load)

Maximum permissible load on the rear wheels of the vehicle.

TRANS. TRANS.

2/3/ – four–speed manual

8 – MT75

D/G – automatic

E – four–speed manual

F – five–speed manual (Type 9)

J/L – five–speed manual (T5)

Q – front–wheel drive, five–speed manual (MTX–75)

T – front–wheel drive, four–speed manual

W – front–wheel drive, five–speed manual

X – front–wheel drive, automatic (CTX)

AXLE PT. AR.

M – 3.14

6 – 3.12

A – 3.36

V– 3.38

8 – 3.56

P – 3.58

Z – 3.59

U – 3.62

3 – 3.64

B – 3.77

4 – 3.82

F – 3.84

D – 3.92

J – 4.06

3 – 4.19

S– 4.25

2 – 4.27

TRIM GARN.

This was a one- or two-digit combination. The first letter was for interior trim colour, the second character denoted seat and trim material.

Sierra

First digit	Trim colour	First digit	Trim colour
0	Pimento Red	M	Mocha
1	Medici Blue	N	Taupe
2	Burgundy	Q	Steel Grey
C	Peat	S	Raven
D	Saxe Blue	T	Truffle
F	Navy	U	Steel Grey
I	Medici Blue	V	Shark Grey
J	Bluestone	Y	non-standard
L	Shadow Grey		

Second digit	Trim material or name	Build date
A	Vinyl	08/82-02/93
B	Fife/Plain Fife	10/84-08/87
D	Truro Strobe/Cashmere	10/84-08/87
D	Truro Strobe/Strobe	03/86-01/87
D	Truro Strobe/Angora	08/87-01/90
G	Focus/Angora	04/90-02/93
H	Space/Angora	08/91-02/93
J	Helix/Plain Helix	01/87-08/88
L	Apollo/Angora	01/90-02/93
M	Lorenzo	08/83-08/88
P	Monaco/Plain Helix	01/87-02/93
Q	Astral/Angora	01/90-02/93
R	Savoy/Cashmere	08/83-08/87
R	Miami	05/92-02/93
S	Halley/Angora	01/90-02/93
U	Halley/Angora	08/87-08/91
V	Spa/Plain Rainbow	08/84-08/87
X or 4	Leather	11/88-02/93
Z	Zolda/Angora	01/90-02/93
1	Astral/Cashmere	01/87-01/90
1	Astral II	11/91-02/93
2	Halley/Angora	08/87-02/93
2	Roma/Cashmere	01/86-08/87
5	Barcelona/Plain Helix	03/88-01/90
6	Astral/Angora	08/87-02/93
6	Astral/Cashmere	01/87-08/87
7	Zolda/Angora	01/90-02/93
7	Zolda II	04/92-02/93
8	Chequers/Plain Chequers	08/88-02/93
9	Madrid/Angora	08/88-01/90

Escort

First digit (colour)

E	Raven with Mallard Green
G	Raven with Imperial Blue
L	Raven or Raven with Polaris Grey
O	Raven with Pimento Red

Second digit (material)

9	Hexagon
B	Flow/Monroe
C	Flow/Monroe (Recaro)
F	Mistral/Delon (Recaro)
P	Acadian/Delon (Recaro)
R	Panache/Angora (Recaro)
R	Panache/Delon (Recaro)
W	Leather

TYPE

Sierra/Sapphire

BBG - three-door hatchback (four-pillar)
BBE4 - three-door hatchback (four-pillar) with four-wheel drive
BED - three-door hatchback (three-pillar)
BEE4 - three-door hatchback (three-pillar) with four-wheel drive
BAC/BAG - five-door hatchback
BAE4 - five-door hatchback with four-wheel drive
BFG - four-door saloon
BFG4 - four-door saloon with four-wheel drive
GBC/GBG - three/five-door hatchback, German market
GBC4/GBG4 - three/five-door hatchback with four-wheel drive, German market
BBE - three-door hatchback (Federal Sierra)
BEF - RS Cosworth three-door hatchback
BFGC - RS Cosworth four-door saloon
BFGC4 - RS Cosworth four-door saloon with four-wheel drive
BNG - estate
BNG4 - estate with four-wheel drive
BNCV – van

Escort

ABL - three-door hatchback
AAL - five-door hatchback
ABL4 - three-door hatchback with four-wheel drive
AAL4 – five-door hatchback with four-wheel drive
ABLC4 - RS Cosworth
AFL – four-door saloon
ANL – five-door estate
ALL – convertible
AVL - van

VERSION (Italy only)

S – basic	P – Ghia
D – L	F – XR4
G – GL	S/D/G/P/F5 – with five-speed transmission

COLOUR/COULEUR

First digit

1   Solar Gold 80/Quartz Gold 85/Magenta 88/Levante Grey 93/Pepper Red

2   Imperial Red 83/Wedgewood Blue 91/Lipstick Pink/Chianti Red

3   Caspian Blue 83/Paris Blue 85/Biscayne 88/Nordic Green 91/Juice Green/ Loden Green

4   Forrest Green 81/Regency Red 84/Nordic Green 91/Mallard Green 92/ Obsidian 93/Med Harvest Gold

5   Glacier Blue 83/Mineral Blue 85/Moonstone Blue 86/Aztec Gold/Amparo Blue/Aspen White/Auralis Blue

6   Crystal Green 81/Moondust Silver 91/Columbia Silver

7   Nimbus Grey 84/Ebony 91/Light Grape

8   Jade Green 83/Olympic Gold 89/Alberto Green/Charcoal Green

9   Graphite Grey 81/Fernwood/Tourmaline Green 93/Spring Green 93/Black/ Heath Brown

0   Champagne Gold 82/Regal Red 87/Matisse Blue/Ontario Blue

A   Black 69/Nantucket Grey/Bright Amber

B   Diamond White 73/Cayman

C   Mistral Blue 86/Verona Green/Amalfi Blue 90/Petrol Blue/Medium Graphite

D   Galaxy Blue 87/Java Blue 93/Panther Black

E   Ceramic Blue 84/Burgundy Red 87/Mid Taupe 93/Dark Aubergine/ Portofino Blue

F   Coral Beige 83/Cameo Beige 85/Maritime Blue 87/Bahama Blue 91/ State Blue

G   Polar Grey 83/Cedar Green 85/Antique Bronze 89/Flambeau Red 91/ Spring Violet

H   Pine Green 83 /Ivory White 86/Imperial Blue 92/Autumn Green

I   Toreador Red

J   Rio Brown 83/Chestnut 86/Bahama Blue 90/Pacifica Blue 90/Cuirass

K   Moonstone Blue 86/Tasman Blue 89/Tourmallard Green/Vermillion

L   Baltic Blue 83/Lacquer Red 85/Aqua Jade 89/Aqua Foam 90/Mica Stone

M   Citrine Yellow 86/Smokestone 90/Bardolino Red

N   Ocean Blue 84/Verona Green 91/Polaris Grey 92/Dark Maroon/ Orange Bronze

P   Sunburst Red 81/Radiant Red 89/Medium Willow

Q   Mercury Grey 87/Cayman Blue 93/Belladonna

R   Cardinal Red 82/Rosso Red 85/Spring Violet 92/Sand

S   Silica Gold 87/Polaris Grey 92/Provence Green 92/Bahama Blue

T   Flint Grey 89/Deauville Blue 92/Electric Current 92/Jewel Violet

U   Crystal Blue 87/Aporto Red 92/Zinc Yellow 93/Mint Green

V   Platinum 76/Strato Silver 76/Balliol Blue 92/Ash Black/Atlantic Blue

W   non–standard

X   Willow Green 87/Nouveau Red 92

Z   Karelia Grey 92/Garnet Red

Y   non–standard

Second digit

Paint model year (2 - 82, 3 - 83 and so on)

K.D SVC. REF

Usually left blank, for use by export assembly country.

OR

EXH. EMISS.

1 – EEC Sweden

2 – high altitude

8 - EEC emission level, fifth amendment – reduced severity

E – combination L+7

M – unleaded fuel capability

Q - O2-sensor controlled (three way) catalyser

U – EEC to US standard 83 (petrol) or 87 (diesel) US requirements

W – German standard exhaust emission

X – EEC emission level, fifth amendment

Build plate

Sierra Mk1

Sierras were manufactured around the world in a variety of factories, including the UK, Portugal and South Africa. But the RS Cosworth was built only at Ford's Genk plant in Belgium. Yes, 500 cars were assembled by Tickford in England (as RS500s) but, as they were based on regular Belgian-made RS Cosworths, their original build plates remained.

Genk cars were equipped with a standard Ford build plate, riveted to the bonnet slam panel, painted in the same colour as the car's bodywork. The information on Belgian body plates was extracted from Ford's EOC (European order card) code, which formed something akin to each individual car's DNA.

The EOC contained (in code form) a complete description of the car's technical features, along with a five-digit sequence number that would later be used for the VIN (vehicle identification number). Each EOC was generated when the dealer (or manufacturer) specified the car in a formal order, and it's highly likely that the build plate was an abbreviated transcription of a paper build sheet for each car. On several Ford models, such build sheets have later been found secreted in the car by careless factory workers, but to date no Sierra sheets have been found.

Early Sierras had plates with two lines of information but in 1985 a third row was added, where the colour code and description was sited.

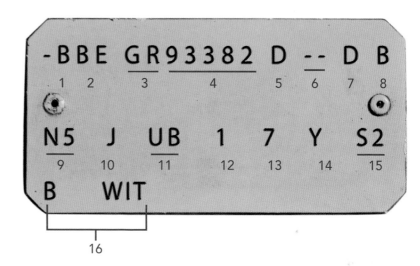

1: Assembly plant

B - Genk

2: Model

BE – Sierra three-door hatchback (type BEC/GBC)

BE – Sierra three-door hatchback/Cosworth (type BEF)

BB – Sierra three-door hatchback (type BBC/GBC)

BA – Sierra five-door hatchback (type BAC)

BN – Sierra five-door estate (type BNC)

3: Manufacture date

Year code	Year	Jan	Feb	Mar	Apr	May	June	July	Aug	Sep	Oct	Nov	Dec
F	1985	J	U	M	P	B	R	A	G	C	K	D	E
G	1986	L	Y	S	T	J	U	M	P	B	R	A	G
H	1987	C	K	D	E	L	Y	S	T	J	U	M	P

4: Serial number

Unique serial number of the vehicle. The sequence number restarted at 00001 every month for all Fords and ended at 99999 depending on the actual number of vehicles/engines produced.

5: Check digit

A single letter here was a so-called check digit, calculated by the factory based on all other codes in the EOC.

6: Special type

Options from the SVO (special vehicle options) list, such as towing hooks or special configurations for commercial use. Unfortunately, a list of options is currently unavailable, although it's unlikely any three-door Sierra RS Cosworths featured a code here on the build plate.

-- (two dashes) = no options.

7: Version

The base version of a Sierra. For example, a Sierra Laser was based on a Sierra L (with a D in this section) but was identified by an additional 'special version' code described below.

S = standard

D = L

G = GL

P = Ghia

F = XR4

8: Drive

The code alternated from one model year to the next, with each year usually beginning in July or August.

	1985	1986	1987
LHD	1	A	1
RHD	2	B	2

9: Engine

JC – 1.3 HC (engine block code JCT)
LC – 1.6 HC (engine block code LCT) or 1.6 HC Econ (engine block code LCS)
LS – 1.6 HC (engine block code LSD) from 10/84
RE – 1.8 HC (engine code REB) from 10/84
NE – 2.0 HC (engine block code NET)
NY – 2.0 V6 HC (engine block code NYT)
NR – 2.0i HC (engine block code NRD) from 04/85
YY – 2.3 V6 HC (engine block code YYT)
YT – 2.3D (engine block code YTT)
PR – 2.8 V6 (engine block code PRT) from 03/84
N5 – Cosworth (engine block code N5B)

10: Gearbox

3 – four-speed Type 3
E – four-speed Type E
F – five-speed Type 9
D – automatic Type C3
G – automatic Type A4LD
J – five-speed T5

11: Market code

Starting with the 1985 model year, market codes were identical for all Ford models and are still applicable today. This is just a small extract of the list.
UB – Great Britain
GK – Germany
IG – Ireland
SU – Switzerland
AK – Austria
FF – France
IJ – Italy
NO – Norway
FD – Finland
NB – The Netherlands
DB – Denmark
ST – Sweden
2B – USA
CB – Canada

12: Sunroof

-        no sunroof
1   sunroof

13: Emissions standard

As found on the VIN plate (where noted).
7 = EEC to ECE level 15.04

14: Special version

W = Laser (based on L or LX)
V = iS (based on L)
Y = Cosworth (based on L, GL or XR4i - all have been seen on the top line)

15: Trim code

As found on the VIN plate. See TRIM GARN. above.
S2 – Raven/Roma and Cashmere cloth

16: Colour

The third line included the colour name in Flemish, for the benefit of the Belgian factory workers, complete with Ford paint code.
B WIT – Diamond White
A ZWART – Black
K MOONSTONE BLAUW = Moonstone Blue

Sierra Mk2/Sapphire

Essentially the same as a 1986-model year Sierra Mk1 build plate, the Mk2 was stamped in three rows. As before, it was riveted to the bonnet slam panel and followed the familiar EOC code. All Sapphire Cosworths were equipped with this type of build plate.

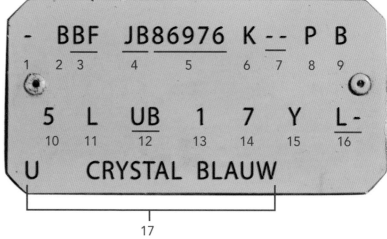

1: Origin of order

-        normal
- 0   special distribution channel

2: Assembly plant

B - Genk

3: Model

BB – Sierra three-door hatchback (type BBG/GBG)
BA – Sierra five-door hatchback (type BAG or BAG4)
BF – Sierra four-door saloon/Sapphire (type BFG or BFGC)
BN – Sierra five-door estate (type BNG)

4: Manufacture date

Year code	Year	Jan	Feb	Mar	Apr	May	June	July	Aug	Sep	Oct	Nov	Dec
H	1987	C	K	D	E	L	Y	S	T	J	U	M	P
J	1988	B	R	A	G	C	K	D	E	L	Y	S	T
K	1989	J	U	M	P	B	R	A	G	C	K	D	E
L	1990	L	Y	S	T	J	U	M	P	B	R	A	G
M	1991	C	K	D	E	L	Y	S	T	J	U	M	P
N	1992	B	R	A	G	C	K	D	E	L	Y	S	T
P	1993	J	U	M	P	B	R	A	G	C	K	D	E

5: Serial number

Unique serial number of the vehicle. The sequence number restarted at 00001 every month for all Fords and ended at 99999 depending on the actual number of vehicles/engines produced.

6: Check digit

A single letter here was a so-called check digit, calculated by the factory based on all other codes in the EOC.

7: Special type

Options from the SVO (special vehicle options) list, such as towing hooks or special configurations for commercial use. Unfortunately, a list of options is currently unavailable.
-- (two dashes) = no options
R9 = commercial estate pack
X0 = towing hitch
W2 = SVO EOC codes 32W and 332

8: Version

The base version of the Sierra. For example, a Sierra Laser was based on a Sierra L or LX, but was identified by an additional 'special version' code described below.
S = Standard (Bravo in some markets).
D = C or L (CL, LX and CLX were identified by a 'special version' code).
G = GL (GLS and GLX were identified by a 'special version' code).
P = Ghia
F = XR4
H = S

9: Drive

The code alternated from one model year to the next, with each year usually beginning in July or August.

	1987	1988	1989	1990	1991	1992
LHD	1	A	1	A	1	A
RHD	2	B	2	B	2	B

10: Engine

LS = 1.6 w/wo cat (engine block code LSE / LSF)
L6 = 1.6 cat (engine block code L6B)
RE = 1.8 w/wo cat (engine block code RED/REF)
R2 = 1.8 (engine block code R2A)
NE = 2.0 w/wo cat (engine block code NES/NEJ)
N8 = 2.0 (engine block code N8A)
N4 = 2.0 w/wo cat (engine block code N4A/N4B)
N9 = 2.0 DOHC w/wo cat (engine block code N9A/N9C)
PR = 2.8 (engine block code PRG/PR7/PR8)
B4 = 2.9 cat (engine block code B4B)
YT = 2.3 diesel (engine block code YTR)
RF = 1.8 TD (engine block code RFA; RFB)
N5 = 2.0 Cosworth (engine block code N5B/N5C/N5D)

11: Gearbox

3 = four-speed Type 3
8 = five-speed Type MT75
F = five-speed Type 9
G = automatic Type A4LD
L = five-speed T5

12: Market code

Starting with the 1985 model year, market codes were identical for all Ford models and are still applicable today. This is just a small extract from the list.
UB – Great Britain
GK – Germany
IG – Ireland
SU – Switzerland
AK – Austria
FF – France
IJ – Italy
NO – Norway
FD – Finland
NB – The Netherlands
DB – Denmark
ST – Sweden
2B – USA
CB – Canada

13: Sunroof

– = no sunroof
1 = sunroof
J = electric sunroof

14: Emissions standard

As found on the VIN plate (where noted).
– = no exhaust emission control
5 = O2-sensor controlled (three way) catalyser
7 = EEC to ECE level 15.04
G = combination for unleaded fuel capability and ECE level 15.04
J = uncontrolled catalyser (a combination code of M = unleaded fuel capability and X = new EEC emission level)
Q = O2-sensor controlled (three way) catalyser
U = emission control to US standard 83 (petrol – three way cat) or 87 (diesel)

15: Special version

3 = Brilliant (German market)
6 = Saphir (German and Austrian markets)
C = GLS (UK market)
F = GLS 4x4
K = Azur (Netherlands and Denmark markets)
N = GLX (UK market)
Q = Saphir with GT pack (in the Netherlands this was simply the GT)
T = Ghia 4x4 Estate (UK market)
U = Finesse/LX from 1989/CLX from 1990 (based on C)
Y = Cosworth (based on Ghia)

16: Trim code

As found on the VIN plate. See TRIM GARN. above.
L- – Shadow Grey/Angora
LQ – Shadow Grey/Angora
SX – Raven leather
S4 – Raven leather

17: Colour

The third line included the colour name in Flemish, for the benefit of the Belgian factory workers, along with colour code. For example:
B WIT = Diamond White
A ZWART = Black
5 MOONSTONE BLAUW = Moonstone Blue
U CRYSTAL BLAUW = Crystal Blue
K TASMAN BLAUW = Tasman Blue
P RADIANT ROOD = Radiant Red
Q MERCURY GRIS = Mercury Grey
Y S.V.O Kleur - special order
For full list of colours see COLOUR/COULEUR in Chassis Plate section (page 162).

Escort RS Cosworth

Escort RS Cosworths (and Escort convertibles) were built by Karmann in Germany using shells shipped directly from a 'body in white' production line. From that point on their assembly was outside the usual Ford manufacturing system, so they featured different build plates with very scant info – just the colour code, model code, production date and chassis number (as found on the VIN plate).

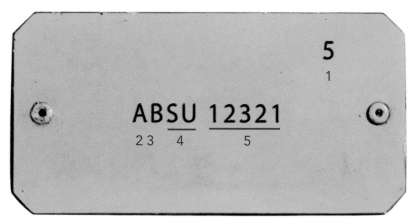

1: Colour code

4	Mallard Green 92
5	Auralis Blue
6	Moondust Silver 91
A	Black 69
B	Diamond White 73
C	Petrol Blue
E	Dark Aubergine
H	Imperial Blue 92
J	Pacifica Blue 90
N	Polaris Grey 92
P	Radiant Red 89
T	Jewel Violet
U	Zinc Yellow 93
V	Ash Black
W	non standard
Y	non standard

2: Model

A   Escort/Orion

3: Body type

B   three-door hatchback

4: Manufacture date

Year code	Year	Jan	Feb	Mar	Apr	May	June	July	Aug	Sep	Oct	Nov	Dec
N	1992	B	R	A	G	C	K	D	E	L	Y	S	T
P	1993	J	U	M	P	B	R	A	G	C	K	D	E
R	1994	L	Y	S	T	J	U	M	P	B	R	A	G
S	1995	C	K	D	E	L	Y	S	T	J	U	M	P
T	1996	B	R	A	G	C	K	D	E	L	Y	S	T

5: Serial number

Unique serial number of the vehicle. The sequence number restarted at 00001 every month for all Fords and ended at 99999 depending on the actual number of vehicles/engines produced.